Secrets of the Executive Search Experts

Secrets of the Executive Search Experts

Christian Schoyen and Nils Rasmussen

AMACOM
American Management Association
New York • Atlanta • Boston • Chicago • Kansas City • San Francisco • Washington, D.C.
Brussels • Mexico City • Tokyo • Toronto

*Special discounts on bulk quantities of AMACOM books are
available to corporations, professional associations, and other
organizations. For details, contact Special Sales Department,
AMACOM, an imprint of AMA Publications, a division of
American Management Association,
1601 Broadway, New York, NY 10019
Tel.: 212-903-8316   Fax: 212-903-8083*

*This publication is designed to provide accurate and authoritative
information in regard to the subject matter covered. It is sold
with the understanding that the publisher is not engaged in
rendering legal, accounting, or other professional service. If
legal advice or other expert assistance is required, the services of
a competent professional person should be sought.*

Library of Congress Cataloging-in-Publication Data

Schoyen, Christian.
    Secrets of the executive search experts / Chrisitan Schoyen and
Nils Rasmussen.
        p.   cm.
    Includes bibliographical references and index.
    ISBN 0-8144-0495-2
    1. Executives—Recruiting.   I. Rasmussen, Nils, 1964   .
II. Title.
    HF5549.5.R44S2944   1999   99-28285
    658.4'07111—dc21   CIP

Printing number

10 9 8 7 6 5 4 3 2 1

Contents

Figures

Part III Online Research (Chapters 9–12)

Part IV Country Profiles (Chapter 13)

Acknowledgments

This book has been made possible thanks to important contributions and guidance from several people in the field of executive search. We especially want to thank Research Director Henrietta Davis and partner Andrew Knox at Korn/Ferry International in Century City, California; Research Manager Justin Carpenter at A. T. Kearney Executive Search in London; and Practice Leader for Ward Howell International's Automotive Group, Doug Smith.

In addition we want to thank the 145 researchers and associates worldwide who have also contributed valuable information on how they each conduct research. These professionals work in a total of thirty countries in three of the leading executive search firms in the world:

- ▲ Korn/Ferry International
- ▲ Ward Howell International
- ▲ A. T. Kearney Executive Search

Thanks to the insight of all these experienced people we have been able to create an easy-to-use and extremely efficient and professional model for executive search research.

Introduction

The goal of this book is to provide human resource professionals and managers with a unique tool that explains how the leading executive search experts work. This book combines the long-kept secrets of the modern executive search experts with today's user-friendly information technology, in a domestic and global perspective. By understanding this work model, you can improve your own routines for hiring new executive, managerial, and professional staff by applying some or all of the methods yourself, or you can simply better understand your search firm and thereby be able to work with them for optimal results.

The recruiting methods described in this book are based on executive search methodology, proven to be the most effective and thorough way to recruit the best talents. Executive search aims at tracking down and recruiting people who are doing a great job in their current companies. Because of their superior performance, they are usually well respected and integrated into their existing work environment, and therefore not actively looking for new jobs. These individuals do not regularly read the job ads in the classifieds and therefore need to be identified and then approached on a direct, individual basis.

Executive search has long traditions, going all the way back to the 1920s in the United States, and with time, the work models have changed from being mysterious to becoming a structured process that can be learned by any qualified person. This change has now opened up a new door in terms of finding the best way to recruit executives, managers, and professionals. In theory, you should always be able to fill your open positions with the best possible talents, as long as you have something attractive to offer them and an effective recruiting strategy.

The focus of this book, executive search *research*—also called the backbone of executive search—is to *identify* and *screen* highly qualified candidates. Throughout time, the profession of executive research has undergone dramatic changes. So far, three distinct phases have taken place. They are referred to as first-generation, second-generation, and third-generation research. In the early days, first-generation research depended largely on personal contacts within the headhunter's limited personal network, also referred to as "the old-boys' network." Later, second-generation research was supplemented by the use of published secondary sources and circulation lists of particular business companies and alumni. Third-generation research is now practiced in most modern search firms, and involves a systematic and creative cross-checking of a variety of sources through various directories (published and online), cold-calling, and telephoning existing contacts. Due to the dramatic changes in research and how it is being conducted, the sources of the names on the target list (list of potential candidates and sources) have to a great extent changed. As the target list contains the names to be contacted in the search, it also becomes the parameter by which the historical changes in research can be measured. In the 1950s, during the early days of organized headhunting, all the names on the target list came from the old-boys' network. Recent surveys show that as many as 85 percent of the names on certain target lists now evolve from original research and published information (names originating from research and not a personal network), and only 15 percent from the old-boys' network. Figure 1 shows the evolution of executive search research in the United States, the most competitive and advanced headhunting market in the world.

Figure 1 The evolution of executive search research in the United States.

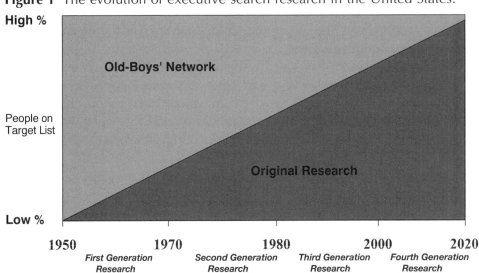

Today's information society enables modern executive search researchers, consultants, and other recruiting specialists to work in a borderless world, with access to information on prospects and target companies at the click of a button. In earlier years, it was necessary to use different interfaces and access gates, but today most information databases can be reached through the Internet. This breakthrough in advanced and user-friendly technology has resulted in faster searches and a broader coverage of markets in a shorter period of time. The challenge that remains, in order to come up with the best available and interested candidates, is to take full advantage of all the opportunities that the information society offers. When we do so, we can expect the first part of the search process to require less time. At the same time, the value of the old-boys' network used for candidate identification decreases.

The new executive search process, also referred to as "fourth-generation research," is strongly technology-driven, something that will become increasingly evident within the next few years. Fourth-generation research will require more interpersonal and technical skills and a more structured way of working than in previous generations of research and, unlike earlier old-boys' headhunting, the techniques can be learned. As a client you will, by watching and learning how to conduct fourth-generation research, realize that modern executive search is not mysterious anymore, but rather a very effective way to recruit based on a proven, logical step-by-step process supported by the effective use of new information technology.

How This Book Is Structured

Part I, "Executive Search Research Methodology," consists of six chapters that explain in detail how to complete a candidate search. The various chapters cover both the basic steps and the written documentation produced. The executive search research process is divided into seven major steps. These steps are explained in detail in the six chapters, which take the process from step one, defining the job, all the way to the final steps, placing the candidate and closing the files. The resources for actual company and candidate research (steps 2 and step 3) are found in Part III, "Online Research." For specific countries that you are working on, please refer to the company profiles in Part IV.

In Part II, "The Executive Search Profession," Chapter 7 explains what to look for when you have decided to use an executive search firm. In addition, you learn what to expect during the recruitment process in terms of follow-ups, written documentation, and quality of candidates. You also get insight to your role during the course of the search and how you and the executive search firm can work together for optimal results.

Chapter 8 presents three superior professionals from three of the world's leading executive search firms—Korn/Ferry International, A.T. Kearney Executive Search, and Ward Howell International—who answer the most frequently asked questions relating to their specific areas of expertise. The whole executive search process is described in detail.

The four chapters that make up Part III, "Online Research," describe a wide variety of online research resources in detail. Part III starts with an overview of the major categories of resources, helping you to select the best tools for each information search. Then, it explains six recommended steps for online research, followed by a selection of the thirty-two most popular business research databases, with a short description of each. The book explains how the two leading commercial online services (America Online and CompuServe) can be used in research and provides an in-depth description of research on the Internet. The latter goes into detail on how to search for information in the Cyberspace jungle and contains an overview of numerous exciting and helpful new research tools that have become available for Internet research.

The country profiles in Part IV give you unique and detailed information to be used in both domestic and international searches. In addition to describing the key directories and databases in several major countries worldwide, each country profile also gives you inside information on cultural factors affecting executive search. The "Culture" section gives information about legal constraints that apply when asking questions of candidates and sources. Information is also provided regarding what countries that are similar so you can broaden your search for candidates. The country profiles also contain a geographic map, a list of major city centers and industries, and key country facts.

Finally, the appendix contains a list of technology and industry terms, Internet statistics, and access providers, and a list of codes for sorting and storing résumés (curricula vitae, or CV). The most common terms used in executive search and within this particular recruitment industry are explained in the glossary. And a listing of human resources and technology books that cover different aspects of the recruitment process can be found in the bibliography.

Part I | Executive Search Research Methodology

1 | Beginning the Search and Defining the Job

To be a good hunter in the recruitment process, you must be both a good judge of character and a good researcher. For research is the backbone of the search process, involved in almost every step. The focus of this book is on research and the resulting written documentation.

The research techniques described in this book apply throughout the world, but sometimes must be adapted to suit the cultural differences in different countries. These differences (and how to deal with them) are explained in each country's "Culture" section in the country profiles in Chapter 13. Also, the directories you use to compile information about companies and people will, of course, be different from country to country (with exception of the global directories provided by companies such as Dun & Bradstreet, Wards, and Gayle Research, which cover almost all countries on just one CD-ROM).

At some executive search firms the recruitment consultant personally does all the research, while other firms have professional researchers who assist in the process. In some firms, researchers participate in every step of the process, while at others they just make target lists, and might not even speak to the potential candidates or sources on the telephone. In some executive search firms, there might be a hierarchy of people involved in the process—research analyst, junior researcher, senior researcher, associate, principal, consultant, and such—with each person having specific duties. In other places there might be just one consultant who does everything. While who does what may differ from firm to firm, the steps presented here are universal, so rather than get involved in division of tasks, we focus on the process itself.

The methodology presented in this book is based on search. As the target group in search is usually higher level executives who, in most cases, are not looking for jobs, the challenge of tracking down Mr. or Ms. Right is a big one. To be successful at executive search research, you must be determined to crack each problem, using all the initiative and imagination at your disposal. If you knock on the front door and get turned away, you should not feel that you are stuck—you just have to climb through the kitchen window. To be successful you have to be persistent, very creative, quick, and extremely professional in your approaches and conduct. Also, keep in mind that research is an art and not a science. While gathering information you must speak to many people—both potential sources and candidates. You must remember to treat everyone you speak to with courtesy and decency, as you never know where you might run into your contacts again. The ultimate goal is to find a sufficient number of qualified and interested candidates, and to complete the process both quickly and professionally. Therefore, it is important that you follow certain basic steps to select the best available candidates.

The flow and logical sequence of the various activities in the executive search research process are shown in Figure 1.1. The way the flowchart works is very simple: The flow keeps going down until the search is filled (search is closed). A key rule is to keep working on finding candidates

Figure 1.1 The executive search process.

If too many prospects or candidates decide to drop out of the process because of lack of sufficient benefits offered or attractiveness of the job, reevalute the position description and requirements or benefits.

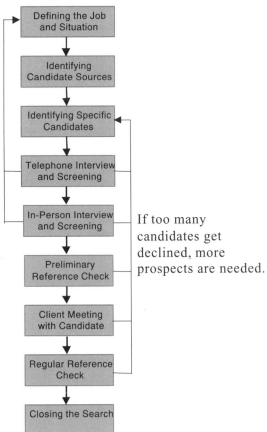

If too many candidates get declined, more prospects are needed.

until the final candidate has accepted and signed. If all the people on the target list have been contacted, new sources and candidates must be identified. If everyone rejects the position for the same reason—for example, too low a salary—it might be necessary to make changes by increasing the salary or lowering the requirements and thereby revising the position specification (see Figure 1.2).

Figure 1.2 The key areas in executive search research.

Basic Steps	Documentation Created
1. Defining the job. Situation Analysis. Meeting of minds between client and consultant regarding what they are looking for.	A written document, the *position specification* describing the full picture—company, position, and requirements. At the same time a *template* with only the requirements is made, which is later used for screening.
2. Identifying candidate sources. Making a task plan regarding the time frame for the search, where to look for the right candidate, selecting industries, what companies to look into, and what individuals to speak with.	An alphabetic *target list* with the names of companies and people you are going to source. The list should be sorted according to company, and alphabetized according to potential candidates' last names. In this format, the calling list can be utilized as a "log."
3. Identifying specific candidates. The process of identifying potential candidates is called *sourcing,* which is best accomplished by speaking to key people who are in the target group and asking them for "assistance."	During sourcing, the comments made by the people being contacted should be recorded in the log, with dates and correct "code." This means if a source, for example, becomes a candidate, the coding and group that this particular individual belongs to will change.
4. Telephone interview and screening. Interviewing potential prospects on the telephone and obtaining the necessary information to decide	Use the template you made in Step 1 and compare it with the prospect's background. It is also

(Continued)

Figure 1.2 *(Continued)*

Basic Steps	Documentation Created
whether they remain on the list. If the candidates remain on the list, begin gathering more information.	helpful to have prospective candidates explain to you how they feel their background fits your position specifications. If it is still not clear whether the prospects are on target, then you can go through the template with them over the phone. These notes should be stapled to the résumé.
5. In-person interview and screening. Verification of facts concerning a candidate by face-to-face interview. Getting a sense of the personality. Finding out more about the candidate through questions and your own judgment to determine whether the person fits and moves to the next level.	Those candidates who are on target should be written up in an extensive report describing personal traits, work history, and personal observations made by the interviewer. The documentation regarding the work history is called a *career brief.* The documentation portraying a more personal picture of the candidate is called the *appraisal.* This document seeks to explain where the person is coming from, why certain choices were made in life, strengths and weaknesses, and the interviewer's assessment.
6. Preliminary and regular reference check. Preliminary checking of a candidate is conducted before the client interview by discreetly speaking to a few people for an insider idea of the person. A regular reference check is conducted after the client interview. At this stage, there is extensive questioning of several people whom the candidate is working or has worked for.	The questions being asked during the regular reference check are basically the same for everyone. All the replies from the references are recorded, as stated, in a *reference report.*
7. Closing the search (closeout). After a successful placement of the candidate, all sources and unsuccessful candidates are contacted to tie up the loose ends. All the necessary documentation is placed in the closing file.	The various people that you have closely interacted with during the search get a letter stating the appreciation for their time and/or interest in the search or position. These acknowledgment letters are called *closeout letters.*

Defining the Job

The first major activity in the search process is defining the job. This step sets the tone for all that follows. Preparing a *job description* is where all the discussions between client and consultant (if the company has decided to use outside help) about job requirements, organizational relationships, and cultural issues are crystallized. So that it does not give people the wrong picture, the job description must be accurate and well written. It is always important to gather information from all parties involved: (1) the person leaving the position; (2) the person that the new employee will report to; (3) coworkers; and (4) people reporting to the new employee. By gathering the necessary information from these four groups, you ensure that the picture of the situation is accurate.

The job description is a written document that should be extensive enough to give potential sources and candidates a clear and informative picture of the company, the position to be filled, and the requirements. Written documentation is a tool for everyone in the process: the company with the recruitment need, the consultant and researcher (if you are using outside help), the client, sources, and potential candidates. It is very important to conduct sufficient research so that you are able to write the documentation, answer questions from sources and candidates, and conduct an extensive search in the market. Keep in mind that even though you might know all the answers to the different topics, you still have to cover everything. The first documentation, which is based on the following required information, is called *situation report* documentation:

The Company

- ▲ Historical background, development
- ▲ Plant and office locations, affiliations, number of employees
- ▲ Organizational structure (organization chart)
- ▲ Product lines, sales volume, market share
- ▲ Profitability; past, current, and projected rate of growth
- ▲ Strengths and weaknesses of the company
- ▲ What is the company culture like?
- ▲ Why has the vacancy arisen?
- ▲ If a person was previously in this position, where did he or she go?
- ▲ What background did this person have?
- ▲ Why has the position not been filled internally?

▲ Is there something unusual about this position?
▲ What efforts have been made to fill the position and why have they failed?

The Position

▲ Title of position
▲ Responsibilities, functions, duties, and accountabilities
▲ Objectives and time frames in which to achieve them
▲ Organization charts of whole company and relevant department or division (showing functional as well as hierarchical relationships)
▲ The challenge and attractions of the job (including compensation package)
▲ What company policies and practices will affect the jobholder?
▲ What are the personalities of the people with whom the jobholder will be in contact?
▲ What are the future opportunities for the person appointed, and over what time scale?
▲ Supervisor and subordinates and their qualifications and experience
▲ Geographic restraints

The Ideal Candidate (Identify the ideal candidate's qualities on two levels: essential and desirable)

▲ Education and paper qualifications
▲ Experience
▲ Language requirements
▲ Personal qualities
▲ Skills required
▲ What type of company culture would you expect the person to come from (or not to come from)?

Target Companies and Positions: Where Might This Person Be Found?

▲ Names and divisions of companies
▲ Geographic locations
▲ Sales volume
▲ Standard Industrial Classification (SIC) and function codes
▲ Number of employees
▲ Possible title(s)
▲ Possible level(s)

Important: Until everything is completely clear, continue to go back to the involved parties to get your questions answered. Make sure that every requested piece of information on the foregoing list is covered.

By now, your understanding of the situation should be good enough for you to write the *position specification/candidate profile* (see Figure 1.3).

Figure 1.3 Position specification and candidate profile.

DIRECTOR, MANAGEMENT INFORMATION SYSTEMS

THE COMPANY

Our client is one of the leading manufacturers of belt buckles in the world and is a publicly held company (NYSE). The company sells its premium products exclusively through its own network of stores. With more than a century-long history of making belt buckles, the company has successfully built a strong reputation in the market-place for being the highest caliber manufacturer of its type.

The company is headquartered in Chicago and owns a total of thirty stores throughout the United States and abroad, all situated in metropolitan cities, with a total of 3,000 employees. The buckles are manufactured at the company's own production and distribution site in Florida. The company also has a mail-order facility based in Chicago. Currently annual sales are reported at one billion dollars (1995), with a high growth rate. The U.S. stores are responsible for 20 percent of the company's sales, while mail order consist of 10 percent, and international of 70 percent. The company has a 70 percent market share.

Our client's biggest challenge is to remain the market leader by being innovative and delivering the highest possible quality, with minimal expenses, and the highest degree of service to its customers.

THE POSITION

LOCATION

Chicago, Illinois

THE POSITION

The Director of MIS will be in charge of managing a team providing the company with strategies, development, and implementation of information systems that are cost-effective, efficient, with current and emerging technologies to support decision-making requirements, goals, and plans. A major focus will be to improve and maxi-mize the use of a newly installed system, which links Inventory, Finance, Sales, and Manufacturing.

The Director of MIS will have a staff of five and report to the Vice President, Finance and Administration.

(Continued)

Figure 1.3 *(Continued)*

RESPONSIBILITIES

▲ Develop and manage the implementation of the company's high-tech information systems.
▲ Determine and recommend for approval information systems policies, standards, practices, and security measures that ensure effective and consistent information processing and the safeguarding of the information resources.
▲ Research and direct the continual upgrading of the information system staff, equipment, and procedures to maintain pace with technological progress, economic change, and business needs.
▲ In an emerging outsourcing environment, manage the relationship with the outsourcing partners.
▲ Create special assignments and projects based on needs of teams from multilocations.

EXPERIENCE AND BACKGROUND REQUIRED

▲ A minimum of ten years business experience with a broad understanding of all business functional areas and their relationships to information systems.
▲ A proven track record of systems project management experience with a blend of technical and business skills.
▲ Knowledge of structured analysis and design to conduct system reviews. Such a review would consider the accuracy and completeness of deliverables in each development phase.
▲ Knowledge of data communication capabilities in order to understand line types, protocols, and equipment used so those characteristics could be considered in system design.
▲ Must have experience in successfully implementing a computer system in a multisite environment that centralized the functions of inventory and finance.

EDUCATION

An undergraduate degree is required, preferably in one of the computer or information technology sciences. An MBA is very desirable, although not required.

COMPENSATION

A highly competitive base compensation plus 50 percent bonus opportunity in addition to client's executive level stock option and benefits programs.

PROCEDURE FOR CANDIDACY: Send résumés or nominations as soon as possible to:

Peter Smith
ABC Headhunting, Inc.
270 N. Canon Drive, Suite 1166
Beverly Hills, CA 90210
Ph.: 310-999-2222
Fax: 310-999-5199

This written documentation, which you will share with potential sources and candidates, should not cover all the information that you put into the situation report documentation. Sometimes you do not want to use the company name in the written documentation that you mail out. It is difficult to conduct this mail-out yourself with full discretion if you are not using an executive search firm. Also keep in mind when creating the document that readers want something that is short and to the point, yet contains enough information to interest them (or screen them out if they do not have the right background). As a rule you should never send out written documentation that contains confidential information. To prevent mistakes and at the same time ensure that you are on the right track, the documentation must always be approved by the new employee's superior before it can be sent out to any potential sources or candidates.

Frequently a search changes direction. Be prepared to change the course if necessary. Keep in mind that anything can change during a search: new reporting relationships, a new compensation scheme, or a new set of performance objectives for the position. You therefore have to be flexible so you can resolve new recruitment issues.

From the situation report you need to make a *template* for the search, which helps you to screen people (see Figure 1.4). With this simplified form, all you need to do when speaking to people you want to screen is to go down the items and write yeses and nos. Getting all yeses means you are on target.

Figure 1.4 Example of template.

#12129   Client: BELT BUCKLE INTERNATIONAL

Position Title: Director MIS

Candidate: _____

Attribute	Y/N	Comment/Description
Ten Years Business Information Systems Experience		
Systems Experience UNIX Based Wang Equipment Cobol Generation Tools		
Novell Networks Tools LAN WAN		
Gateway Experience		
EDI Experience		
MFG/PRO Experience		
Installation/implementation		
Project/Team Management Experience		
Change Experience		
Outsourcing Management Experience		
Industry Experience Types of Companies		
Education		
Compensation		

2 | Identifying the Candidate Sources

It is important to prepare a formal task plan to guide yourself through the search for Mr. or Ms. Right. This plan serves as a road map in developing the proper approach to conducting research suitable to the particular assignment. The task plan need not be voluminous or complicated. Its purpose is to define the various activities and sources of information to be used in completing the research.

Most task plans consist of at least four major elements:

1. Selecting likely industries
2. Identifying target companies
3. Sourcing for specific individuals
4. Time schedule

Selecting Likely Industries

The first step is to select likely industries. You should look first at competitors of the company for which you are recruiting. But keep in mind that other related industries or, in some cases, totally unrelated industries can also be likely sources for the talent(s) that you are seeking. These should be discussed with all parties involved in the search. A wide selection of target industries will broaden the pool of potential candidates. But focusing on more than just one industry can be very time-consuming. To best understand where to look for candidates, it is helpful to think of circles representing places to look. This idea, called the *logic of concentric circles*, is represented in Figure 2.1. As the main goal is generally to find the best possible candidates in the shortest period of time, when selecting likely industries, it is best to concentrate on the center of the logic of concentric circles where direct competitors are located, then similar or parallel industries. Finally,

Figure 2.1 Logic of concentric circles.

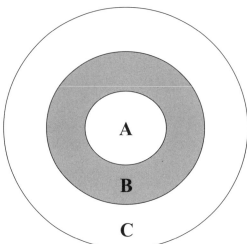

if this is not sufficient, look at companies that utilize the product or service provided by the client company for which the search is being conducted.

A good place to start digging for information when selecting target industries and likely industries where your prospects might be located is the library. Modern libraries not only have vast amounts of information on companies, but also trained information specialists who can be extremely helpful. These modern librarians are usually experts at finding the appropriate industry codes for your search, in addition to having available information sources for free. A listing of libraries that you can use in each country can be found in the respective country profiles in Chapter 13.

Identifying Target Companies

If you are using an executive search firm, you must understand that some industries are dominated by one or two major companies, which may be off-limits (previous or present [within the last two years] clients of the executive search firm). If this is the case, then use the logic of concentric circles: First look at parallel industries; then look at companies that utilize the product or service. Be aware that a professional headhunter can always source someone at the client company, just not recruit anyone.

When identifying target companies, you will frequently find that subsidiaries are listed only by name and location. Sometimes they are not even listed. Because your Ms. Right could be in a subsidiary not listed, you need to do some digging. Investigate the annual report of the parent company. You can obtain the information from this report either by getting online and checking out the company's Web site or by calling and asking them to send the annual report, which should have the appropriate addresses. When you have them on the phone, you must get them to tell you what you need to know. The second step is to call the subsidiary and conduct the regular identification (ID) work described in Chapter 3, to obtain the names and titles of the people who interest you. When you receive the annual report, you can double-check the information to ensure its accuracy. Sometimes the annual report contains information about key executives at the different subsidiaries.

Sourcing for Specific Individuals

The third major element of the research task plan is to track down specific individuals who might be appropriate candidates. In this part of the process you are very dependent on using published reference books and directories and speaking to third parties (sources) to identify potential candidates.

Once the research task plan has been developed and reviewed by all involved parties, it can be used both to guide the research process and to monitor progress. Based on this task plan it should be possible to estimate the amount of time required to complete the various parts of the process (see the discussion under "Time Schedule").

The different sources that you can use in the search include:

▲ Direct competitors (see concentric circle)
▲ The respective association for the industry
▲ Your own network (previous searches)
▲ Journalists representing industry magazines or newspapers or other experts

Many people feel that one of the most important sources, and a place that should be contacted immediately, is the appropriate association for the particular industry where the search is being conducted. This source will know of the different directories that exist, including potential membership books. Because sources are the experts, they can be helpful in pointing you in the right direction. In large countries such as the United

States, directories exist that list all of the associations in the country, while in smaller countries such as Norway or Sweden, you must look in the yellow pages of the telephone book.

After the target industries have been selected, you must identify specific companies where potential candidates can be found. It is important to understand how the company size affects the search and at what level your target person is located. If the company with the recruitment need is looking at a target company of the same size, the target person in this company should be located one level down. On the other hand, if your target company is smaller than the company for which you are recruiting, you can focus on the same-level position. When the company for which you are recruiting is extremely popular to work for, such as Harley Davidson, these rules do not necessarily apply. Normally the thinking is that you approach people to whom you can offer something better. In other words, put yourself in the shoes of the candidates. Why change jobs? What is the catch? Keep in mind that the various companies might be using different titles for the same position. If you are dealing with just a few companies, be careful not to contact too many people in the same company without some preresearch.

If possible, all target industries should be identified with the Standard Industrial Classification (SIC) code. For a complete breakdown and explanation of each SIC-code group, consult the *Standard Industrial Classifications Manual,* published by National Technical Information Service (NTIS). It is also important to keep in mind that certain industries or segments are so specialized that you will not be able to find the exact SIC code. In that case, you have to go for the parent group and then do a manual sorting. (*Note:* At this writing, the SIC codes are being replaced with NAICS [North American Industry Classification System] codes. Manuals for both SIC and NAICS codes can be obtained through the NTIS Web site at www.ntis.gov/sic and www.ntis.gov/naics, respectively.) As a rule, the more selective you are in your search, the more selective (specific) your results will be. In order to be specific, you should, if possible, know:

▲ SIC code (industry code; found by looking up the company for which you are recruiting)
▲ Size of the company (range)
▲ Geography (location of target company)

Important: When looking for target companies, use more than just one directory or source. Keep in mind that one directory might be missing important information that you can find in another directory.

All countries have published directories with key information on the major companies in the respective country (there is an extensive listing with description in each country profile in Chapter 13). The information providers in each country sometimes offer a variety of media where you can access their company information. The most common media are:

▲ CD-ROM
▲ Books
▲ Internet

In addition, sometimes the providers offer manual consulting services, meaning that for a certain cost they can do the search job for you (finding companies).

Time Schedule

The fourth element is the time schedule. Every step of the process must be completed as quickly as possible. But, it is still important to set goals as to when you should complete each step. The faster you get going, the better you feel. A fast start-up is the goal. It is important to concentrate on compiling the target list before you start the calling, as this will save

Figure 2.2 Time schedule.

Search Definition (2 days)	Target List (2 days)	Sourcing (10 days)	Candidate Development (6 days)	Interviews and Closing (ongoing)
Activities: Interview key people at the client company to get an accurate picture of what to look for.	Activities: Create list of all the companies and people you are going to source. ($\frac{1}{2}$ day of directory search, $1\frac{1}{2}$ days of ID work)	Activities: Contact everyone on target list. Leave a maximum of two messages.	Activities: Follow-up and development of prospects (including rejections)	Activities: Interviews by consultant and client, then closing of search when candidate accepts.

you time. Then, if you plan to undertake a mailing, it should be done immediately. If you plan to ease up, it should not be until after the mailing. The average time frame for each step in the search process is shown in Figure 2.2.

Note: In every search it is important to work backward from the completion date. This means that if you are using an external executive search consultant and he or she has promised that you will be presented with a candidate four weeks after the start of the search, the executive search consultant should meet that person at the latest three days before that date. This in turn means that the individual must have been identified and fully developed seven days earlier (telephone interview before the face-to-face interview). In order to meet this goal you must have approached all the people on the target list at least once in less than two weeks from the start of the search. Only in the first parts of the search do you have full control over time and process. It is harder to control the activity that goes on after the prospect has been interviewed face-to-face, because this is when the major decisions for both parties have to be made. It is always difficult to predict how much time people need to think things over, and how many people you need to see before you make a decision. Also, the negotiations between your company and the candidate regarding terms can sometimes be lengthy.

3 | Identifying Specific Candidates

The executive search method requires you to find a small group of outstanding individuals who have interest in pursuing the opportunity that you are presenting to them. It is important that the search is comprehensive. You must utilize various sources of information, including all available published directories relevant to the search, as well as industry contacts. You should also conduct extensive original research.

The first place you should start looking is in your file of previous searches. These sources may identify as many as several hundred potential candidates. But, only a small number of these people will be interviewed in person. The goal when making calls is to find quality; the bottom-line goal is to come up with the best possible candidates. How many you call or interview is less important than who you come up with. It is therefore of great importance to make quality calls. Your goal should be to come up with no more than five qualified and interested candidates at the final round. However, in order to get these numbers, you have to interact with many people.

Documentary sources are the starting point in this process. If you use an executive search firm, it should have its own extensive libraries of directories, trade journals, and publications in order to target companies and potential sources and prospects. Be aware that almost all of this information can also be found at a modern library. The higher the level of the search, the more likely you are to find a good amount of published material (directories) that will be of great help. The rule when using published material is that people high up on the corporate ladder are the easiest to identify.

Often you will find that no published material exists about your prospect—you will not even find the person's name in the listings. The best (and only reliable) way to get what you want is by picking up the phone. This process of identifying candidates is called *ID work* (identification work).

ID work can be time-consuming, and thus demands persistence and a high level of creativity. A good starting point is company directories. In most cases you succeed in finding the companies through these directories. The information that you often lack is the name or even the correct title of the person you are seeking. How long the name search will take depends very much on whom you are seeking and what codes or rules the receptionist or secretary has to follow. If you are seeking the director of manufacturing or director of human resources (HR), it will be a straight shoot. But if you try to map out a sales department, it will be trickier. To avoid wasting time, always try for the easy names first. This means you should start out with the line, "Who is the director of HR?" Do not represent yourself; just ask the question. If you are asked why you want the information, just say that you do not know yourself as you are just an employee who has been told to do a job. This plain, straightforward approach should get you as many as 80 percent of the missing names on your list. If you focus you should be able to get the appropriate names and titles of as many as sixty to eighty people a day. For the remaining 20 percent, just try a day later with a new tack such as, you are sending a letter from your boss who is traveling and you can not remember the name and title of the person to whom you are to send the letter. On this second round, you should be able to obtain most of the remaining names. If you still have not gotten everybody, on day three you can try something like: You are calling from a consulting company and you are putting together a list of speakers for a particular symposium, and you have been told that a particular person at company X is a terrific guy, but you are not sure of his name and title. By now you should have gotten all the names.

Sourcing

Sourcing is the process of locating names of possible candidates by referral from others (or themselves, when contacted). You generally have to contact many people to obtain names. Some of these may be found unsuitable quickly because they do not meet the job description requirements. Sourced names that seem to be suitable are added to a list of potential candidates for further investigation.

The first people to telephone in your source search are those who know about relevant industries and companies, such as association executives, academics who have specific knowledge about industries and key companies, accountants, attorneys, investment bankers, journalists, and business acquaintances. Or they may be people brought to your attention by third parties.

Sourcing calls are made primarily to obtain names of individuals who appear to meet the qualifications for the job that you are seeking to fill. Sometimes you call an executive you have reason to believe may be a potential candidate. Other times, the sourcing call's purpose is to obtain the names of as many potential candidates as possible. It is also a good idea to try to get additional source names from individuals called.

After making a sufficient number of sourcing calls, you should have obtained the names of potential candidates (who will be further investigated), as well as additional sources. Names of five or more potential candidates might be obtained with a single source call, along with the names of one or two additional sources. After a number of calls have been made, you should have a network of names.

Sourcing calls make up a good deal of the workload in the search assignment. It is important to note clearly on the call list which potential sources have been contacted, so that future work, when needed, can proceed based on leads not followed up the first time. It is up to your own professional judgment when enough sourcing calls have been made.

Sourcing in Small Versus Big Markets

For maximum efficiency, small markets and large markets call for different methods. One reason for this is that you usually have many more target companies to hit in a large market. In a small market, often with just a handful of target companies, you cannot afford to do many wrong source calls in a company, or stir things up. You have to hit your target right away if possible. Wrong calls can make the word go around, and your target can easily lose interest because he or she does not feel special. Sourcing techniques must be adjusted according to the marketplace, the existing culture, and the situation at the time.

Timewise, the most efficient way to conduct research in larger markets such as the United States, Germany, and the United Kingdom is the straightforward approach explained in this book, where you concentrate first on finding candidates who are qualified, and you do not conduct reference checking until much later. This method often includes extensive use of mailing before calling.

In smaller markets such as Ireland, Norway, and Sweden, a helpful way to source is by careful reference checking, as you not only want names, but also would like to know beforehand who the best candidates are. In this method, it is helpful to speak to someone who just left your target company, and who happened to work in the department you were targeting for prospects or potential candidates. The goal should be to find someone (source) who is one level above your potential target's. If this source is helpful, he or she can provide you with quality names. This method of tracking down candidates is generally too time-consuming to use in larger markets.

Both approaches are being mixed in small and big markets, although there is a tendency to lean toward a certain way to conduct the search in the specific market as explained.

Finding Sources Who Left the Company

Talking to people who recently left the target company can help you tell the rising stars from the falling ones early in the search process. Keep in mind that it is important who your source is: A statement from a boss who recently left the company usually has a lot more validity than one from a secretary. There are two basic methods you can use to find your source:

1. *Cross-check directories.* Look at the executives listed in a current directory, and compare them with those listed in an earlier edition of the same directory. Names that were previously listed but are not in the newest edition are good potential sources. Next, phone the company and ask for the missing people. Pretend that you think they are still there. Tell the switchboard operator or the person in the department that you are speaking to that you used to be friends with the person, but you lost touch over the years. Keep in mind that if you get the HR department on the line the game is over, because they generally will not give out a forwarding number.

2. *Connect with someone in the department that you are targeting.* Tell the person at your target company that you are looking for someone that you met a while back who had told you he used to work with the target company until recently, but had recently started elsewhere. If he or she asks you why you want to know, say that it is very personal and out of respect for the person in question you do not wish to disclose any further information on the matter. You are not 100 percent sure about the name, but you think that it may be Jim or Peter. In most cases the person will try to help you out by giving you different names of people who have left if you just keep probing. This method should only be used if nothing else works. You should always use your real name and the company that you are calling from, if you are asked. Never pretend that you are someone else,

as you can get involved in legal complications. Be persistent, polite, quick, and positive.

Mailings and Source Letters

Mailing the position specification to potential sources and candidates is a practice that both private companies and several executive search firms stick to religiously, while others ban it. Even some of the most prestigious executive search firms with top-notch positions do mail-outs. To obtain the best possible results, certain basic rules should be followed:

1. *Protect the confidentiality of the firm.* The company name should be left out if possible (this is of course difficult if the company with the recruitment need is conducting the mailing). If the recruitment is official, the position specification can be very detailed. If the opposite is the case, then you need to be careful about what information you present, as you do not want anybody to be able to guess what company it is. This confidentiality can only be ensured if an external executive search firm is conducting the mail-out.

2. *The source letter must be well written.* Get to the point quickly, and stick to the basics. Be sure that there are no grammatical errors in the letter. Mistakes indicate sloppiness and give an adverse impression about you, the sender. Every source letter must be addressed to the receivers as sources. If you plan to mail a position specification to somebody at his or her workplace, be aware that the mail will likely be opened by a secretary or assistant before it reaches the target. This means that you cannot afford any misunderstandings. Even though you try to reach a target that you feel could be a great candidate, still write to him as a source. If you already have spoken to somebody who has shown great interest and wants to receive the mail at home, you can use a so-called potential candidate letter. Keep in mind that this kind of letter can never be sent to someone's work address.

3. *The receivers of the mail-out are all the people on your target list.* Each mailing (envelope) should contain a source letter and a position specification.

4. *Never wait for your target group to call you.* Right after the creation of the target list and the mail-out, start calling. You can never afford the luxury of waiting for the mail to reach the targets.

Note: Do not call anybody before you have created the target list. It will, to a great extent, slow the process later in the search if you have to stop because you did not make a complete list in the beginning.

The Proposition

Before making any calls, it is important to make sure that you can do a good job selling both the job and the company. You must practice to the extent that you can do the pitch well and at the same time sound convincing. Do not start calling before you have it down right, as you get only one chance to make a first impression.

A good way to make sure that you get the pitch right is to write down what you want to say and practice it until you know it by heart. It will also be of great help to have this script next to you when you are working on several searches simultaneously. Let someone who is also working on the search listen to your sales pitch before you start making calls. This will help ensure that what you are saying is correct.

When making the pitch, do not trick your target by lying, just to get him on your hook. If you do so, it will only backfire later in the process. Put yourself in the shoes of the listener. Be able to explain why your listener should be interested in the opportunity. You must be able to sell the position, which means finding a good way to trigger the listener's attention. Keep in mind that any negative points may cause the target to decide too rapidly against what may actually be a very good opportunity.

Before you start to make calls, it is helpful to speak to someone who really knows the field for which you are recruiting. Preferably, this person should not be a candidate, as you want to determine the golden nuggets that will make someone interested in what you have to offer. Also, try to practice your pitch with this expert so you can get some feedback and make necessary adjustments.

Calling the Target List

If you are using an outside executive search firm, the source call typically opens with the recruiters or researchers identifying themselves and their organization and asking for assistance in getting the names of prospective candidates. Usually, the job is described in general terms including the projected compensation range. This small amount of information makes it possible to screen out inappropriate candidates. If the person has been previously identified as a possible candidate, there may be some discussion of this possibility as well.

The executive search consultants and their researchers use different techniques to get data from a source or to get prospective candidates to volunteer their own names. The specific technique is not as important as the end result of securing names through forthright and ethical means.

When speaking to people you should have the following information handy:

- ▲ A questionnaire (see the section "Defining the Job" in Chapter 1) to be used during the source calls
- ▲ The position specification/candidate profile (see example in the section in Chapter 1 "Defining the Job")
- ▲ Situation report documentation (see the section "Defining the Job" in Chapter 1) and organization chart of the client company
- ▲ A list of potential candidates and sources (target list)
- ▲ A one- or two-paragraph synopsis of the client company and opportunity (the pitch)

Sourcing calls can often be time-consuming, depending on the circumstances, your personal style and technique, and the interest and receptivity of the individual called. The overall number of calls will depend on the complexity of the search and professional judgment as to when enough names have been secured. One good rule to follow is that you should not stop searching before a candidate has accepted and signed the papers.

A major obstacle when calling is that most of the people you aim for will not be reachable. The closest you will get to them is through their voice mail, which means you are dependent on them calling you back. Therefore, when you leave the message, make sure that it will get their attention. Keep in mind that there might already be other voice-mail messages from other recruiters when you leave yours. You want people to call you back, so make sure that you do not sound like a sales representative from a telemarketing firm. But also keep in mind that there is always a risk of a secretary or an administrative assistant listening to the recordings on the voice mail. You could be badly burned if you leave a message giving the impression that Mr. X is job hunting. A good rule, therefore, is to approach everyone as sources when contacting them the first time, and always when leaving messages. You should always leave a message when you have the opportunity. An example of a message left with a voice mail or secretary could be:

"This is John Smith from Jones International in Los Angeles calling. I am seeking your assistance in regards to an MIS director search I am currently conducting for Belt Buckle International, based in Chicago. [*If you cannot use the name of the company, use a phrase like 'a leading manufacturing company producing belt buckles, based in an attractive city in the Midwest'*] Please call me at your earliest convenience at (555) 555-5555."

If your company is conducting all the calls itself, it is difficult to maintain full discretion. If full discretion is required, it is always better to have an outside source to assist you in the search.

Dealing With Secretaries and Switchboards

Switchboard operators are often the first line of inquiry when you call into a company. Some switchboard operators will talk freely about executives in their firm, while others will be very suspicious and might even transfer you directly to your target. Therefore, it is very important to be prepared for the worst. Also keep in mind that when you have made it through the switchboard, you can probe anywhere in a company for information. Be aware that you can get any information you want as long as you have what it takes: persistence, smarts, the right personality, and the requisite set of skills.

Some basic rules:

▲ Try to get the direct extension of the potential candidate and not his or her secretary's.
▲ Sound self-confident; be decisive when talking to the secretary.
▲ Be put through by a colleague if possible.
▲ Tell the secretary that you are seeking Mr. or Ms. X's assistance due to his or her great network in the field, to find someone for a position (you only say this line if you are being asked).
▲ Call the candidate later in the evening or early in the morning when the secretary might not be in.

There will always be several people who do not call you back. To make sure that you do not waste your time when calling, make it a rule to cover all the names on your call list at least once. Then start from the beginning again and go for round number two. Stop approaching people after leaving two messages if they have not called you back. They are blind shots and are not worth pursuing—you want motivated people as well as qualified. Most likely they are not interested in the opportunity you are presenting. But, if for some reason you know that someone is extremely appealing, you can always go a little further. If you compare it to fishing, you know that sometimes you have to fight a little harder for the big ones. But it is worth it if you catch one.

Direct Telephone Contact (Some Rules)

When you get through to the source or to potential candidates, keep in mind that these people probably get a lot of calls from people like you.

So you have to grab their attention quickly. When you speak, be as positive as possible about the assignment. Keep in mind that attitude is as important as presentation. The opening dialog could contain the following information:

- ▲ Name
- ▲ Executive search consultant or in charge of recruitment at Company X
- ▲ Currently looking for a director of manufacturing

Build up a personal relationship in the first few sentences

- ▲ Be short and direct; don't waste the candidate's time with explanations.
- ▲ Be aware that you have something to offer.

After the pitch, ask if the person would like to hear more, based on the brief information. If you feel that the person could be a candidate, mention to her that she has been highly recommended, which is why you are calling. Keep in mind that most people like to be flattered.

At this point, explain that you have heard great things, but you do not know details of her background. Before she gets a chance to answer, state the basic requirements for the position that you are looking to fill. At this stage you use the template shown in Figure 1.4. Then pause, because this is when you will get the feedback that lets you know whether the person is a possible candidate. By this firm and direct approach you will, after a maximum of three to five minutes, know if you want to continue talking to the candidate. If you sense a potential fit, your time on stage has come and the work begins. You now not only must describe and sell the opportunity, but also get as much information as possible about the individual. This should be done by calling her at home after work. If she appears to be on target and is open to listening, keep in mind that most candidates will not say yes in the first three minutes of the conversation, as switching jobs is not like buying dinner. As this is the starting point of a relationship, you have to be the prospect's friend throughout the process. With this attitude, you will be well respected even by the ones you reject.

If you do not know beforehand whether your contact is a source (i.e., someone who can recommend names to call) or a prospect (i.e., a potential candidate), you might close your pitch with some of these questions:

- ▲ "Do you know anyone who might be qualified and interested in something like this?"

▲ "Is this an opportunity that would be appropriate for someone with your background?"

▲ "Would you be interested in learning more about this opportunity?"

▲ "The next step would be for us to get some information on your background. Can we do that while we're on the phone right now?"

Repeat anything that is not clear. Try the statement, "My understanding of what you are saying is. . . ." or "Am I understanding you correctly when you say. . . ?" Very often the person you are speaking to might not have a résumé. If such is the case, ask him or her to prepare one. At the same time, keep in mind that the best way to get the information you need accurately and quickly is to get it over the phone. This is typically the best way to sketch someone's background.

Whenever a source refers someone, always ask for permission to use the source's name. Do not use the name if you are not sure that doing so is all right with the source. It is better to call the source back, just to double-check that you have permission. The source should certainly appreciate your conscientiousness about a matter as important as using his or her name.

You should also know that if you already have the names of prospects, sources are usually more forthcoming than if they must give the names. Ask the source to rank them and to tell you who is bad and who is good. This procedure works well with sources who just left a company or are still there.

In order to determine if you are dealing with the right candidates, you need to know where in the organization they stand. Therefore, it is important that you flesh out the organizational chart and clarify reporting relationships. You should ask your prospect for the titles of:

▲ His or her boss
▲ The boss's boss
▲ All direct reports and the number of people reporting to each of them
▲ Peers reporting to the same boss

If a candidate is not interested in the opportunity you present, always find out why. It may be something that can be dispelled. If not, source him for other potential candidates. If neither, leave your name and telephone number—always try if possible to get information on him or her for future reference. No matter what the outcome is, always be polite and understanding. Most likely you will need to speak to your contact again at a later point.

Documentation (Recording Information)

When searching for the right candidate, you will deal with many telephone calls and with a lot of information pertaining to each call. To make sure that you are in full control of the situation, be sure to write everything down, including information such as:

- ▲ Person to speak to (full name, address at work and home, telephone numbers, title, company)
- ▲ Details of the conversation, with time and date
- ▲ When to follow up again, with time and date
- ▲ What category the contact is (see the section "How to Use the Codes" in this chapter)

Documentation is one of the key elements that you need to master. You can never afford to be lazy with documentation, or you will lose the control you need in order to complete the search. Everything that you record must be identified with the year and the search. When you record summaries of the conversations you have with prospects and sources, it is very important not to generalize. Always get to the essence. Ask yourself why for every action you take. If someone declines, for example, it is not sufficient to say that he or she did not want to pursue. You have to record why he or she declined. If someone is very rude and behaves in a way that does not fit into the company's culture, you have to be specific. You could record: "He was very rude, which is why he is being declined. He made several remarks about people he worked with as being stupid and ignorant with intelligence on the level of a cow. He called his present boss a birdbrain." Even when someone is being interviewed, you should make conclusive notes. And again, you have to be specific.

If an executive search firm is involved, the researcher should pass the information or problems on to superiors; otherwise they will assume everything is fine. Furthermore, it is always better to address a problem sooner rather than later. If your sources and prospects are making the same remarks over and over, it is important to record them. This way, you can document why the original compensation package needs to be increased, with comments from such-and-such—including titles and companies—ideally with information about their current compensation, plus how much it would take to talk seriously about the job. Remember that if it becomes necessary to have the job upgraded, it is important to have a good deal of data to support this move. This is just one example of why it is of such great importance to be very good at recording information throughout the course of the search.

The main purpose behind putting everything in writing is to make things easier for yourself and at the same time enable you to make maximum use of the information that you gather. You must therefore not only write down everything of importance, but also organize it so you can easily retrieve what you need. If you are using professional executive search firms, be aware that one individual consultant might be working on as many as seven or eight searches simultaneously, so the need for keeping full control of what is going on is especially great. The bottom line is that you need a good system, and you must stick to it if you are going to control the information flow. The tools described later in this chapter should help you in getting organized. But, before you start, it is important to have a system to organize every step of the process, the big overall picture. This is why there is no substitute for the log, or the cycle of the candidates, and the search folder with the candidates.

Phone Log of Source or Prospect Call Sheets

Phone log and prospect call sheet documents track everyone you called in a particular search. It is helpful to organize the log when you start calling, by last name, especially if you do not use a computer system and utilize a so-called call sheet. If you use a computerized system, it is easy to run lists organized both by company and by last name. This allows you to review at a glance everyone you have spoken to at a given company or by last name. You do not have to write everything in full sentences. The main thing is to write down the most important facts, in an understandable manner. For example, if a prospect sounds good but is not interested, find out what it would take to get her interested: compensation, responsibilities, opportunities, job satisfaction, and whatever else is important. Be sure to write it down in the log. Everyone you speak to regarding a specific search should be recorded in the log. To make the log easy to retrieve at a later point, identify it with a number that pertains to the particular search. That numbered log will contain only individuals whom you have called or plan to call in reference to that particular search.

How to Use the Codes

To keep track of what stage or group the people in a search belong to at any given time, it is very important to code everyone in the log according to his or her status. This method is very common at the leading executive search firms. The codes presented in this section are being used by Ward Howell International and many other firms. As a rule, you should change the coding (group) when you have a good indication of the next event that is going to take place. This means that if, for example, someone you speak to (coded CLM, or *called and left message*—these codes are explained in the cycle of candidates in Figure 3.1) tells you that he or she could be interested, the code should be immediately changed to PSP (*prospect*). You do not have to wait for the résumé to arrive to change the code. The same goes for a prospect you have decided to interview. Even if the date has not been set, he or she immediately should be grouped as INV (*interview*). This code again should change right after the interview to either CND (*candidate*) or INQ (*interested but not qualified*).

By religiously sticking to the log and the coding, you will quickly be able to tell where you stand at any point during the search. But, in order for this system to work, you must always make good notes, and always make sure that your contacts have the right coding. You will quickly be able to make reports that tell you how many candidates you have, how many you have called, how many declined, and so forth.

Manual Versus Computerized Log

At most major executive search firms, people use computerized systems, but many people at smaller firms still use manual systems such as the old-fashioned call sheets (also called *contact sheets*). The main objective with any system is that you record the information that you need and make the system work in the best possible manner. If you use the manual method as the log, you need to make sure that you use the same kind of call sheet for everyone (see the example call sheet in Figure 3.2). It is also of great importance that you only have one contact (person) for each call sheet. You then need to organize every contact sheet alphabetically. All contact sheets should remain in a binder assigned to the particular search. The advantages with a manual system are that you do not need a computer,

Figure 3.1 The cycle of candidates.

CIP—At the beginning of a search, all people you plan to contact should be coded CIP (*contact in progress*) and thereby treated as sources. Once called, they change codes.

    CLM—When you have tried to make contact but have only been able to leave a message, use CLM (*called—left message*). When connection is made, the code changes.

      SRS—If somebody can provide help or assistance, they become *sources*. The code does not change after someone has become SRS.

      CNI—(*Candidate not interested*) When somebody is not interested and does not want to help out with names of potential candidates.

      PSP—Anyone who is interested and submits their paperwork (résumé) or gives their background over the phone becomes a potential *prospect*. After you have completed the development of a prospect, the code changes (*potential search prospect*).

        INQ—Someone is interested, *but not qualified.*

        INV 1—The prospect (PSP) appeared to be qualified for one more round in the process and has been scheduled for an *interview* with the search firm.

        INV 2—The prospect has been *interviewed* but a decision has not yet been made whether he is going to proceed. If the contact is not presented to the client, the code does not change.

          CND—A prospect who meets the requirements and appears to be a good match for a particular position and gets presented for the client as a *candidate.*

            PLC—The successful candidate who accepts the terms so that there can be a final agreement made between the two parties becomes the *placement.*

Figure 3.2 Example of call sheet.

CONTACT SUMMARY

Date: _____ Search #: _____

Name: _____

Title: _____

Bus.Tel.: _____ Home Tel.: _____

Mobile: _____

Pager: _____ Other: _____

Company: _____ From: _____ To: _____

Address: _____

City: _____

State: _____ Zip: _____

Source: _____ OK to mention: Yes   No

Compensation

Base: _____ Bonus: _____ Total: _____ Other: _____

Previous Employment

Title: _____

Company: _____ From: _____ To: _____

Title: _____

Company: _____ From: _____ To: _____

(Continued)

Figure 3.2 *(Continued)*

CONTACT SUMMARY

Education

School: _____ Degree: _____ Year: _____ Major: _____

School: _____ Degree: _____ Year: _____ Major: _____

School: _____ Degree: _____ Year: _____ Major: _____

Personal

Home Address: _____

_____

City: _____ State: _____ Zip: _____

Birthday: _____ Spouse: _____

Children: _____

Other Information: _____

Status

Initial Contact Date/Summary: _____

_____

_____

Résumé Received: _____ Résumé Current: _____ Interview Done: _____

Presented Client: _____ Interviewed Client: _____ Reference Rpt: _____

Offer Extended: _____ Offer Accepted: _____

Remarks (include contact code): _____

_____

_____

Figure 3.4 Example of report screen.

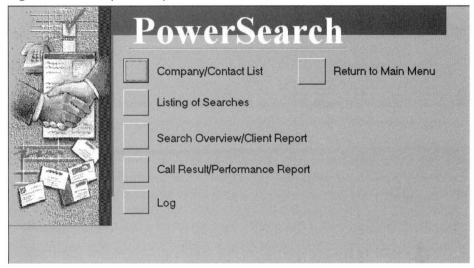

the searches (see Figure 3.4). The various reports available in PowerSearch are:

▲ Company/Contact List: A listing of all the target companies and target people attached to the particular searches. The list can be sorted in alphabetical order according to companies or people. The list gives you the person's full name, address, phone number, company, title, contact code, and last date when spoken to.

▲ Listing of Searches: A complete listing of all searches open and closed, with name of client, search number, title of position, and starting/ closing date for the search.

▲ Search Overview/Client Report: A control report that on one page presents an overview of all the developed prospects attached to each search. The report shows only name, title, and company for the developed people who are on the way to becoming the candidates or have been interviewed. If declined after the interview, they are automatically erased from the report. Next to each person there is a date when the person was developed. The report lists the status of all the searches going on in the office or that pertain to a particular consultant. The purpose is to show the bottom line of what you have accomplished at any given point by listing names of qualified people on each search.

▲ Call Result/Performance Report: This report allows you to monitor specifically what work has been done by each researcher or consultant during a set time period. You can choose any time period and track down how many calls each person in the office makes during this time and, of course, the results achieved. The report can be run by people or search number. For example, if you want to monitor a researcher's work for the last five days, you can get the bottom-line facts, such as how many calls the person has made on each search. You can also get information such as how many new prospects and candidates have been found and developed in the same time period.

▲ Log: This report gives you a listing of all the people who either have been or will be contacted for a particular search. Contact codes and all comments recorded are presented.

Candidate Backgrounds (Résumés)

During the Search

The résumés of interested candidates should be filed alphabetically by name in a folder or binder for the particular search (or if you have the capability, scanned into the computer system and filed there), while the search is being conducted. As this folder is the heart of the search, it is of great importance that there is only one candidate search folder for each search. It is also very important that all original paperwork (résumés) stays in the folder. If someone wants a candidate's paperwork, he or she must make a copy (or print one, if the résumé is in the computer). The best binder to use is one that is alphabetized so you can enter people according to their last names. Also, be sure to mark (code) all the candidates who have a fit, and those who decline, so you can quickly separate the two groups. On the top of the front of the folder, you need to make a sticker with the following information:

▲ Search number and client name (company)
▲ Title of position

The search folder works as a control tool, indicating whether you have done your job. If you do not have any candidates in the search folder, you need to work harder. If you still have candidates in the folder long after the search, it means that you have not closed out people and followed them up as you were supposed to.

After the Search

After the search has been successfully completed, the candidate's background should go to one of three different places:

1. *CND file.* All the candidates who become final candidates should be alphabetically organized with appraisal, reference report, and all other paperwork in a special drawer or cabinet for candidates (CNDs). These candidates are considered to be the most important ones, except for the placement. Because they have gotten so far in the process to become finalists, they are usually excellent candidates. Their personalities and skill sets might be perfect for a subsequent search. In addition, these people could become excellent sources for future searches, if you maintain a good relationship with them. After all, you basically gave them an opportunity to improve their lives by inviting them to participate in the search process.

2. *General filing cabinet.* Potential candidates who have an interesting background, but did not become CNDs, should be filed according to industry (alphabetically) in the general filing cabinet. When filing résumés, it is important to mark each with that person's industry and function group. For a filing system to work well it cannot be too detailed. See Appendix for example codings that can be used. *Note:* A similar coding system can also be used for the electronic system. Most leading executive search firms such as Ward Howell International have created categories that have been based on the SIC codes.

3. *Waste basket.* Résumés of people who did not become CNDs and who do not have an interesting background should be thrown away.

Company File

The company file includes organizational charts, lists of names and published company research, including directories, annual reports, and so forth. The purpose for creating this file is that you might need this information at a later point if you need to look into these companies again. A separate set of industry and function files should be maintained so you can find information according to topic.

4 | Interviewing and Screening

When calling potential prospects, it is of great importance to be able to screen people, to separate the gold from the silver. It is very important to be good at screening, so that you avoid wasting your own time and, of course, the time of the people that you contact. Not all identified potential candidates will have equal credentials for the job. It is therefore very important to sort the right candidates from the wrong ones as early as possible in the process. This is of great interest not only for yourself, so you do not have to waste time on unproductive interviews, but also in the interest of the candidate, who also does not want to waste time. There are basically two different screenings or telephone interviews that take place when you hook up with someone who could be the right one:

1. The first interview, called *basic screening,* is conducted when you want to figure out if someone is a fit. This is when you are using a template.
2. The second telephone interview, called *development of a potential candidate,* is conducted after you have decided that someone appears to be on target, but you need more complete background information in order to have an accurate picture. It also enables you to get right to the questions and the essence of the candidate when later interviewing this person.

Basic Screening

In trying to decide whether to go further with a candidate, you will sometimes find that the candidate's written presentation (résumé) does not clearly state what you need to know. By comparing the requirements listed in the template you prepared at the very beginning of the search with the candidate's résumé, you should, in at least half the cases, be able to tell if somebody should continue in the process. But, there will always be people you need to question by phone in order to screen them. In some cases you will even deal with people who are afraid to submit a résumé (even if they are very interested). When this is the case, you just have to get everything you need over the phone so you can create your own complete résumé on the prospect. During the telephone interview process you always need to ask the same questions, so it is very helpful to use the template.

If the person in question has received the position specification/candidate profile, keep in mind that you can ask him to take the page with requirements listed and match them up with his own background, in writing. When doing this, the person has to be specific. If you choose to do the matchup at this point, you should not ask the prospect to do the matchup after the face-to-face interview.

Candidate Development

The development of a potential candidate interview is used when you want to flesh them out, after knowing or believing that they are on target. The information that you gather is basically what you need in preparation for the in-person interview. By following the checklist below, you should be able to gain enough information to write a career brief before even meeting with the candidate (see the example in the section "Written Presentation of Candidates"). By obtaining every piece of background information before meeting someone, you will find it easier to spot the weak spots or potential gaps in the career history or moves that appear to be happening. You can and should, basically, by having someone "developed" before the meeting, be able to cut to the meat. In developing a candidate workup, you should obtain the following information about prospects that you plan to interview:

Checklist for Candidate Development

☐ Education and work experience, dates with gaps reconciled
☐ Succinct organization descriptions—what business, scale for each company
☐ Position titles
☐ Organizational chart (above, on line, and below)/reporting relationship
☐ Size of the department, division, or group responsible for

☐ Position responsibilities
☐ At least three major accomplishments in each position
☐ Motives for interest in position
☐ Reasons for job change
☐ Personality
☐ Compensation; age
☐ Thoughts on why this prospect might be a good candidate
☐ Accomplishments relating to the specific responsibilities enumerated in the spec
☐ Details of source(s) by whom mentioned
☐ Level of interest and obstacles

When covering the foregoing information for a prospect, remember to write down the search number, log number, date, and year as well. If the next step is to interview the prospect, make a copy of the information covered and place the original in the search folder and the copy in the interview folder.

The Face-to-Face Interview

Even if you are able to find highly qualified candidates purely by working the phone, everything must still be verified by a face-to-face interview. A candidate is not guaranteed the job even if he or she has the right work experience, education, and excellent references. Just as important is the personality of the individual in question. This can best be experienced through a face-to-face interview. There are also certain questions that are best asked of somebody when you meet him or her in person. The same goes for uncovering certain weaknesses. Someone with good interview skills should be able to obtain the necessary information in short order. In order to be a successful interviewer and thereby get the results that you want, you need to:

▲ Be well prepared (study the write-up and comments that you earlier obtained over the telephone).
▲ Know what questions to ask (know what you need to probe on), and do not be afraid to ask them.
▲ Have a very good understanding of what your company's needs are.
▲ Understand the personalities of the people with whom the candidate will be working.

When you spend time with someone, you usually get a certain gut feeling about him or her. This gut feeling should become an important part of the process. During the entire interview, let the candidate do most of the talking. Try to stick to the 80/20 rule; ask questions 20 percent of the time and you will be able to listen 80 percent of the time. It is very important to know in advance what you are going to say and ask, because this enables you to dedicate the greater part of your time to listening. Always use the assessment report (see Figure 4.1).

An interview should be handled professionally from both sides. This means that a confirmation letter should be sent to the prospect's home address with information on time, date, and place. After all, you are the one who contacted the candidate. When the potential candidate shows up, certain factors can affect both parties:

The Prospect's Expectations

▲ The prospect should not have to wait. If the interview is to take place at 2:00 P.M., then that is when everything should get started.
▲ The prospect should get the feeling that the interviewer is well prepared and has spent time reading the written material (résumé, write-up, etc.).
▲ Information about the further process, the next step (follow-ups when promised) is of great importance.

The Interviewer's Expectations

▲ The candidate is expected to be on time.
▲ The interviewer expects to meet someone who is polite, eager, and well groomed. Many candidates unfortunately do not realize that if their behavior or dress is off the wall, the interview is really over before it has even started.

The interview should follow the flow of the written candidate presentation. After some social chatting, it is important to figure out what the candidate was like through high school and college and what events in the candidate's youth might have shaped his or her career. Also attempt to cover the different personal events during the candidate's career, such as a divorce or health problems, and of course areas of interest at the present time. If the client likes to go mountain climbing, it is nice to have a candidate who also enjoys mountain climbing.

During the interview, look constantly for personal impressions such as posture, self-assurance, presence, enthusiasm, ego, aggressiveness, abil-

Figure 4.1 Example of assessment report.

☐ **NOT PASS**   ☐ **PASS**

ASSESSMENT REPORT

Candidate's Name:	Search number:
Title:	Telephone number:
Organization:	Address:
Consultant:	Date:

Breakdown of points:
3 points = Very good   2 points = OK or borderline   1 point = Not strong enough

▲ Problem solving: Score (1–3) =

    Strengths:

    Weaknesses:

▲ Communication: Score (1–3) =

    Strengths:

    Weaknesses:

▲ Motivation: Score (1–3) =

    Strengths:

    Weaknesses:

▲ Interpersonal: Score (1–3) =

    Strengths:

    Weaknesses:

▲ Administrative: Score (1–3) =

    Strengths:

    Weaknesses:

▲ Final assessment of candidate (comments):

ity to get to the point quickly, ability to articulate accomplishments, memory, quick mind, personality, sense of humor, and other traits. Good questions to ask are: How would your present boss describe you? Are there any personal factors that could affect your employment? When conducting the interview you can never be lazy about making notes. Another important rule is to try to stick to open-end questions (unless you want to clarify whether the candidate has certain skills or background required for the position, which can be answered with yes or no). When you ask questions, do not show signs of agreement. To get the most out of the time, do not comment at all. Just listen very carefully, and ask the right questions. (Remember that in some cultures, it is illegal to ask certain questions—check this out for the country in which you are interviewing people.)

Basically five different areas need to be covered in the interview. They are:

1. Problem-solving skills
2. Communication skills
3. Motivation
4. Interpersonal skills
5. Administrative skills

The list of questions provided in the example that follows is merely a guideline, including the five groups in the previous list. Sometimes certain questions are more important than others, all depending on the situation. Always keep in mind the purpose of the interview: to determine whether the candidate is a good match for your client's needs. Therefore, it is very important to keep the position requirements very central when asking the questions. As you have only a certain amount of time available for the interview, all the preparation and homework must be done beforehand. Before meeting with somebody you should have sufficient information to be able to write the career brief on the candidate. This preparation also enables you to focus on potential weak spots to a greater extent, and to get an opportunity to focus on the person's personality and potential abilities, thereby enabling you to make an accurate assessment. After the interview, you should be able to answer the three crucial questions:

1. Is the candidate able to do the job?
2. Is the candidate willing to do the job?
3. Is the candidate going to be manageable?

Time Frame

Never try to make a marathon session out of the meeting. Do not chit-chat more than necessary. Spend a maximum of ten minutes to break the ice. Always get to the point when you speak. Keep in mind that you are in charge. To make sure that you cover everything, you need to tell the candidate up front how many minutes you have available and what you need to cover. (The meeting should last from one to two hours—maximum.)

Documentation You Should Bring to the Interview

When interviewing someone, you should always bring the following information, which, of course, has to be studied beforehand:

☐ The candidate's résumé with notes from the development.
☐ A list of comments and initial questions based on telephone contact and the résumé. You should know what specific areas you need to probe in order to feel that you have a complete picture of the candidate.
☐ A list of interview questions (the list in this chapter can be used as a guideline).

When you have finished, pull back and consider with the candidate the implications of what he or she has just told you. Spot any gaps in necessary experience and discuss these. It may be that you mutually come to the conclusion that the job is not a fit. If a candidate is on the borderline, you can honestly say, "You realize that in my terms you would be on the 'light' end of the candidate scale, although this does not necessarily disqualify you completely." If this is the case, he or she will no longer be the number one candidate, but more of a reserve, unless the requirements change in favor of the prospect in question.

Matchup is a technique used by leading headhunters to build a case for a candidate. It basically means that you ask the person you just interviewed to prepare (at home after the interview) and submit in three-quarters to one page the reasons why he or she should get the job. This information can also be of great help when writing the candidate report. You will also get a feel for the candidate's motivation for the position.

Immediately after the interview, while everything is still fresh, you should prepare the assessment report. This report is basically a one-page summary of the interview, where you list the strengths and weaknesses of the candidate on the five previously mentioned areas. This report is also where you list, in a few sentences, why you think this candidate fits or does not fit the particular position.

Sample Interview Questions

If candidate has not been developed, this has to be done first; see previous section "Candidate Development."

General Start-up Questions

1. Draw the organizational chart of your present company, including your specific department. What is your role?
2. What indicators measure your performance within your current position?

Approaches to Problem Resolution

3. Were you ever in a situation where you had too many things to do in the time available? How did you handle it?
4. What kinds of decisions are most difficult for you?
5. Do you discuss important decisions with anyone?
6. Imagine a situation where you find yourself without the specific technical knowledge to perform a task essential to a project. What would you do?
7. Imagine you are asked to set up a task force to investigate the advantages of using temporary office workers in your company. If there were no precedent for establishing such a task force, how would you do it?
8. If you had to interview someone for a position on your staff, and you lacked the technical depth to understand their competence, how would you handle the interview?
9. What major problems have you identified in your current position that were previously overlooked, and what have you done about it?
10. What kind of people do you feel represent a challenge to work with and how do you best deal with them?
11. What was your biggest challenge this last year at work, and how did you reach a solution?
12. What was your worst mistake during the last year, and what did you do about it?

13. What has been the toughest decision you have made in your career?
14. In terms of problem resolution would you describe yourself to be more analytical or intuitive? Give specific examples.
15. How do you react if someone criticizes the work you have done? Give specific examples.
16. What notable successes have you had in problem solving for your company?

Communication Skills

17. How would your boss describe you?
18. How would your closest friends and family describe you?
19. How would you describe yourself in terms of weaknesses and strengths?
20. In considering important career questions, what impact does your closest family play in the decision making?
21. What do you do for relaxation, or what means a lot to you, besides work?
22. If you could start again, what would you do differently?
23. Do you consider yourself to be more or less creative than your boss and coworkers? Give examples.
24. How do you tell your boss or board of directors that the action is wrong, or at least that they are going in a direction with which you are in total disagreement?
25. What business or social situations make you feel awkward?
26. How have you dealt with an angry or frustrated customer? Tell me about it.
27. How do you turn things around when the initial impression of you is bad?
28. Was there ever a time when your timing was bad? Tell me about it.
29. What is the most memorable mistake you have made in dealing with people?

Motivation

30. Why are you interested in this particular opportunity, and why should we hire you?
31. How do you motivate people?
32. What are three examples of major projects you initiated at work, or in your spare time, that you did not have to do, within the last two years?

33. Tell me about your workday. When do you start and when do you finish?
34. If you rank yourself in terms of college, how did you do in regard to grades and ranking?
35. What mission or thinking do you follow when you work?
36. Do you ever find it necessary to go beyond the call of duty to get the job done?
37. What have you done to become more effective in your career?
38. When the pressure is on, where does your extra energy come from?
39. Do you ever take work home?
40. What kind of initiative do you take in a challenging situation? Give me an example.
41. What means more to you in the job—money or personal growth?
42. Recount when you made a major change. Why did you do it and how did it work?
43. Was there a time when you failed, but came right back again? Give me an example.
44. With regard to your job, where do you see yourself five years from now?

Interpersonal Skills

45. Do you socialize with your coworkers outside of work, and why?
46. Have you laid off many people during your career? When doing so, how have you done it?
47. In what way do you give subordinates feedback?
48. When recruiting new people, do you look for specific characteristics? If so, what are those characteristics?
49. How do you work with new and weak members of your group?
50. Who is the best manager that you know of and why?
51. How do you deal with employees who are strong performers?
52. Getting the job done involves gathering information and input from others. How do you do this?
53. What is the toughest communication problem you have faced?
54. Have you ever verbally convinced someone of an approach or an idea? Tell me about it.
55. How do you perform as a speaker or motivator in front of large and small groups? Give specific examples.
56. When has your verbal communication been important enough to follow up in writing?

57. Are there situations better suited to written communication?
58. What do you admire and dislike the most, and why?

Management/Administration

59. How would you characterize your management style?
60. What is the limit of your management responsibilities? Explain the types of decisions that are beyond your authority.
61. How would you prioritize your work schedule during a busy week?
62. To what degree do you give people freedom at work? How do you ensure that it does not get out of hand?
63. Are there certain tasks that a manager can never delegate? If so, what are those tasks?
64. Do you consider yourself to be replaceable? What would happen with the day-to-day business at your company if you decided as of today to not return to your job again?
65. As a manager have you changed your organization, and why?
66. How do you inspire your subordinates?
67. How are you with discipline in terms of your employees? What do you do to ensure that efficiency is kept at a high level and that people follow the orders you give them?
68. How do you discipline people (nonperformers)?
69. What are the most common problems or challenges that you are facing in your job? How do you deal with it?
70. Do you consider yourself to be better at strictly planning and *then* delegating or the other way around?
71. How would you rate your management skills to the former manager in your position, and why?
72. How would you react if one of your workers told you that you were wrong in one of your decisions?

Written Presentation of Candidates

Career Brief

After a candidate proves suitable in the interview the next step is to create a written candidate report (see Figure 4.2). (If you are using an executive search firm to assist you, it should to present you with a complete written report before you even see any candidates.) The written presentation basi-

Figure 4.2 *(Continued)*

___

After two years as an ISM he was again promoted to more responsibility as the Director of Information Systems and Distribution Operations. This job has been the most challenging in his career. For the first eleven months he averaged eighty hours a week, due to cleanup of the mess left to him by his predecessor. His favorite and best assignment at this position has been to implement AS/400 warehousing systems at four regional locations. During this process John also attended evening school for two years, which resulted in him getting a Bachelor Degree in Management Information Systems in 1995. His current situation as Director of Information Systems and Distribution Operator is the reason for wanting to pursue the opportunity at Belt Buckle International. John strongly feels that he cannot move further up the ladder in the organization. As well, he feels it is time to change scenery.

ASSESSMENT OF STRENGTHS AND WEAKNESSES

Perceived Strengths

John believes some of his strengths are:

▲ Proven leadership abilities
▲ Strong technical skills and a solid programming background
▲ Thinking ahead
▲ Getting along easily with others
▲ Good at strategy development

Based on my own assessment, John offers the following:

▲ Good interpersonal skills
▲ Good financial judgment in regards to expenditures
▲ John appears to be a solid person with good values
▲ Good sense of humor and likeable personality

Potential Weaknesses

▲ At times John talks too fast and uses too many technical words.
▲ He has never had the amount of responsibility that the position at Belt Buckle International requires.
▲ It appears that he at times can lose his temper.
▲ At times he can be a little egocentric.

(Continued)

Figure 4.2 *(Continued)*

PERSONAL CHARACTERISTICS

John seems to be a person with good interpersonal skills and solid values. He said that some of his personal values include honesty, integrity, and treating others fairly and well. John said he is the kind of person who thrives in an environment where there is a great deal of change. He also said that he enjoys working closely with other people and welcomes opportunities for leadership. If he were to leave Murphy Books he would like to work in an environment where people want to change and grow. John would like an intellectually challenging environment where people also enjoy their work. Further he would like to work for an organization that relaxes its investments in information systems technology. John feels that his biggest limitation for the job is having to move again.

His wife works part-time at the local grocery store. Their daughter, at three, is planning to start kindergarten next year.

VERIFICATION OF CREDENTIALS

The following information has been verified by direct contact with the appropriate sources:

▲ Academic credentials
▲ Employment
▲ Preliminary reference checks

Peter Smith   Los Angeles, June 3, 1998
Consultant

cally reflects the interviewer's observation about the candidate and his or her fit for the position. This presentation consists of two parts. The first part is a detailed *career brief,* which is basically a very detailed résumé, fully written out. This document is filled with facts and includes extensive details about the work history. It is always helpful to start out by writing the career brief to ensure that you get the basic information documented first. Make sure that sufficient information is included. Always be very specific. Every sentence should be short and precise. The career brief should include the following information on the candidate (in chronological order):

- Age, marital status
- Full name and address with phone numbers at home and work
- Educational background (degree, institution, location, month and year finished)
- Professional experience (for each position):

  - Name of company
  - Sales dollars or number of employees
  - Department or division size (sales or number of employees)
  - Reporting relationship
  - Company products or services provided
  - Most important accomplishments (sectioned in bullet points—a minimum of three for each position)
  - Dates for starting and ending each position
  - Compensation (complete information on what the salary package includes)

Career Appraisal

The second part of the candidate presentation is the *career appraisal,* which in a storylike way takes you through a person's life from cradle to grave. This is a more personal way of giving the client insight into the candidate, including personal observations of the candidate's personality. The appraisal normally covers the following four areas.

Section One

The appraisal should start out with a paragraph that introduces the candidate, to help the reader to understand where he is coming from. It basically means to follow in the footsteps of the candidate from childhood to the finish of his higher education. Try to answer:

- ▲ Where did he grow up?
- ▲ What was the family situation?
- ▲ What did the parents do?
- ▲ Where did he go to college, and why was this decision made?
- ▲ What did he study and why?
- ▲ How did he do in college?
- ▲ What interests did he have outside of school?

Section Two

The middle paragraphs review highlights and accomplishments in the candidate's career that are not included in the résumé. These paragraphs normally include tasks and achievements relevant to what the client wants (matchup in requirements) in the position for which he is searching, why the candidate made employment changes—essentially the highlights of the candidate's career. It is important to finish by explaining what the candidate is presently doing, and if not presently employed, why. You should also include comments on why the candidate might want to leave his or her present company (if employed) and why he or she is interested in this particular position. When writing this paragraph start with the first job and finish with the present one.

Section Three

The next paragraph should summarize your personal impressions of the candidate in regard to strengths and weaknesses (relate this to the particular position for which the candidate is being considered). This is your assessment based on your interaction with the candidate. Start out by listing the perceived strengths and finish with the perceived weaknesses.

Section Four

The last paragraph is about personal attributes and characteristics, such as personality, mobility for the position, and any obstacles: the candidate's wishes or expectations (what will make him or her accept the position), the candidate's own perception of his or her own weaknesses. Information on the candidate's family situation should also be included with information on what each member is doing.

5 | Reference Checks

Once you have identified potential candidates who are both motivated and appear to match the requirements for a specific assignment, you have done only a part of the job. You not only want to find who appears to be the right person for the job, but also to make sure that he or she is. If you bought a $300,000 house, you would surely have crawled underneath the house or had someone to do it to have the piles checked out. If not, the house could cost you even more. You cannot afford to overlook any information. Extensive research and reference checks can help you sort out the rising stars from the falling ones.

The best guide to what an executive will do in the future is to look at what he or she has done in the past. This means tracing his or her progress—childhood, school, college, and business career—in detail, month by month. You will be looking for evidence of recurring habits (traits) that make the executive a good employment risk. You have to check out the specific achievements with each employer, reasons for joining and leaving, how he or she got along with colleagues and superiors, and salary history. All this information can easily be obtained by following the steps in the executive search research model explained in this chapter. By learning the steps and applying them in a professional manner, you can minimize the risk of a wrong placement.

Academic claims should always be verified. This can be done by calling or writing to the candidate's college to check whether he or she graduated, and in what year. All you need is the candidate's full name and social security number. You should also check the candidate's credit report and any criminal record. As all of this checking is very personal, it is very important to obtain the candidate's authorization to conduct the check. Many researchers also choose to conduct an extensive news search by Lexis & Nexis and Info-Track (if in the United States) to check to see whether the person in question has been mentioned in the media, and if so, why. In summary a potential candidate is checked in secrecy by:

- ▲ Preliminary reference check
- ▲ Regular reference check
- ▲ Academic claims verified
- ▲ Credit
- ▲ Criminal record
- ▲ News search

Most of the candidates who are in the process already have a job and feel happy about their situation. Nobody knows that they are considering other opportunities except you. If someone at his or her current job knew anything, the candidate would be at risk of losing that job or standing. To avoid this (and the resulting enemies and bad reputation that will kill you in the marketplace), you have to follow certain procedures. Remember that all it takes to cause a problem is one wrong telephone call or an unfortunate phrasing during the course of a reference check.

Because the reference check is a sensitive matter, you should be very careful with reference checking people before they have become the final candidates. Protecting the confidentiality of discussions with an employed candidate must be an absolute priority for both you and the potential new employer. But, as your interest is to weed out the wrong candidates, you want to get some kind of feedback from the marketplace about your candidate. You do so by the preliminary reference check, which is based on light conversations with a couple of people who know of your candidate. The extensive regular reference check is done later when the candidate is at least one of the finalists.

Unemployed candidates or those whose decision to leave their current position is known can be asked for reference names immediately. Candidates who have been approached about a new position, however, will often request that reference checking be delayed until later, when both parties have expressed an interest in proceeding. But the other checks, such as verification of academic records, credit, criminal record, and news search, should always be completed at the point where you feel that someone appears to become a final candidate. If you are using an executive search firm, you should expect the firm to have done this before you are being asked to meet someone.

Résumé Inflation

Résumé inflation is a term that is frequently used in the context of reference checking. It means:

"Intentionally misrepresenting, distorting, or otherwise providing less than truthful information in one's résumé or in a job interview for purposes of personal career advancement."

In 1985 Ward Howell, one of the oldest and largest executive search firms in the world, conducted an extensive study on the subject of résumé inflation (see Figure 5.1). The survey was based on interviews conducted with more than 500 executives in general management positions in large and medium-sized companies. In addition, more than 250 human resources (HR) and personnel specialists in large and medium-sized companies who had experienced résumé inflation also participated. Recent updates of the study show that the numbers are just as valid today.

Preliminary Reference Check

The preliminary reference check preferably should be approved by the candidate, although this does not always happen. Speaking to one or two references for a few minutes just to get a thumbnail sketch should suffice for this check. You must be extremely cautious with your phrasing. You would very much like to know if you have a diamond or nickel candidate, but you also would hate to lose this person because you make a mistake. Months of work can be wasted with one wrong phone call. The people you speak to during the preliminary reference check should not be too close, or under any circumstance a superior at the current company. If possible you should avoid people in the prospect's company at this point. It is best to speak to someone to whom your candidate previously reported. Here is an example of how to properly phrase such an inquiry:

"My name is John Smith and I am calling from company X [the name of the company that you are recruiting to]. I am contacting you because I am trying to find out more about one particular individual you know. Do you happen to have a few minutes available right now?"

"Yes."

"This call concerns Mr. Dick Jones. Before we start, I want to inform you that Mr. Jones has not contacted us nor is he in a recruitment process of any kind. As a matter of fact we have never even spoken to Mr. Jones. The reason for this call is that the individual's name, on a couple of occasions, has surfaced and we therefore want to try to get a thumbnail sketch on him, as we one day might have an assignment that could fit with his background. It is also of great importance that you do not tell anybody

Figure 5.1 Statistics.
Table 1   Executive Experience with Résumé Inflation During the Past Year

	Percentage of Executives
Who have discovered instances of résumé inflation	26
Who have not experienced the problem	74

Table 2   Executives Encountering Misrepresentation

Job Area	Percentage
General Management	33
Personnel	31
Finance, Accounting, Control	29
Marketing	27
Manufacturing and Production	17
Engineering and R&D	13
All others combined	24

Table 3   Falsified Components of Employee's Credentials

Résumé Claim	Percentage of Respondents With Falsification
Academic credentials	62
Compensation history	43
Responsibilities in previous positions	42
Accomplishments in previous positions	34
Criminal record	25
Interpersonal relationships	15
Professional licenses	10
Dates of employment	7
Management style	7
Credit history	6
Reasons for leaving previous position	5
Problem-solving abilities	4
Omitting job from employment history	3
Military record	2
Family relationships	2

These three tables should help you understand the great importance of running extensive checks on candidates before you take them on board. You cannot afford not to run the checks.

Source: Ward Howell International, 1985.

about this conversation, as the individual has not been contacted and also is not being considered for a position."

After the introduction you can ask questions like:

- ▲ How long have you known Mr. Jones, and in what capacity and how often did you interact with him?
- ▲ What is your impression of him as a person and as a worker? How did he perform?
- ▲ What do you consider his strong points to be?
- ▲ Would you rehire him or recommend him for other similar positions?
- ▲ Does Mr. Jones have any particular limitations or weaknesses?

Regular Reference Check

The regular reference check is where you really pick a candidate apart. This check may take sixty minutes or longer. To be successful, it requires a lot of effort from not only the referee, but also you. You must be prepared and know what to ask. The regular reference check should be extensive and thorough, because this is the last chance you get to make discoveries that support or weaken the candidacy of the person in question. When asking somebody to spend up to one hour to give information about a candidate, keep in mind that this person is doing you a big favor. Such people usually have a busy schedule. Therefore, you should adjust according to their needs and conduct the reference check at a time convenient for them. You should ask them what time is the most convenient. If they tell you that they do not have the time when you call, just make a phone appointment for later. If you cannot reach your reference and have to leave a message, state your name and firm and that you are calling to conduct a reference check. Never leave the name of the candidate, as this is a violation of the candidate's privacy.

Sometimes, references are reluctant to give out negative information. Some companies have an official policy not to give out information beyond dates the person worked there, for legal reasons, and you might not be able to obtain more information, especially from HR personnel. By using a professional telephone manner combined with a familiarity with the candidate and an understanding of the new position under consideration, you usually can encourage other references to be candid. References should be told the specifications of the new position and asked to comment upon the suitability of the candidate for such an opportunity. Past compensation, dates of employment, reasons for leaving, and other confirming data should be obtained as a part of the process.

When seeking a reference, it is very important that you speak to people who can give you the information you need. These references should be from the last three companies. The most recent references are the most important. You should talk to the closest supervisor to whom your candidate reported, the closest coworker, and someone who reported directly to your candidate. You should aim for this selection as a minimum. The candidate might suggest additional references who know his or her work. If you speak to someone in the last group make sure that he or she is not related to the candidate or a best friend. During an extensive reference check you might end up speaking to as many as twelve people! It is better to talk to too many people than too few. It is also important to remember that each search is different, and so is each candidate, so the questions you ask the reference must take into account the requirements of the position and any particular concerns that might exist. You may develop a slightly different guide for each candidate on the same search.

When contacting the references, you should follow a written guideline. This guideline should be kept in front of you to ensure that all concerns are covered and that you do not get sidetracked. With practice, you can become very skilled at conducting a reference check. But even if you have not done a check before or for some time, with a good guideline or list of questions handy, you do not have to worry, even if a reference call comes right in the middle of something else. Another key rule is, always ask the most important questions first in case the conversation becomes very short.

The reference check is supposed to help you uncover or strengthen any uncertainties about the candidate. Always ask for examples, and probe if you hear something out of the ordinary. For example, if you hear about a weakness, keep probing and get other references to comment, and be sure to get examples. Of course, everything you hear should be documented, because you will need to make a written report after speaking to all the references.

You should follow certain guidelines in order to get the information that you need and at the same time leave the references with a professional impression. At the beginning of any conversation with a reference you should identify yourself and the candidate in question, and inform the reference that your candidate has asked (or at least given permission) for you to contact the reference. The first information that you want to get from the reference includes:

▲ Full name (including middle names)
▲ Address at work and home (including phone numbers both places)
▲ Current title
▲ Relationship to the candidate

   ▲ How long has he or she known the candidate (dates)?
   ▲ What kind of relationship (work or private)?
   ▲ How did they work together (sketch up the setting with titles) and how long?
   ▲ How frequent was interaction?

After confirming the nature of the reference's relationship to the candidate, you can start asking the questions that will enable you to gain more insight into your candidate.

Following is a list of some suggested areas that you should cover when conducting a reference check. Also remember to ask open-ended questions. Never lead the reference by asking close-ended questions, that is, questions that can be answered with yes or no.

Reference Report

All the information that you get from the reference check must be written down. Out of all the information you obtain, you need to create reference reports. If you are using an executive search firm, it will present you with these reports before you make a final agreement with a candidate. The reports are a result of the information gathered from all the references (see Figures 5.2 and 5.3). Each statement should contain at least five reference briefs. Each brief should contain the following information:

▲ The relationship to the candidate
▲ Comments on specific skills, expertise, and achievements
▲ Personal characteristics, attributes, and management style
▲ Relationship with superiors, subordinates, and staff
▲ Comments on why the candidate would be a good fit for the position
▲ Areas that need improvement (weaknesses)
▲ Comments on any domestic, personal, or financial difficulties that might interfere with the candidate's performance
▲ Thoughts on why the candidate is considering the position
▲ Other comments on the candidate

Figure 5.2 Reference questions.

Candidate's Name:	Search number:
Reference's Name:	Date and year:
Title:	Telephone number:
Organization:	Address:

1. How long have you known the candidate (CND) and in what capacity?

2. Comment on the performance of the CND. What were the CND's major accomplishments?

3. What are the CND's major strengths? Weaknesses? (If no response, probe areas that could use development.)

4. Comment on CND's relationships with superiors, subordinates, and peers.

5. Describe the CND's management style.

6. Why might the CND be considering a move at this time?

7. Have there ever been any domestic, personal, or financial difficulties that would have interfered with the CND's work?

8. What is your assessment of the CND's suitability for the position?

9. Is there anything else we should know about the CND? Do you have any specific advice to give to the CND's future employer?

Reminder: Thank the reference. Assure confidentiality. If appropriate, tell the reference that you will let him or her know the outcome of the search.

SAVE THIS FORM AND INCORPORATE INTO DOCUMENTS

_____

Consultant's Name

Figure 5.3 Confidential reference report.

ABC Headhunting, Inc.

CONFIDENTIAL REFERENCE REPORT OF CANDIDATE

JOHN HARRISON

FOR THE POSITION: DIRECTOR, MANAGEMENT INFORMATION SYSTEMS WITH
BELT BUCKLE INTERNATIONAL, INC., CHICAGO, ILLINOIS

DATE: 03/20/98

CONFIDENTIAL: This report has been prepared for the use of the Belt Buckle International. It contains confidential information. Its distribution should be controlled and limited to the executives concerned.

Candidate: J. Harrison/Ref.: R. Hummel

John Harrison

1. Mr. Rafer Hummel
Senior Consultant
Computer Systems Inc.
999 Colorado Avenue
Santa Monica, CA 90401
310-999-1111 (p) 310-999-6666 (w)

Mr. Hummel is currently a senior consultant at one of the leading computer consulting firms in the country. He has had this position since leaving Murphy Books, in Momence, Illinois, in January 1990. At Murphy Books Mr. Hummel was the manager of MIS, and thereby Mr. Harrison's direct boss during the time period Jan. 1986 to Jan. 1990. Mr. Hummel interacted with Harrison on a daily basis for a total of four years. They had a purely working relationship and did not know each other before they started to work together, nor did they keep in touch later.

When asked about Harrison's skills, expertise, and achievements, the reference made the following comments:

Mr. Harrison is a strong technical person. He is a hands-on person who is not afraid to get his hands dirty in order to get the job done. In addition, he is dependable and can always be counted on to complete his work. Mr. Harrison's greatest achievement was to not only realize that the company had a poor order entry system, but also to create a new electronic system with his own initiative. Without guidance and letting the new added workload affect his daily assignments, he spent his weekends for a total period of three months to come up with the new electronic order entry system, which is still in use today.

(Continued)

Figure 5.3 *(Continued)*

2. **When asked about Harrison's personal characteristics, attributes, and manage-**
   ment style, the references made the following comments:

He is a true team player with an always positive attitude. He did not have a staff at
the time, but it was noticed by the management that Harrison had strong leadership
and people skills, and it was just a matter of time before he climbed the corporate
ladder in the firm. He was always creative and had the ability to connect with people
from all different walks of life. Harrison is not only a hardworking person, but also
a compassionate human being. One event in particular took place that showed what
kind of person he was and that gave him great respect by his coworkers; another
person in the same department who had the same job as Harrison at the time went
through difficult times due to a serious illness his wife had. Every week there would
be a day or two when the coworker did not show up at work because he did not
succeed to pull himself together. With no complaint Harrison would take over his
work. Mr. Harrison's added efforts did not affect his regular performance and after
a period of six months the coworker's wife recovered and everything went back to
normal. If it had not been for Mr. Harrison, the coworker would probably have been
fired. But, Harrison is an upright person. If a coworker did not perform and there
was no reason for him not to, Harrison would not hesitate to tell his coworker to
straighten up and get to work. The same went for situations where the management
treated subordinates poorly. Harrison is also a fun person, outgoing, has a good sense
of humor, and is very professional.

3. **When asked about Harrisons's relationships with superiors, subordinates, and**
   staff, the reference made the following comments:

He was extremely easy to work with and he had an excellent relationship with both
peers and superiors. He always worked with people rather than against them. This
was clearly demonstrated when a new coworker came into his department and was,
for no reason, being hostile to Harrison. Instead of going behind his back and reporting the situation directly to his superior, he worked with the new person. The end
result was that the new worker eventually came around and with time the hostility
went away.

4. **When asked about Harrison's suitability for the position at Belt Buckle Interna-**
   tional, the reference made the following comments:

His excellent track record speaks for itself and proves that he should have no problems
whatsoever to do a great job. Due to his capability to pick up new things easily and
adapt quickly to new environments, it should not take him long before he will be
up and running in his new position. It also appears that the responsibilities at Belt
Buckle International are of similar nature to his current position, the only difference
being a slightly larger staff at the new position. Due to a good network in the field,
Harrison is, to my knowledge, the best person in the marketplace for the job. If the
opportunity were there, I would rehire Mr. Harrison in a second. As a matter of fact,
I tried to recruit him a year ago for a consultant position at Computer Systems Inc.

5. When asked to comment on areas of improvement, the reference made the following statements:

He needs to have a good supportive staff; otherwise he might push himself too hard because of his high expectations and commitment. Harrison will at times take on too much work, not just for himself but the whole department. He can also at times be a little too direct with people around him and be impatient with nonperformers who do not do their best.

6. When asked to comment on any domestic, personal, or financial difficulties that may interfere with Harrison's performance, references responded with:

At one time he went through a hard time with a relationship to his alcoholic father, but it did not interfere with his performance at work. He is a professional and is excellent at separating personal life and work. If something took place in his personal life it would be hard to tell as he always exceeded his expectations at work.

7. When asked about why Harrison would be considering the position at Belt Buckle International, the reference made the following comments:

The position at Belt Buckle International appears to be a step up careerwise and Mr. Harrison is very ambitious. There is also reason to believe that he is somewhat frustrated at his current company, as the MIS department is not getting the necessary financial funding and support. He is also very career-oriented and it appears that there is no room for further advancement at Murphy Books.

8. When asked if there was anything else we should know about Harrison, references made the following comments:

He is a very driven person. When he sets his goals he works until he reaches them. He is a very special person and there are only good things to say about him. He always made a strong positive impression on people and is a very good employee. The company that gets him is very fortunate.

9. When asked what advice the reference would give Harrison's future employer, the following comments were made:

It is important that he has a good staff around him. Otherwise he will try to do everything by himself.

At the beginning of each reference report, state who the reference is, and his or her relationship to the candidate. Take the comments you get from each reference and systemize them underneath the area where they belong. Write everything down just as the reference said it. If several references say the same thing, you should still write it down. Also, be sure to write down specifics. Keep in mind that the purpose behind the reference report is to enable both you and the client to make a sound judgment regarding the candidate. If something negative comes out of the reference check, you have to probe to get the specifics.

The reason for making separate reference reports is to make sure that you make the right decision by ensuring that you get answers in each area that you need to cover. Certain executive search forms merge all the remarks into one document so you do not know who said what. But for many it makes a big difference if a subordinate or someone's superior made a specific comment. When making the report it is important not to be tempted to cover up someone's weaknesses in order to close the search. If you do, it will most likely blow up in your face later.

6 | Closing the Search

When you have completed the identification, screening, interviews, reference checks, and presentation of the best-qualified candidates in the process, the search usually has come to an end. Unfortunately only one candidate gets the job after hundreds of phone calls, which is why executive search is also called *the business of rejection.* It is important not to consider the search complete until the final candidate agrees to an offer. Be aware that if the candidates are not treated professionally, because of delays, poor treatment, or unskillful negotiations, it is very possible that they might realize that they are happier at their current company. It is important to treat everyone as you want to be treated yourself.

It is also important to have a good backup plan in case something goes wrong. This means that you have to keep the other finalists "warm" in case your final candidate drops out. You can tell the other finalists that you need a few more days to make a decision.

When the best candidate has been chosen, it is important to move quickly and notify the candidate immediately. Make sure the client provides the candidate with a written offer that states the compensation agreed upon and starting date. It is important that there is no delay in the presentation of terms and conditions.

Closing Out Candidates and Sources

When closing a search it is important to confront and deal with all those you have been in touch with during the course of the search, in addition to the final candidates. Many of these people gave you helpful information; others were interested and sent their résumés to you, while others functioned as references for candidates. All of these people have one thing in common; they interrupted their busy schedule to give you the time of day. To close a search does not only mean to have placed somebody successfully, but also to have closed out everyone who somehow participated. To become good at this last step, all you have to do is put yourself in the shoes of the participants. What kind of courtesy would you expect if you had sent off your résumé filled with excitement? You would expect a prompt follow-up one way or another. A letter stating that you did not measure up would do. If someone became a candidate but was rejected, he or she should receive both a letter and a phone call. If you gave information about candidates, you would expect a thank-you letter. When a search is over, a letter should therefore be sent to the participants, with content matching the nature of the participant. All of these letters need to be sent to the home address of the people you interacted with. This is one of the reasons why it is crucial to keep good notes throughout the search, so you can easily track down all the people who should receive a letter from you. When you have closed the search, there should not be any loose ends or anybody wondering about anything relating to the search. The folder used to organize prospects should also be emptied (refer to the section "Candidate Backgrounds" in Chapter 3).

Closeout File

Every search should, after completion, have a closeout file. This should be entered in your filing system according to the search number assigned. On the outside on the top front of the file, you should place a sticker that reads:

▲ Search Number   Client Name (company)
▲ Title of position

In the closing file, the minimum information should be:

▲ Printout of the final log (a list of all people called with comments and correct codings)
▲ Position specification
▲ Source letter
▲ Career brief and appraisal of placement with exact information on final compensation package accepted

The whole purpose behind making a good closeout file and keeping the paperwork well organized is to prevent you from having to reinvent

7 | Working With an Executive Search Firm

When your organization needs to recruit a new person or replace someone, it is important to determine as early as possible who is going to do the recruiting. This book is meant both as a guideline for yourself if you want to do the recruiting, and as a control tool if you decide to hire an executive search firm to assist you. If you outsource the job to a search firm, there are several things you should know.

Categories of Recruiting Firms

The knowledge and methods presented throughout this book are based solely on executive search, as this is generally accepted as the most thorough and effective way to recruit someone. But there are actually three main categories of recruiting firms: employment agencies, contingency recruiting firms, and retainer executive search firms.

Employment Agencies

Employment agencies normally specialize in filling clerical and staff support positions. The fees are often fixed, and are always lower than those of the executive search firms. Agencies may charge the employee, the client, or both for its services. There are many agencies worldwide. Many are private; some are government sponsored.

Contingency Recruiting Firms

These firms' fees are dependent on the success of an assignment: If the recruiting firm does not find a candidate to fill your position, they do not charge you. Contingency work was common in the early days of headhunting, especially in the United States, but search firms now work primarily on a retainer basis. Some contingency firms are similar to employment agencies except that they usually do not charge the candidate for their services and they normally work with positions at a higher level than employment agencies, namely lower and mid-level management positions.

Some contingency recruiting firms focus on providing services similar to those of the retainer firms, but these face a big challenge in the potential loss of their investment in man-hours (on the average, a retainer firm spends 150 man-hours per assignment) if they should not be able to fill their clients' positions. This means that contingency firms have to take a number of shortcuts in areas such as research, documentation, and interviewing, which ultimately may result in filling a position with a less-than-ideal candidate.

Therefore, you should consider a contingency recruiting firm if the positions you hire for are not so critical that you necessarily need to have the most qualified available people filling them.

Retainer Executive Search Firms

Retainer executive search firms are the most thorough and usually most expensive type of executive search firms. A firm is paid in stages during the search, and the payments do not depend on successfully finding a suitable candidate. You pay fees from the beginning of the assignment without any guarantees that your company's vacant position will be filled. However, retainer firms are the most professional and thorough, and if there is a highly qualified candidate out there, these firms are the most likely to find that person and bring him or her to you.

Because of the high nonrefundable fees involved, there usually are a number of contractual issues to be settled before the executive search firm takes on the assignment:

- ▲ Can you get a discount if you are hiring people for several similar positions (multiples) at the same time? In this case, the search firm can save time by continuing to search for the additional candidates within the same framework they have already defined.
- ▲ What if you need to cancel the assignment (e.g., a great candidate shows up on your door unexpectedly or the position is terminated due to a reorganization) after the search firm has started working?

▲ What if the search takes too long? (This does not necessarily mean that the search firm is doing a poor job; it may mean that it is very difficult to find a qualified person.)

▲ What if the executive found by the search firm is hired but then leaves after a short period of time? (If this happens within a year of the hiring date, most executive search firms will find a replacement for you free of charge—you only have to pay for expenses.)

▲ What if the position requirements change substantially after the search firm has started working?

If you make sure these situations are covered in the contract between you and the search firm, a lot of potential confusion or conflict can be avoided later.

How Much Will It Cost?

While employment agencies usually have simple, fixed charges, executive search firms normally calculate their charges based on the annual compensation that goes with the position they are helping to fill. For the retainer-based search firms the total basic charge is generally from 30 to 35 percent of the annual compensation. In addition, search expenses such as phone charges, travel to meet with candidates and the client, and meals with sources and candidates are added to the bill. Other executive search firms will give you a fixed quote after discussing the assignment with you.

The actual billing methods vary (see Figure 7.1). Some firms may ask for 20 percent of the basic charge up front and then spread the rest over the next few months. Other firms charge 33 percent at the beginning of the assignment, 33 percent halfway through the search, and the rest on completion. In Europe, it is normal practice that the last amount is paid only after the candidate has signed the employment contract.

If, after discussing the assignment with you, the executive search firm sees that the search will require more resources than normal to complete (such as a search covering several different countries), it might increase its charges due to the increased workload.

Figure 7.1 Examples of billing methods.

| | Start | Week 2 | Week 4 | Week 6 | Week 8 | Week 10 | Week 12 |
| | $17,000 | | | $17,000 | | | $17,000 |

Example 1

| | Start | Week 2 | Week 4 | Week 6 | Week 8 | Week 10 | Week 12 |

Example 2

$10,000 $6,660 $6,660 $6,660 $6,660 $6,660 $6,660

(Example based on a person with $150,000 in annual compensation and a search that takes twelve weeks. Phone, travel, and other expenses are extra.)

How to Select an Executive Search Firm

Choosing the right executive search firm can be difficult due to the many companies in the market. Throughout the United States and the rest of the world, there are so-called boutique firms (smaller local firms) and international chains consisting of a large group of search firms linked together in the same network. The large chains are easy to locate, as they frequently appear in rankings and industry magazines or newsletters like the *Executive Recruiter News,* published by Kennedy Information (800-531-0007 or 603-585-6544).

The top international search firms listed subsequently are on the list merely because of their size in terms of revenue and number of consultants. All state that they conduct their searches with the same universal high-quality approach, so it is wise to conduct reference checks not only of the candidates involved in the process but also of the executive search firms that you are considering. The local boutique firms frequently use the selling point of being the personal kind of headhunter and not the large factory type.

The following international executive search firms are considered to be the top ten, based on their revenue (see Table 7.1).

Table 7.1 International executive search firms.

Firm	Revenue[a] ($ millions)	Number of Offices
Korn/Ferry International	301.1	71
Heidrick & Struggles	258.0	50
Spencer Stuart	244.7	40
Amrop International	187.0	79
Russell Reynolds Associates	184.3	33
Egon Zehnder International	181.9	46
Ray & Berndtson	117.3	42
Ward Howell International	104.7	60
H. Neumann International	81.8	43
TranSearch International	68.0	60

Source: Executive Recruiter News, March 1998. Kennedy Information, LLC, New Hampshire, U.S.A.
[a]Figures are 1997 worldwide consolidated revenues.

When considering buying the services of an executive search firm, also ask yourself if you are buying their work methods or a specific individual's expertise. Normally, you would like to get a combination of the two. If you are interested in working with the so-called top-notch headhunters in the United States, it is possible to obtain information on some of these through the book *The New Career Makers,* by John Sibbald, published in 1995 (third edition), which can be ordered through Kennedy Information (800-531-6544 or 603-585-6544). This book presents profiles on 250 outstanding individuals within the field, nominated by clients and peers. The individuals are indexed by twenty-one functional and forty-three industry areas of specialization. Keep in mind that there are also other excellent headhunters out there who are not listed in the book.

The most frequently used—and easiest—method of finding an executive search firm is through the grapevine or your own private network. Very few companies are willing to experiment with a headhunter who does not have a good reputation. If a search firm has done a good job for someone that you know, then at least you get some kind of security. Buying the service of an executive search firm is difficult because what you are buying is trust and not a tangible product like a car or a new suit. Therefore, it is very important to investigate whether your headhunter is a good bet.

Even if an executive search firm is recommended, those recommending it might not have extensive experience with search firms and therefore do not know what to expect. This means that a mediocre headhunter can get a high recommendation because of ignorance in the marketplace. It is important to listen to recommendations but still be very critical. You should also always consider more than just one executive search firm.

After all, you are going to have to pay them a large amount of money and give them lots of trust to do the job.

For the U.S. market, *The Directory of Executive Recruiters, Corporate Edition,* published by Kennedy Information in 1998, gives you updated information on more than 10,000 individual recruiters at almost 6,000 offices in North America. The book has indexed the consultants and firms by industry specialties and functional expertise. When selecting a firm, you also must decide if your needs are local or international. If the search is international, then you need someone with international capabilities, but if your recruitment needs are local, a boutique firm could be as efficient as a large firm with international affiliations.

When deciding on an executive search firm, you should obtain the following information from the firm during the meeting:

- ▲ Presentation of the credentials of the firm and its employees. Ask for written material presenting both the people you are dealing with and their consultants.
- ▲ History, size of the firm, and who its clients are.
- ▲ The firm's fees, methods of payment, and the required time it takes to solve the search.
- ▲ Guarantees and rules for off-limit that it can provide.
- ▲ After explaining your needs, ask how the firm would handle the assignment (basically how it would conduct each step and the different timelines). Get details on the most critical part of the search, the research phase, and find out how the firm gets information on candidates who are not coming from their old-boys' network or filing cabinet.
- ▲ Get a minimum of five recent references. Inform the firm that you want the references from searches conducted within the last few months. Also ask for permission to pick references yourself from the client list that you were presented with. From this list pick one or two companies that are similar to yours.
- ▲ Get an example of a typical position specification, target list, candidate report, and reference report.

Here are questions to ask the executive search firm's references:

- ▲ Why was the particular executive search firm selected?
- ▲ How much time did the firm need to complete the search(es), and how many qualified candidates did it come up with?

▲ What kind of positions did the firm recruit to, and what was the success rate for each position?

▲ How often were you updated during the course of the search on what was going on?

▲ How was the quality of the written material that the search firm provided, such as the position specification, candidate or assessment reports and the reference checks?

▲ On a scale from 1 to 10, how would you rate the firm that you used (10 being the best score).

▲ Was there something during the process that you were not happy about?

▲ How did the firm participate in the final negotiation?

▲ Are there any other executive search firms that you have heard good things about?

After meeting some executive firms that you feel comfortable with and that meet the requirements listed previously, you should be able to select the right firm to assist you.

Working With the Executive Search Firm

After selecting an executive search firm you must confirm in a contract what you as a client are buying and the financial obligations and terms that are involved. After the contract has been signed, the firm should provide the following within ten working days:

▲ Position specification (see the section "Defining the Job" in Chapter 1).

▲ Complete list of target companies, prospects, and sources that will be contacted (see Chapter 2).

▲ Time schedule for the telephone screening, and when you can get feedback on candidates who appear to have both the required qualifications and motivation for the position. This is the step before the consultant conducts the face-to-face interview (see the section "Time Schedule" in Chapter 2).

▲ Time schedule for when you can expect to receive the first candidate reports and meet with candidates (see Chapter 2).

Your Role in the Search Process Versus the Executive Search Firm's Role

As a client, you are concerned not only that you get a good candidate in place, but also that your executive search firm conducts the search with speed and high-quality market research. Even though you are the client, you should arrange to be available for the executive search consultant to ensure that misunderstandings and delays are prevented. Keep in mind that your search is most likely not the only search on your consultant's agenda (this is also a good sign). Therefore, it is unrealistic to expect any quicker time span than what has been described in this book. Shortcuts mean a faster process, but also a risk of not getting what you want. The result, in such a case, could be having to start all over again, greatly lengthening the process. However, if the executive search firm has not taken on too much work and is up to date on how a search should be conducted (as explained in this book), you should be able to get a final candidate presentation four to six weeks after the official start-up date.

During the search you might feel that you have no control over what is going on, or what is not going on. This book shows you what to expect. Keep in mind that every modern search firm works on a computer system and therefore can give you updated information with current status at any point during the search. Modern headhunting is based on hard work with a predefined strategy and work method, and not like the old days when the success rate of the search depended on how many close friends you might have (old-boys' network). The old-boys' network is a helpful supplement, but original research and published information will always be the basis for the highest success rate. Based on these facts, you should be able to get speedy updates throughout the search regarding its status and what to expect. You should expect the extensive documentation detailed in this book to be available from a high-quality executive search firm.

There are different approaches to the final interviews. Some executive search firms believe that the candidate reports provided to the client are so thorough that it is safe to let the client meet the candidates by himself or herself. One argument for this approach is that candidates behave more freely than when a third party is sitting in on the meeting. Another school of thought is that the consultant can help the candidate sell himself or herself at the final interview. It is also possible that you as the client are not used to interviewing, and therefore might not be able to obtain the necessary information. Also, the consultant can help you sell the position and your company. Whether you have a consultant present is up to you.

to market job opportunities. From proper briefings with consultants, or, much better still, face-to-face with the client, the researcher will have a much better understanding of the position and the associated dynamics—he or she will probably feel more affinity to the client and will want to get the job done rather than try to sell another soulless typewritten proposal. In essence, when the job "comes alive," the researchers are at their most effective.

A further tangible result of this style of participation is that the research team has much more to say; they gain better ideas of how to market the position and whom to pitch it to.

3. *What message do you leave when you cannot get hold of someone?*

Messages left with personal voice mails and secretaries should be clear and succinct; leave your name, company, and enough of a clue to suggest it may be a headhunting call. Use your judgment on each call but *never*, as with all calls, fabricate an untruth. It is very important that you clearly state in the message that you are seeking assistance. You do not want someone to lose his or her job because you did not get your message right. When leaving a message on voice mail, you can also make the position for which you are hiring sound extremely attractive. If you must leave a message with a secretary, keep it extremely simple just to make sure she or he does not get the opportunity to convey it incorrectly.

4. *How do you deal with difficult switchboard operators and secretaries?*

This is a two-part problem: (1) making sure you get through to the person, and (2) making sure you identify the *right* person to be contacted.

Unfortunately there are no magic solutions to getting around a secretary who has been told not to put calls through. There are many methods, but none are foolproof. Voice mail and gaining direct lines are probably the most obvious solutions.

Switchboard operators are becoming very aware of their role in defense of the organization, and in many cases they are not given the information we need in terms of job title or description to avoid the risk that they will pass this detail on. Departmental secretaries are more useful, but again there are no guarantees that they will be helpful or accurate. More fruitful research can be conducted from department to department, which requires researchers to think about the people they need to identify and to understand their position in the structure.

5. *How many do you call on a given search, and when do you stop or reduce the number of calls?*

Researchers should make as many calls as required to be able to understand the dynamics of the market—the key players and industry trends, for example, as well as identifying and approaching suitable candidates. Our experience suggests that quality work targeting the most *likely* sources of candidates pays dividends as opposed to a more volume-oriented smile and dial approach.

Calls on assignments should be seen in terms of opportunity cost; there are always competing needs for resources, so it makes commercial sense for researchers to make fewer but more accurately targeted approaches.

Volume calling is still an integral part of executing the assignment. However, excessive calling may suggest a weak search strategy or a fundamental question mark over the attractiveness of the position, which needs to be addressed with the client.

6. *How do you decide if someone is right or wrong?*

You should employ a series of "filters" to refine the short list of potential candidates. There are a number of key drivers that a researcher should recognize as being nonnegotiable; these are often macroskills such as the possession of specific product knowledge or functional expertise. Clearly in the filtering process we need to eliminate all those without these key core skills.

The more difficult part of the process is the fine tuning—conducting a telephone interview and trying to develop the conversation so that high-value questions in terms of the person's past performance and motivation can be addressed. Ultimately, the process relies on judgment that is conditioned by having executed a good number of assignments, ideally in the same or similar industry. If in doubt, discuss with the consultant or client.

7. *If someone appears to be "on target," what do you do next with him or her?*

First of all I try to get them to send me their résumé or curriculum vitae (CV). If the time line is tight, then it is very important to just develop the CV over the phone. In most cases the résumé that you receive from a candidate or prospect lacks information that you are seeking. Therefore, if you have the time, the results usually get better when you put it together yourself. After gathering the prospect or candidate's background information I arrange a face-to-face interview.

8. *How do you organize your information?*

Each call is logged on the in-house database. Progress reports are derived directly from this system and put into a user-friendly format. Above all, researchers or consultants should produce a report that not only shows the raw data of names contacted or identified but also some form of structure; a logical line of argument that reflects a strong methodology.

10 | Professional Online Databases

Professional online databases usually require a fee from the user and are normally controlled by companies specializing in information collection, organization, and retrieval. Some are available through the Internet (usually with a password and user ID to enable the company to collect fees), while most have direct dial-up access via specific phone numbers. The advantage of direct dial-up is, of course, that you can avoid all the traffic on the Internet, and retrieve information faster. Possible disadvantages include the need for special software (and sometimes hardware) from the database company, and that long-distance phone calls might be required to get connected (depending on where your office is located, of course).

For more information about available online databases, check the Online 100, *Online Magazine*'s field guide to the 100 most important online databases (www.onlineinc.com). Many of these services contain overlapping information, so in many cases subscribing to any one of them can give you all the information you need on a regular basis.

Online databases have been around for more than a decade. But only in the last few years have they started to connect their databases to the Internet. Today, thousands of databases are available to researchers and other people with specific information needs. Many database providers act as umbrella organizations for a large number of databases, thus allowing you to maneuver around and make multiple searches once you have set up an online connection to the provider. The cost of doing searches in the different databases varies, but for the most part the price ranges between $15 and $40 for one to five articles or profiles. (If you are unsure about some of the technical expressions used in the following pages, please see the Appendix.

Figure 10.1 lists some of the most popular and comprehensive professional databases for business research. Each one is also included with more detailed information in the more comprehensive list on the following pages.

Figure 10.1 Major international online databases.

Company	Product/Service	Address
DataTimes	DataTimes provides more than 5,000 leading information sources for research and intelligence gathering. The information network covers regional, national, and international newspapers, magazines, real-time newswires, trade publications, financial information, newsletters, and broadcast transcripts	DataTimes Corporation Parkway Plaza, Ste. 450 1400 Quail Springs Pkwy. Oklahoma City, OK 73134 Ph.: 800-642-2525 or 405-751-6400 Web address: www.datatimes.com
Dialog	One of the most comprehensive services for all subjects, with unsurpassed collections in business news, business research, and companies. Its new KR BusinessBase product is designed for easy use by business professionals.	Knight-Ridder Information Services, Inc. 2440 El Camino Real Mountain View, CA 94040 Ph.: 800-234-2564 or 415-254-8800 Web address: www.dialog.com
Disclosure	Disclosure is a source for financial and business information on companies across the globe. And with Info Centers located in 20+ major business centers around the world, it provides personal research services.	Disclosure Inc. 5161 River Rd. Bethesda, MD 20816 Ph.: 800-945-3547 or 301-951-1300 Web address: www.disclosure.com

Company	Product/Service	Address
Dow Jones News/ Retrieval	Probably the strongest collection of finance and investment resources. Dow Jones has now also released a new front end software that makes it easier to access its content for any level of user.	Dow Jones & Company P.O. Box 300 Princeton, NJ 08543-0300 Ph.: 405-751-6400 Web address: www.dowjones.com
Dun & Bradstreet	Duns Financial Records Plus contains history, operations, and selected financials for nearly two million U.S. private companies.	Dun & Bradstreet Information Services Three Sylvan Way Parsippany, NJ 07054 Ph.: 800-223-1026 or 201-605-6500. Web address: www.dnb.com
LEXIS-NEXIS	Considered the best U.S. and international business news, with additional research and company strengths.	LEXIS-NEXIS 3445 Newmark Dr. Miamisburg, OH 45342 or P.O. Box 933 Dayton, OH 45401 Ph.: 800-544-7390 Fax: 513-865-1666 Web address: www.lexis-nexis.com
NewsNet	A strong collection of business news and business research databases. It can be accessed with Baton, a specialized graphical user interface.	NewsNet 945 Haverford Rd. Bryn Mawr, PA 19010 Ph.: 800-345-1301 or 215-527-8030 Web address: www.newsnet.com

ABI/INFORM
UMI/Data Courier
620 S. Third St., Louisville, KY 40202-2475
800-626-2823 or 502-583-4111
Web address: www.umi.com
Popular access providers: CDP Online, Data-Star, Dialog, EPIC, ESA-IRS, FirstSearch, Infomart, Knowledge Index/CompuServe, LEXIS-NEXIS, Orbit*Questel, STN

ABI/INFORM contains full text and abstracts from leading journals across the entire spectrum of business and management. The focus of many of the journals reflects current trends and methods in all management functions, including management practice, human resources, marketing, finance, computers, R&D, and technology.

ABI/INFORM also includes key journals from major industry and service sectors, with a special focus on banking, health care, insurance, real estate, and telecommunications. The service abstracts more than 1,200 journals, many of which are important foreign periodicals. ABI/INFORM's emphasis is on significant mainstream discussions of business issues and trends.

Associated Press
Associated Press
50 Rockefeller Plaza, New York, NY 10020
212-621-1500
Web address: www.ap.org
Popular access providers: CompuServe, DataTimes, Dialog, NewsNet, LEXIS-NEXIS, PRODIGY (AP Online)

The Associated Press (AP) is wide in scope and constantly updated with news, business, sports, and feature information. AP provides current general, business, and feature news from the United States and the world. It is considered a major supplier of general and topical news worldwide. The company has more than 140 bureaus in the United States and nearly 100 abroad. Virtually every U.S. newspaper, and more than 15,000 newspaper and broadcast outlets around the world, draw upon and contribute to AP for news and feature content.

AP carries general and political news from all over the world, with particularly good coverage of local, state, and national U.S. news. Its business wire provides news and commentary about companies, markets, and finance worldwide. AP also offers a number of special topic databases that concentrate on different business, political, and international subjects.

Business Dateline
University Microfilms International
620 S. Third St., Louisville, KY 40202-2475
1-800-626-2823 or (502) 583-4111
Web address: www.umi.com
Popular access providers: CompuServe, Dialog, Dow Jones News/Retrieval, EPIC, LEXIS-NEXIS, Infomart

Business Dateline contains the full-text articles of hundreds of regional business publications from the United States and Canada. The 350 separate periodicals cover virtually every business center in both nations. The service is a unique source for hard-to-find information about small private

Figure 10.2 Business Wire screen.

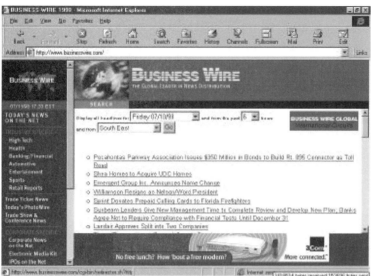

companies, entrepreneurial and start-up ventures, and branches of larger corporations. It emphasizes agriculture, banking, electronics, health care, hospitality, real estate, and transportation sectors. Besides company and industry news, it always covers general business, including market and management trends, economic climates, and business environments.

Business Wire (see Figure 10.2)
Business Wire
44 Montgomery St., San Francisco, CA 94104
800-227-0845 or 415-986-4422
Web address: www.businesswire.com
Popular access providers: America Online, DataTimes, CompuServe, Dialog, Dow Jones News/Retrieval's Market Monitor, Dow Jones News/Retrieval, LEXIS-NEXIS

Business Wire is a major conduit for press release information, with instantaneous distribution channels to print, broadcast, and online media worldwide.

The database contains the complete text from thousands of U.S. corporations and other organizations. More than 12,000 corporations from the United States and a number of nonprofit and public organizations such as hospitals and government bodies make up the membership body of Business Wire. The members themselves supply their press releases to

Business Wire, which in turn supplies the information to national, local, and foreign newspapers, TV and radio stations, PR and investment firms, and two dozen online database services.

The press releases typically contain new product announcements, merger information, acquisitions and strategic partnership agreements, executive changes, and earnings, dividends, and other public financial reports. The information also often gives useful background data on company, product, and persons.

Company Intelligence
Information Access Company
362 Lakeside Dr., Foster City, CA 94404
800-321-6388 or 415-358-4643
Web address: www.informationaccess.com
Popular access providers: Data-Star, DIALOG, LEXIS-NEXIS

Company Intelligence has good summaries, which include background and current news on U.S. and foreign public and private companies. These brief profiles, along with article references from business periodicals, provide a good overall and current picture of a company.

Profiles on 130,000 U.S. public and private companies come from an online version of Ward's Business Directory. These records include information about line of business and officers. Facts on 30,000 foreign companies come from directories published by Graham & Trotman, a British firm. Article citations are drawn from the Information Access Company family of databases.

Corporate Affiliations
Reed Reference Publishing
121 Chanlon Rd., New Providence, NJ 07974
800-323-3288 or 908-665-2861
Web address: N/A
Popular access providers: DIALOG

Corporate Affiliations describes corporate ownership linkages among large U.S. and foreign corporations. It concentrates on larger businesses, with a requirement for inclusion of $10 million in annual revenues. It describes 117,000 companies, of which 15,000 are ultimate parents. It includes all New York Stock Exchange (NYSE) and American Stock Exchange (AMEX) companies, all over-the-counter (OTC) companies, large U.S. private companies, and large non-U.S. companies. It is also a standalone directory of businesses, containing key data on financials, operations, and officers integrated into the basic ownership records. The database has a separate record for each company, whether it is an affiliate or a parent. Each record contains two types of information: description of the company's own operations, and its linkages to other family members.

DataTimes Newspapers
DataTimes Corporation
Parkway Plaza, Ste. 450, 1400 Quail Springs Pkwy.
  Oklahoma City, OK 73134
800-642-2525 or 405-751-6400
Web address: www.datatimes.com
Popular access providers: DataTimes, Dow Jones News/Retrieval

DataTimes has expanded its content to become a major source of national and international information, but its large collection of local news remains its most distinctive content. This database includes the full text of more than five dozen local and regional U.S. daily newspapers, representing medium and large cities throughout the United States. DataTimes often has the most thorough coverage of local business news, economic conditions, small companies, and local subsidiaries of large corporations.

Dialog Papers
Knight-Ridder Information Services, Inc.
2440 El Camino Real, Mountain View, CA 94040
800-234-2564 or 415-254-8800
Web address: www.dialog.com
Popular access providers: CompuServe, Dialog, Knowledge Index/CompuServe (selected papers)

The Dialog Papers database is a unique resource for general and business news at the grassroots level. It includes the full text of more than sixty U.S. urban and regional newspapers. These newspapers are particularly valuable for local business, economic, and company news. They are also an important source for company information, especially for small companies and subsidiaries or branches of corporations.

Disclosure
Disclosure Inc.
5161 River Rd., Bethesda, MD 20816
800-945-3547 or 301-951-1300
Web address: www.disclosure.com
Popular access providers: CompuServe, Data-Star, DataTimes, Dialog, FirstSearch, LEXIS-NEXIS, Dow Jones News/Retrieval. EDGAR Plus, which contains financials and textual data, is available online from Disclosure Inc.

Disclosure has detailed financial and operating data on every important U.S. public corporation. It includes approximately 12,000 corporations traded on the NYSE, AMEX, NASDAQ, and other OTC companies.

A major advantage that Disclosure has over other public company databases is the large number of companies it contains.

Dow Jones News
Dow Jones & Company
P.O. Box 300, Princeton, NJ 08543-0300
405-751-6400
Web address: www.dowjones.com
Popular access providers: Dow Jones News/Retrieval, CompuServe, Dow Jones
    News/Retrieval's Market Monitor

Dow Jones Text Library (see Figure 10.3).
Dow Jones & Company
P.O. Box 300, Princeton, NJ 08543-0300
609-520-4000
Web address: www.dowjones.com
Popular access providers: Dow Jones News/Retrieval, DataTimes (excluding
    Dow Jones publications)

Dow Jones Text Library is one of the most inclusive group databases and draws upon the resources of Dow Jones as well as other major elec-

Figure 10.3 Dow Jones Text Library screen.

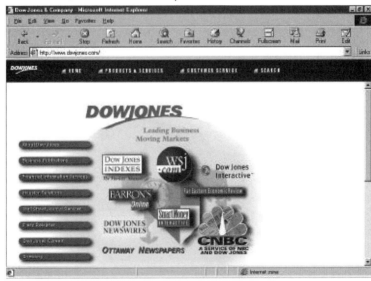

tronic publishers. The service contains the full text of hundreds of leading business magazines, newsletters, newswires, and newspapers. The library combines several Dow Jones publications with important business databases from other major business database providers including a large set of U.S. and foreign newspapers and newswires from around the world (such as *Business Wire, PR Newswire,* the *Washington Post,* and foreign publications). The Business Library includes more than 200 business, trade, and industry journals in numerous manufacturing, service, and retail sectors. Information Access Company's Newsletter Database has hundreds of specialized newsletters providing detailed coverage of industry sectors. Dow Jones provides *The Wall Street Journal,* Dow Jones News Service, and *Barron's.*

This exceptionally wide-ranging collection makes Text Library a fundamental source for virtually every business research topic. Because of their diversity, the Text Library databases, when searched as a collective group, are especially valuable for covering a topic from every angle.

Dun & Bradstreet Reports
Dun & Bradstreet Information Services
Three Sylvan Way, Parsippany, NJ 07054
800-223-1026 or 201-605-6500
Web address: www.dnb.com
Popular access providers: Dialog, NewsNet, WESTLAW. Also available from
    Dun & Bradstreet

Dun & Bradstreet Reports consists of several database files called "reports." The Business Information Report (BIR) and Payment Analysis Report (PAR) contain specific information on the operations, finances, and payment practices of millions of U.S. business establishments. The reports cover more than ten million public and private companies, including subsidiaries and branches. They describe company background, lines of business, officers, facilities, organizational status, and corporate structure.

Dun's Financial Records Plus
Dun & Bradstreet Information Services
Three Sylvan Way, Parsippany, NJ 07054
800-223-1026 or 201-605-6500
Web address: www.dnb.com
Popular access providers: DataTimes, Dialog, Dow Jones News/Retrieval. Also
    available from Dun & Bradstreet

Dun's Financial Records Plus contains history, operations, and selected financials for nearly two million U.S. private companies. With this financial and operating information, which can be found nowhere else, it is an essential resource for researchers.

Dun's Global Families Online
Dun & Bradstreet Information Services
Three Sylvan Way, Parsippany, NJ 07054
800-223-1026 or 210-605-6500
Web address: www.dnb.com
Popular access providers: Dialog, Dow Jones News/Retrieval. Also available from Dun & Bradstreet

Dun's Global Families Online is probably the best service for tracking the links of the world's corporate families. It describes the corporate family relationships among more than thirty million active and inactive business establishments worldwide. More than 300,000 corporate families in 200 countries are described. The service indicates the corporate family relationships—ultimate parent, headquarters, branch, divisions, or subsidiary.

Several different report formats are available from the database. Depending on which one you choose, they can include company résumé, SIC codes, top executive and corporate family relationships, and more.

Dun's Market Identifiers
Dun & Bradstreet Information Services
Three Sylvan Way, Parsippany, NJ 07054
800-223-1026 or 201-605-6500
Web address: www.dnb.com
Popular access providers: Data-Star, DataTimes, Dialog, Dow Jones News/Retrieval, Prodigy. Also available from Dun & Bradstreet

Dun's Market Identifiers contains key operating and financial data on millions of establishments, and it is considered the most comprehensive database of U.S. businesses. It has descriptive, operations, and financial data for ten million U.S. business establishments. The company profiles include subsidiaries and branch locations, and information about key executives, line(s) of business, and more.

Globalbase
Information Access Company
362 Lakeside Dr., Foster City, CA 94404
800-321-6388 or 415-358-4643
Web address: www.informationaccess.com
Popular access providers: DataTimes, Data-Star, Dialog

Globalbase is a major extension in the supply of international business data. The service provides access to hundreds of specialized business periodicals, representing important markets around the world.

Globalbase abstracts significant articles from hundreds of industry-sector trade publications worldwide, especially the United Kingdom, Western Europe, and the Pacific Rim nations. It abstracts from trade papers and journals articles dealing with companies, products, markets, and technologies. It focuses on several sectors, including transportation, forest products and packaging, food and hospitality, chemicals, electronics, energy, cosmetics, and health care.

Globalbase is not truly international because it has very little coverage from North America, Latin America, Africa, the Middle East, and Central Asia. Its strongest areas are the United Kingdom and Western Europe, and in 1994 it expanded with many new publications in these areas and also added a number of titles from Scandinavia and the Pacific Rim countries from South Korea to Indonesia (Japan receives little coverage).

Global Report
Automatic Data Processing
111 Wall St., New York, NY 10005
212-657-3597
Web address: N/A
Popular access providers: CompuServe, and from the service provider itself (Automatic Data Processing)

Global Report incorporates several disparate databases into one simple, consistent interface that quickly provides current information about markets, companies, industries, and countries from around the world.

The service has current analyses and reporting, including real-time news and financial data, for markets, companies, industries, and economies worldwide.

Global Report's main providers include Comtex, Extel, and Knight-Ridder for general and business news; Citibank, Financial Times, and Quotron for finance, quotes, and prices; Business International and the Economist Intelligence Unit for political and economic analysis; and S&P's for company information. Global Report has four sections—news, companies and industries, countries, and markets. Companies and industries includes country- and industry-specific stories from wires, quotes from Quotron and company overviews. S&P's provides detailed profiles for 10,000 U.S. and hundreds of major foreign corporations. Countries has news arranged by region and country.

International Dun's Market Identifiers
Dun & Bradstreet Information Services
Three Sylvan Way, Parsippany, NJ 07054
800-223-1026 or 210-605-6500
Web address: www.dnb.com
Popular access providers: DataTimes, Dialog, Dow Jones News/Retrieval. Also
   available from Dun & Bradstreet

International Dun's Market Identifiers is considered the most comprehensive directory of the world's businesses. The service provides operating and financial data on millions of companies worldwide, excluding the United States. These data are merged with public-domain information to create a directory of four million companies outside the United States. The database is a companion file to Dun's Market Identifiers, which covers U.S. businesses. The international file covers the rest of the globe:

- ▲ Africa and the Middle East—100,000 companies
- ▲ Asia-Pacific and Australia—250,000 companies in 40 countries along the Pacific Rim, including Australia and New Zealand
- ▲ Canada—550,000 companies
- ▲ Europe—3 million companies
- ▲ Latin America—200,000 companies

A typical company record includes company name, address, telephone, top executives, line of business and SIC codes, sales and number of employees, international corporate family linkage, and more.

INVESTEXT
Thomson Financial Services, Inc.
22 Pittsburgh St., Boston MA 02210
800-662-7878 or 617-345-2000
Web address: www.investext.com
Popular access providers: CompuServe, Data-Star, DataTimes, Dialog, Dow
   Jones News/Retrieval, NewsNet, LEXIS-NEXIS, and directly from Thomson
   Financial Services through its I/PLUS Direct online service

INVESTEXT is the sole online provider for thousands of research reports prepared by analysts at leading investment banks and brokerage firms. These are full-text reports about companies and industries. The 300 firms that provide reports include well-known houses from Wall Street, other regional firms in the United States, and important foreign firms.

Company reports cover thousands of firms, from large corporations to small, high-growth start-ups. Most are publicly owned entities of significant investment interest. Industry reports are divided into fifty-three categories, covering both service and industrial sectors.

Figure 10.4 Kompass Databases screen.

The name "Kompass" and the Kompass logo are registered trademarks and are the property of Kompass International. All rights acknowledged.

Knight-Ridder/Tribune Business News
Knight-Ridder/Tribune Business News
790 National Press Bldg., Washington, DC 20045
202-383-6134
Web address: www.knightridder.com
Popular access providers: America Online, Dialog, Infomart, NewsNet. The Knight-Ridder/Tribune Financial Newswire is supplied to a number of other current news services.

Knight-Ridder/Tribune Business News provides current business, financial, market, and corporate news worldwide, from a variety of newswires and newspapers. The service is particularly strong at the grassroots level. It concentrates on financial and commodities markets around the world and local business centers around the United States.

Kompass Databases (see Figure 10.4)
Kompass International Management Corp.
Rutisstrasse 38, Zurich-Gockhausen 8044, Switzerland
41 1 820 3495 or 41 1 821 4664
Individual (country) databases may have different primary publishers.
Web address: www.kompass.com
Popular access providers: Dialog

Kompass databases is considered the world's most comprehensive set of international buyer's guides. It contains brief profiles and specific product and service listings for thousands of companies around the world. The primary focus is on business-to-business trade, particularly in manufacturing, industrial, and related service sectors.

For each company there is a short profile and detailed product information. Basic company information includes résumé, lines of business, names of principal officers, languages spoken, and more.

The Kompass databases covers the following regions:

▲ Asia and the Pacific—300,000 companies in Japan, China, India, Australia, and other Pacific Rim nations
▲ Canada—35,000 companies
▲ Europe—390,000 companies in 12 European countries
▲ United Kingdom—110,000 companies

There are also plans to provide coverage for Africa and the Middle East, Eastern Europe, and Latin America.

Newsletter Database
Information Access Company
362 Lakeside Dr., Foster City, CA 94404
800-321-6388 or 415-358-4643
Web address: www.informationaccess.com
Popular access providers: Data-Star, CompuServe, DataTimes, Dialog, ESA-IRS, Dow Jones News/Retrieval, STN

Newsletter Database contains nearly 600 business and industry newsletters in full text. They provide analysis and reporting about technologies, companies, products, and markets in a number of industries. The concentration is on industries where the pace of technical, market, and regulatory change is so great that a continual flow of current information is necessary in order to stay on top of the business.

The service has especially strong clusters in telecommunications, computers and electronics, environment, medical care, energy, publishing and broadcasting, international business, finance, aerospace, defense, and materials science. The newsletters are divided into forty-eight industry categories. Many newsletters are available online well before distribution by mail, especially those published weekly or monthly.

NewsNet
NewsNet
945 Haverford Rd., Bryn Mawr, PA 19010
800-345-1301 or 215-527-8030
Web address: www.newsnet.com
Popular access providers: NewsNet

NewsNet has a strong focus on specific topics and is in the forefront of online newsletter databases. The service has the full text of more than 600 business and industry newsletters. This type of publication is especially important to the numerous industries characterized by rapidly evolving technologies, business environments, and legal and regulatory climates, or those where executives, planners, researchers, and public officials must stay well informed. Thus NewsNet's Newsletters cluster in industry sectors where current information is considered of particular value, such as telecommunications, international business and affairs, electronics and computers, finance and accounting, energy, environment, publishing and broadcasting, health care, aerospace, and defense. All the newsletters are sorted into thirty-four broad industry categories.

NewsNet also contains several major classes of business information, including company profiles from S&P and several business and general newswires.

NEXIS
Reed Elsevier plc
9443 Springboro Pike, P.O. Box 933, Dayton, OH 45401
800-543-6862 or 513-865-6800
Web address: www.lexis-nexis.com
Popular access providers: LEXIS-NEXIS

NEXIS is considered by many researchers to be the "mother of all databases," and it remains unsurpassed based on its comprehensive, full-text coverage of current general and business news. The service contains the full text of 2,300 newspapers, newswires, magazines, newsletters, and broadcasts covering general and business news worldwide. To cover news and analysis of business, finance, and dozens of industry sectors, NEXIS has incorporated other major databases into its own roster of sources.

Note: LEXIS-NEXIS also owns the LEXIS unit, which is a leading provider of online legal research materials and information products to legal professionals, small and large law firms, sole practitioners, and law schools.

PR Newswire
PR Newswire
1515 Broadway, New York, NY 10036
800-832-5522 or 212-596-1544
Web address: www.prnewswire.com
Popular access providers: Dialog, NewsNet, DataTimes, Dow Jones News/Re-
    trieval's Market Monitor, Knowledge Index/CompuServe, Dow Jones News/
    Retrieval, LEXIS-NEXIS

PR Newswire is the biggest supplier in distribution of press releases. It contains the full text of press releases from thousands of North American corporations, U.S. government bodies, associations, and other groups.

Approximately 75 percent of the contributors to PR Newswire are U.S. and Canadian corporations. Their press releases are often the first and sometimes sole source for several kinds of business information, including product announcements, executive changes, alliances, and a variety of financial reports. PR Newswire records contain contact names, ticker symbols, states, and industry sector and subject descriptors.

PROMT
Information Access Company
362 Lakeside Dr., Foster City, CA 94404
800-321-6388
Web address: www.informationaccess.com
Popular access providers: DataTimes, Data-Star, Dialog, LEXIS-NEXIS,
    Orbit*Questel, STN

PROMT is an acronym for Predicasts Overview of Markets and Technology, and it indicates that the database contains information about markets, companies, products, business, economy, and technology. It is often the first and only place to turn for comprehensive research in all of these areas, and it is a favorite of many business researchers.

PROMT includes abstracts, excerpts, or full text for 1,200 key journals and reports covering general business, industrial, service, and public sectors. Its periodical list includes business magazines, newspapers, trade journals, and newsletters from around the world. These range from news and opinion leaders like *The Wall Street Journal, Fortune,* and the *Economist* to hundreds of specialized sector titles like *Retread News* and *Beverage Weekly.* PROMT stands out with a rich variety of sources including limited distribution market research studies, Securities and Exchange Commission (SEC) registration statements, and company annual reports. The service is updated daily.

Reuters (see Figure 10.5)
Reuters Ltd.
85 Fleet St., London EC4P 4AJ, England
071-250-1122
Web address: www.reuters.com
Popular access providers: DataTimes, Dialog, NewsNet, LEXIS-NEXIS, America
    Online (newswire)

Reuters provides current general and business news from around the
world. The Reuters network includes more than 1,200 journalists in 100
bureaus located in forty-seven countries. With its worldwide span, Reuters
is particularly strong in news occurring throughout Asia, Africa, and Latin
America. Reuters also maintains a strong presence in news centers in North
America and Europe.

Reuters is a leader in general and specialized business reporting. In
addition to regular news reports, it also contains analytical stories about
companies, markets, countries, and economics.

Reuters TEXTLINE
Reuters Ltd.
85 Fleet St., London EC4P 4AJ, England
071-250-1122
Web address: www.reuters.com
Popular access providers: Data-Star, Dialog, LEXIS-NEXIS

Figure 10.5 Reuters screen.

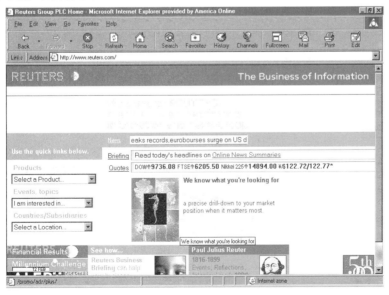

Figure 10.6 Standard & Poor's corporate descriptions screen.

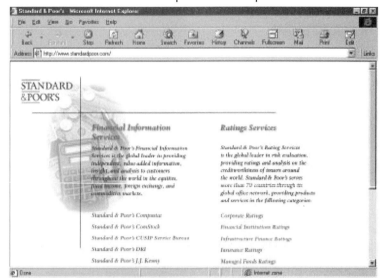

Reuters TEXTLINE is a news and business database of unsurpassed international scope. It contains the full text and abstracts of principal and general business news sources worldwide. Coverage includes Eastern Europe, Central Asia, the Middle East, Africa, and Latin America, as well as traditional industrialized regions such as North America, Western Europe, and the Pacific Rim.

In addition to excellent coverage of general business news, TEXTLINE provides in-depth reporting and analysis for several industry sectors by including trade journals and newsletters about finance, insurance, marketing, and high technology. Databases include Marketing and Advertising Research Service (MARS), Aerospace/Defense Markets, and Technology and Computer Database.

TEXTLINE is particularly information rich for the United Kingdom and Western Europe, whereas coverage of North America is relatively thin.

Standard & Poor's Corporate Descriptions Plus News (see Figure 10.6)
Standard & Poor's
25 Broadway, 14th Floor, New York, NY 10004
212-208-8300
Web address: www.standardpoor.com
Popular access providers: Dialog: Corporate Descriptions Plus News. The Corporate Descriptions and News databases, mounted separately, are on Data-Times, Dow Jones News/Retrieval's Market Monitor, Knowledge Index/CompuServe, LEXIS-NEXIS, and NewsNet.

Figure 10.7 Thomas Register Online screen.

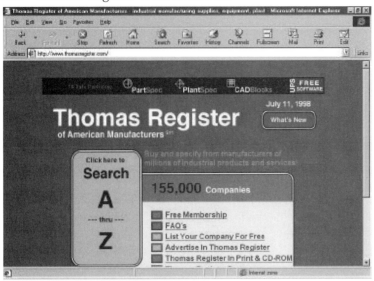

The Corporate Descriptions Plus News database is considered the most important of all the online databases provided by S&P. It provides retrospective and current financial and operating data for thousands of public companies. It covers more than 12,000 companies traded on different U.S. stock exchanges.

Most of the information in an S&P record is derived from public company filings with the SEC. S&P converts these into a detailed corporate description, including lines of business, officers, subsidiaries, and a detailed company description.

The Plus News section of the database is Standard & Poor's Daily News, which is company information obtained from the SEC, the exchanges, company press releases, newswires, and newspapers.

Thomas Register Online (see Figure 10.7)
Thomas Publishing Company
One Penn Plaza, 250 W. 34th St., New York, NY 10119
212-290-7291
Web address: www.thomasregister.com
Popular access providers: Dialog

Thomas Register Online lists the products and trade names of thousands of North American manufacturing companies. It includes millions of individual products manufactured by more than 150,000 companies in the United States and Canada. The database contains more information about the actual product lines of manufacturers than can be found in any other comprehensive company directory, most of which concentrate on financial data and have only summary product coverage. Besides product information and a company résumé, records may contain other company data, including number of employees, officers, assets, and sales.

Trade & Industry Database
Information Access Company
362 Lakeside Dr., Foster City, CA 94404
800-321-6388 or 415-358-4643
Web address: www.informationaccess.com
Popular access providers: DataTimes; Dow Jones News/Retrieval; LEXIS-NEXIS:
    T&I ASAP only; Data-Star: T&I Database and T&I ASAP; Dialog: T&I Database
    and T&I ASAP (merged into one file); Knowledge Index/CompuServe: T&I
    Database (abstracts only); CompuServe

Trade & Industry (T&I) Database is one of a handful of databases that reflexively come to mind when considering research in the area of business. T&I Database contains citations and abstracts from business and industry publications. Trade & Industry ASAP has selected full-text articles. Some supply the broad perspective in general business, management, economics, finance, and governmental relations. The majority, however, are key trade publications covering numerous manufacturing and service sectors. Approximately 20 percent of T&I's source publications are foreign, with a strong emphasis on Western Europe and the United Kingdom.

Worldscope
Worldscope/Disclosure Partners
1000 Lafayette Blvd., Bridgeport, CT 06604
203-330-5261
Web address: www.worldscope.com
Popular access providers: DataTimes, FirstSearch, LEXIS-NEXIS, Dow Jones
    News/Retrieval

Worldscope contains operations, financial, and stock data on leading companies worldwide. Worldscope concentrates on the most important public and private companies in the most active markets. It covers 11,000 companies in forty countries in North America, Europe, Africa, Asia, and Australia. Industries covered include manufacturing, transportation, financial, and high tech.

The company profiles have the most important facts for researchers, for example, business description, product and geographic sales by segment, market value, number of employees, principal officers, annotated news headlines from news services, and more.

11 | Commercial Online Services

Commercial online services differ from the professional databases in that they are much more comprehensive. Rather than just specializing in giving you access to information about companies, industry reports, and news, the commercial online services usually also offer you:

- ▲ Access to a large variety of information from connected databases
- ▲ Access to listservs and newsgroups
- ▲ Access to the Internet
- ▲ Areas where you can chat (live online) with other people
- ▲ Bulletin boards where you can post questions or information
- ▲ E-mail
- ▲ Other services

The cost of subscribing to commercial online services has generally gone down over the years. Most online services now offer pricing plans for both fixed-hour access and unlimited access. For example, five to ten hours of access per month typically cost less than $10, and unlimited access is often offered for about $20 per month (which is similar to the price many Internet access providers charge for unlimited Internet access per month).

Web Sites of Popular Online Services

The following list is by no means comprehensive, but it shows some of the largest online services that have emerged (and survived) over the last few years. The address in parentheses after each service provider is the World Wide Web address where you can connect to the service or read more about it. America Online (AOL), CompuServe, and Microsoft Network are among the largest and most famous online services today.

America Online (www.aol.com)
CompuServe (www.compuserve.com)
DataTimes (www.enews/clusters/datatimes)
Europe Online (www.europeonline.com)
eWorld (www.eworld.com)
Genie (www.genie.com)
InfiNet (www.infinet.com)
Los Angeles Times–Washington Post News Service
   (www.newsservice.com)
MCI/NewsCorp (www.delphie.com)
MedioNet (www.medio.net)
Microsoft Network (www.home.msn.com)
NewsBank (www.spider.newsbank.com)
Presslink (www.presslink.com)
Prodigy (www.prodigy.com)
The Well (www.well.com)

Example of Information Search on America Online

AOL is currently the largest—and also considered one of the most user friendly—of all the different online services.

Major areas on AOL are Today's News, Personal Finance, Clubs & Interests, Computing, Travel, Marketplace, People Connection, Newsstand, Entertainment, Education, Reference Desk, Internet Connection, Sports, Kids Only, Woman, Music, Health, and Games.

The directory of services has been designed to help you search AOL for areas that might interest you. It includes such information as a graphical picture of the area, a description, and the keywords to use. There is also a button on each screen entitled "GO," which will take you straight to the area.

To give you an idea of how easy it is to look for information in some of the larger and more established online services, a description of an information search using AOL's search feature called AOLFind follows. You can search for a specific word describing what you are looking for. For instance, type "automobile" in the search line and then click on the Find button or press Enter. This will bring up anything that AOL might contain about automotive companies.

You can also search for more than one word at a time. To search for several words at once, be sure to type "AND" or "and" between words and phrases. This makes your search fairly specific. For example, "automotive and manager" will bring up everything that contains both words. You can expand your search by putting "OR" or "or" between words and phrases: "Automotive or manager" will bring up everything that contains the word "automotive" or the word "manager." Use "NOT" or "not" to eliminate items that you do not wish to search for. For example, "automotive not Europe" will bring up everything regarding automotive that does not include Europe references. When you have finished typing your search criteria, click on the Find button or press Enter to bring up a listing of areas in AOL that contain the word(s) you are searching for.

News Search on AOL

If you would rather not wade through the sections of the newspaper or are too busy to catch the six o'clock news, News Search can help you stay on top of current events without leaving your computer. News Search allows you to find specific and up-to-the-minute news articles by searching feeds from the Associated Press, Reuters, Business Wire, PR Newswire, and SportsTicker. All you have to do is type in a word or phrase related to the topic you are interested in and News Search presents you with a list of relevant articles.

Searching Company News on AOL

A thirty-day archive of articles from the Reuters, PR Newswire, Knight-Ridder, and Business Wire newswires is available from Company Research. You can get up-to-date news on corporations from Company News as well as from The Online Investor. The latter offers informative, understandable guides to more detailed online information resources and links to company Web sites. It is a great way to get company news without accumulating useless piles of paper.

Comparison Between AOL
and CompuServe

In addition to AOL, CompuServe also clearly stands out when it comes to number of users, the amount and quality of content, and company stability. Following, we evaluate and compare the content of the services provided by the two companies in respect to three distinct areas that will be helpful to you when researching companies where you might find talented candidates for your open positions:

1. Business and Financial News
2. Business Research
3. Company Information

To enter a specific area on CompuServe, enter the command "Go" plus a keyword: for example, "Go Worldnews." Similarly, on AOL, you enter a keyword to go directly to an area of the online service. For example, "Hoovers" will take you to the Hoover's Online area with company information.

Business and Financial News

Both CompuServe and AOL feature continually updated news from a number of major newswires and online newsmagazines.

CompuServe provides access to most newswires, including Associated Press (Go AP), Reuters, CNN, PR Newswire, Business Wire, and several foreign newswires (Go Worldnews). Using its Executive News Service (Go ENS), you can create a customized search profile that automatically runs searches of several major newswires, including Reuters, AP, Dow Jones, and UPI.

CompuServe also gives access to more than fifty newspapers from large and medium-sized cities across the United States, which are useful for researching local markets, small companies, and other local business news that are often overlooked by the national press (Go Newspapers).

AOL receives information feeds from Reuters, Knight-Ridder/Tribune Business News, PR Newswire, and Business Wire (Go Topnews). The stories are sorted by category—top stories, industry news, and so forth—by AOL editors and integrated into a single news service for AOL users.

Overall, CompuServe has a larger selection of newswires, U.S. papers, and a strong international coverage. AOL's news service is convenient for picking up the top stories.

Business Research

News services usually lack the depth and detail needed for heavy research into companies, industries, markets, technologies, and trends. For a good level of analysis, you need newsletters, magazines, journals, and trade papers.

CompuServe has a very good research source in the Business Database Plus (Go BUSDB) and Global Report (Go GRP). Business Database Plus offers full-text articles from hundreds of journals and newsletters that together provide solid reporting and analyses on virtually any industry or business topic. Global Report is a gateway service with company descriptions, news, and market and country analyses. This service is excellent for research on international markets and economies.

AOL has online versions of many leading publications, such as *BusinessWeek* (BW), *Inc.* (INC), *Home Office Computing* (HOC), and *Worth* (WORTH). Conversely, CompuServe has *Fortune* (Go FORTUNE), *Forbes* (Go FORBES), and *Money* (Go MONEY). These electronic magazines have months or years of back issues, and all issues are usually quickly and easily searched in one operation by keyword.

The online versions of business magazines such as *Forbes* or *Business Week* often have extra material not found in the printed version, along with bulletin boards and real-time chat areas that connect you with other readers. Currently, CompuServe has the most depth with its Global Report and Business Database Plus.

Company Information

Both CompuServe and AOL have a number of good databases for researching large U.S. companies. For corporate profiles and financials, both offer Hoover's Company Profiles and Disclosure SEC databases. Both of these services provide their own versions of the data that public companies submit to the Securities and Exchange Commission (SEC). They cover organization, areas of operation, top officers, and financials for thousands of companies.

CompuServe and AOL also provide access to the actual EDGAR database of SEC filings. Be aware that EDGAR is very much a collection of raw data, and it takes a bit of time to get a clear picture of the information in the database. Disclosure and Hoover's contain all the essential data from a company's SEC filings, organized into a single easy-to-understand report. Both AOL and CompuServe also have databases covering historical, current, and projected stock performance and earnings. Neither is very well equipped for researching private companies (although you do have access to such information through online press releases, short profiles in Hoover's, and by using the online services' Web gateways to search the Internet).

AOL's version of Disclosure (COMPANY RESEARCH) has the benefit of including profiles of thousands of large foreign companies. AOL also has two other databases that cover company stock performance (both found in COMPANY RESEARCH). These are The Morningstar and First Call. In addition, AOL offers twenty-minute-delayed and three years of historical stock quotes. CompuServe has more thorough information on U.S. corporations, as well as gateways to foreign and private company databases on other online systems. It has two versions of the Disclosure database—an abridged version with summary descriptions and financials (Go BASCOMPAN) and the complete version with more in-depth financial and operating data (Go Disclosure). CompuServe also has Standard & Poor's Profiles (Go S&P), which contain background, operations, and financial data on nearly 5,000 U.S. companies. The I/B/E/S (Go IBES) database provides earnings forecasts for public companies. And, similar to AOL, CompuServe provides twenty-minute-delayed current quotes, and its historical quotes database goes back twelve years.

Links and Other Features

Links to the Web

Links to the World Wide Web are found throughout the business areas in both CompuServe and AOL, providing an almost seamless link between their own resources and Web-based resources. Their Web browsers are automatically started by clicking on a Web site link. This Web integration should in many cases (except possibly for money-saving reasons) be good enough so that you do not need a separate Internet service provider for your Internet research. The most prevalent difference between the information sources located within the online services and those located on the Web is that the latter can be slower because of the sometimes high traffic on the Internet compared to direct-dialed online services. Another major difference is the actual organization of information. On AOL and CompuServe, you will benefit from common user interfaces in the different areas and the same way of using different resources, whereas on the Web each site usually has its own design and method of use. Currently, AOL has somewhat better integration of Web links from within its different information areas.

Gateways

In this context, gateways are direct links from an online service to an external database. CompuServe offers several gateways to research databases in a number of areas. Be aware that as soon as you enter one of the gateway services, the meter starts running in addition to the basic CompuServe charges. However, the extra cost is not more than what it would be if you hooked up directly with the separate database service.

Many external databases are reached through IQuest, an intelligent gateway to numerous online services operated by Telebase Systems, Inc. IQuest is a good way to link to private company databases, market research reports, and other specialized resources. Knowledge Index provides simplified and low-cost searching of many business databases on DIALOG, but is only available at off-peak hours. Global Report provides news, financial market, and economic information, and is especially valuable for its strong international coverage.

12 | Using the Internet as a Research Tool

With its explosive growth of information providers and users, the Internet (also called the information superhighway, cyberspace, and the infobahn) has become a tool that can no longer be ignored by anyone in the human resources field. The wealth of information becoming available on the information superhighway covers virtually every topic. This chapter focuses on how and where to identify candidates for your company's open positions by finding information about other companies and their employees. As discussed in this chapter, this type of data is often provided by a number of different sources that are hooked up to the Internet: companies, universities, online newspapers and magazines, individuals, discussion forums, to name a few. The following short description of the Internet highlights the basics of the information superhighway.

A Short Description of the Internet

The Internet is a global network of more than 12,000 smaller computer networks. In mid-1998 it was estimated that the Internet supported about 129.5 million users worldwide (for more information go to www.nua.net/surveys/how_many_online_world.html), and it has been predicted that it will have a 5–10 percent monthly growth rate for some time to come.

The most popular and dominant resource on the Internet is the World Wide Web (often referred to as WWW or the Web), and it is the fastest-growing part of the Internet. The World Wide Web has become very popular because of its capabilities to display colors, graphics, pictures, sound, and video to users. Most businesses that set up sites on the Internet choose the World Wide Web because of its graphical user interface and multimedia capabilities, its ease of use, and because of its enormous popularity.

Internet Bandwidth

One of the biggest issues on the Internet right now (and probably for several years ahead) is that of bandwidth. There is a clear limit to the amount of data that can be transferred through our telephone lines. Transmitting text usually does not pose any problems with speed, but as soon as high-resolution pictures, sound, or video is transmitted, things can really slow down. This affects everybody using the Internet, including yourself when you are doing online research, because at certain periods of the day, the usage of the Internet is so heavy that every task you do is slowed down to a crawl, often causing several minutes of waiting to retrieve information that normally only takes a few seconds to access. Industry gurus such as Microsoft's chairman, Bill Gates, have predicted that fast access speed on the Internet probably still lies several years in the future.

Online Research Resources

A plethora of Internet sites provides access to human resources, company, and industry information. The following is a short description of the different resources that can be accessed online.

▲ *Newsgroups* are information forums, which currently number more than 10,000, covering topics from sex to accounting. If you are looking for a top talent within the field of aerospace engineering, you can closely watch newsgroups in that area and see who is contributing and what their specialties and professional interests are.

▲ *Listservs* used for marketing purposes can also be used to collect information on competitors and to keep up to date on industry advances. All you need to subscribe to a listserv is electronic mail with a connection to the Internet. Almost all listservs are free of charge.

▲ *WWW sites,* which provide search engines (a search engine is a program that helps you search for information on the Internet) such as Yahoo (www.yahoo.com), Excite (www.excite.com), and Lycos (www.lycos.com), provide the best starting points for researching suppliers, competitors, and customers.

▲ *Forums* in online services can be good starting points for finding companies and people in special areas. For example, in the many forums for discussion of different information technology, there are often experts

Figure 12.1 Overview of common research resources on the Internet.

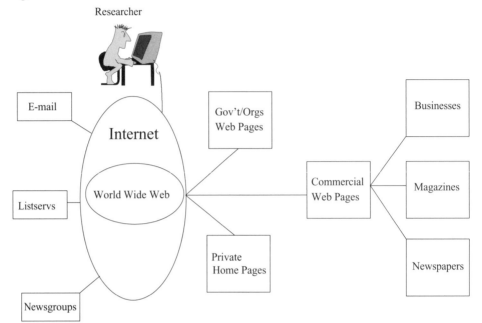

who post news, questions, and answers to one another. An increasing amount of hiring takes place as a result of people being found in these forums (see Figure 12.1).

Note: As you browse the Web, newsgroups, listservs, and online forums, keep in mind that the accuracy of information provided can vary. While some Internet resources are monitored for content and accuracy, many others are open for anybody to post his or her unedited information. You should therefore always carefully consider content from the Internet, unless you know that the source is reliable.

How to Get Connected to the Internet and Online Services

It has become easy to tap into the information superhighway because the number of access providers has exploded and hardware and software have become more powerful and easier to use. Figure 12.2 shows what you need to get online.

If you decide to get an account with one of the commercial online services, it will provide you with all the necessary software. Both regular Internet access providers and the commercial online services might also have some sort of running fee, generally per minute you are connected. Usually this expense is fairly low; however, it might vary in different countries.

Figure 12.2 Example of hardware and software needed for online research.

Equipment	Price Estimate	Comment
Personal computer	US$ 1,000–2,000	
Modem	US$ 100–300	Min. 33,600 bps modem is recommended
Software:		
▲ Internet browser	Free–US$ 100	Included in, for example, Windows 95/98
▲ E-mail program	Free–US$ 100	Included in, for example, Netscape, Windows 95/98
Internet/online access:		
▲ Internet account	US$ 10–30 per month	Sometimes also fee for time used
▲ Online account	US$ 5–25 per month	Hourly plans and unlimited use plans

How to Find What You Are Looking For

We have described the Internet in general, and some of the main resources that can be useful in locating and researching candidates and companies where you might find them. Now, let us look at how you actually find the information of potential interest to you.

If we assume that you have the necessary equipment and software to connect to the Internet, and that you use the World Wide Web (where most information on the Internet now is located and accessed), you will then use a browser to maneuver around on the Net. There are several ways to access information on the Internet:

1. Access a Web page containing a list of hot links (hyper links) to different information sources.

2. Connect directly to the information source (if you already know the Internet address).
3. Use a search engine to search for keywords (name, topic, etc.), and then check out the different responses returned to you.
4. Use intelligent agents, which continually will search for information for you, usually based on keywords that you have provided, and then deliver it back to you as e-mail or as a dynamic news service.

Connecting Directly to the Information Source

If you already have the address of a WWW site you can enter it in the address field of your browser and access the site directly. Many Internet users actually keep an electronic address list (also called bookmarks) in their browser with all their frequently used Web addresses. This allows them to quickly access sites whenever they need to, and they do not have to go around and remember the often very awkward WWW addresses.

Using a Search Engine

Search engines on the Internet have a similar function to the computer catalogs you use in libraries to locate books, magazines, and newspapers. The search engines are databases that contain indexes of information residing on a large number of computers that are linked to the information superhighway. Search engines have user-friendly interfaces that allow users to find potential useful information quickly and easily. Following is a list of some of the most popular and powerful search engines on the Internet:

- ▲ Alta Vista (www.altavista.com)
- ▲ Excite NetSearch (www.excite.com)
- ▲ HotBot (www.hotbot.com)
- ▲ Infoseek (www.infoseek.com)
- ▲ Lycos Search (www.lycos.com)
- ▲ Magellan (www.mckinley.com)
- ▲ MetaCrawler (www.metacrawler.com)
- ▲ WebCrawler Search (www.webcrawler.com)
- ▲ Yahoo Search (www.yahoo.com)

The companies behind the search engines all try to differentiate themselves by offering slightly different features, but the core functionality is the same: to help you find information on the Internet.

Yahoo is considered to be the leading search engine, but there are currently more than 100 search engines on the Internet, and the number seems to be growing all the time. The trend seems to be that they get corporate sponsors, and that they then can provide the search service for free to the user.

Searching the World Wide Web

The World Wide Web is the dominating information source on the Internet. There are a number of search engines, and most are used in a similar way. Here is how they work:

Search Engine Example—WebCrawler

WebCrawler understands plain English and is programmed with novice users in mind, so you don't need to be a master of Boolean search syntax to unleash its power (see Figure 12.3).

Connect to the Internet and start your Web browser. Enter www.web crawler.com in the address field in your browser.

Figure 12.3 WebCrawler screen.

WebCrawler is a trademark of Excite, Inc. and may be registered in various jurisdictions. Excite screen display Copyright © 1995–1999 Excite, Inc.

To use WebCrawler's Search feature, you just need to be able to describe what you are looking for with a series of words or a phrase. Type those words into the search box, click on the "Search" button, and WebCrawler will find resources on the Web. Below are two examples of simple WebCrawler searches. Enter the text and click on the "Search" button to try the query.

Example 1: *manufacturing.* This search will return Web pages that contain the word "manufacturing." It will rank them according to how often the word "manufacturing" appears in the Web page.

Example 2: *manufacturing and auto.* This query will return Web pages that contain both the word "manufacturing" and the word "auto."

Example 3: *"automobile manufacturing."* Please note that there are quotation marks around the query. Using quotation marks when you have more than one word in your query will return Web pages that contain all the words in the query in exactly the order you entered them. This allows you to be much more specific in your searches. If you enter several words in a query and do not use quotation marks around the whole expression, WebCrawler will return Web pages that contain one or more of the words. This can, in many cases, lead to a large number of search results that are not specific enough to be useful.

How to Get Results

After the result of a search is returned to your screen, WebCrawler lets you choose whether you want to see just the titles of the Web pages it lists for you, or a title and a summary for each Web page. You can select *titles* or *summaries* from the line right above the search results.

Titles. This short format gives you a list of titles of Web resources that match your query.

Summaries. This detailed format provides titles plus summaries, Web addresses, numerical relevancy scores, and the option of viewing similar pages for each result returned. The summaries allow you to read a few lines of text from each Web site to help you decide whether to click on the links.

Search Examples

If you are not sure what to type in the search box to get good results, here are some examples of WebCrawler searches that work, and why they work.

car automobile usa america
This example is a good search because it is specific, in both the type of industry and the location. Including synonyms or partial synonyms for automobile (car) and USA (America) gives WebCrawler more related terms to match documents against so you cast a wider net and do not miss relevant pages.

employment jobs resumes career
If you're trying to find employees on the Internet, this search will give you the information you need. This search relies on a series of synonyms to capture the various employment-related information that is available.

automobile manufacturing car "safety manager"
If you are trying to find information about safety managers in the automobile industry, this search might produce the information you are looking for. As with the previous examples, including synonyms for what you are looking for means that you will not miss relevant results that are described using different terminology. The quotation marks around the phrase "safety manager" filter out resources about managers in general and information about safety.

Improving Your Results

Focusing Your Search
If you got too many results or the results were not as specific as you want, here are some ways to focus your search results.

Put quotation marks around phrases or words that must appear next to each other in your results. Example: Putting quotes around the words "space shuttle" filters out pages about outer space and those about various spaces closer to home, returning only pages that pertain to the space shuttle.

Eliminate or replace generic or commonly used words with unique terms, or add words that make your original description more specific. Example: The very general word "program" is a term that adds noise. Noise means that you give the search engine information that is too general, so it usually returns with a large number of irrelevant results that are of no use. There are lots of programs out there—television, software, and so forth—so removing "program" from your search words will produce more focused results.

Learn from your results. Often by scanning the results of your original search, you will discover one that is close to what you want. The title or content of that page can give you ideas for terms that better describe what you are looking for.

Broadening Your Search

If you got too few results or did not find what you were looking for, try adding synonyms for your original words. Example: If your search on bed and breakfasts in Northern California produced too few relevant resources, try bed and breakfast inns "small hotels" in Northern California. Check your spelling. A single misspelled or mistyped word can turn an otherwise well-defined search into a dud.

Advanced Searching

Do not let the animated User Interface fool you. Underneath a user-friendly exterior lies a powerful search and retrieval technology that supports a full range of Boolean search operators to keep expert searchers happy. Figure 12.4 shows examples of Boolean search operators and how to use them. The queries are entered in the same search box on WebCrawler as any other search queries you do there, and they let you broaden or narrow your searches depending on your use of operators.

Figure 12.4 Boolean search operators.

Operator	Example	Finds
AND	gardening AND vegetables	pages that include both of the words, e.g., pages containing both gardening and vegetables.
OR	whales OR cetaceans	pages that include either of the words or both, e.g., pages containing whales OR those containing cetaceans OR those containing both whales and cetaceans. (Note: WebCrawler performs OR searching by default so it is not necessary to explicitly specify an OR search.)

(Continued)

Figure 12.4 *(Continued)*

Operator	Example	Finds
NOT	science NOT fiction	pages that include the first word but not the second, e.g., pages containing science but NOT fiction.
NEAR	arthritis NEAR/25 nutrition	pages in which both words appear within twenty-five words of each other in either direction, e.g., pages containing the words "arthritis" and "nutrition" within twenty-five words of one another. If you do not specify a range, as in the example, budget NEAR deficit, the search will return pages in which the two words are next to each other (in either order).
ADJ	global ADJ warming	pages in which the two words appear next to each other in that order, e.g., pages containing global warming. ". . ." "all you can eat" pages containing the phrase, e.g., only those documents containing the phrase "all you can eat." For two-word phrases such as animal magnetism, "animal magnetism" and animal ADJ magnetism have the same effect.
(. . .)	Homer NOT (Simpson OR Alaska)	pages containing the first word NOT either of the other two, e.g., pages containing Homer but NOT Homer Simpson or Homer Alaska. Parentheses simplify the creation of complex queries and can be used in combination with any of the search operators on this list.

The Excite Search Engine

What Is Excite Search?

Using some search engines to search the Web is like asking a librarian for information on a topic and being given a large number of card catalog cards to sift through on your own. Excite takes search technology one step further by using a unique concept-based approach to search. Like most search engines, Excite Search looks for Web pages (also known as pages) containing the exact words you entered into the query box. But Excite also looks for ideas closely related to the words in your query (see Figure 12.5).

Suppose you search on the terms "financial manager budgeting." In addition to finding sites containing those exact words, the search engine will find sites mentioning "financial analysis" and "executives." The search engine can figure out that relationships exist between words and concepts—that the term "manager" is related to "executive" or that the term "budgeting" is related to "financial analysis." It learns about related concepts from the documents themselves, and learns more from each new document it indexes. This procedure is called *concept-based searching*.

Figure 12.5 Excite screen.

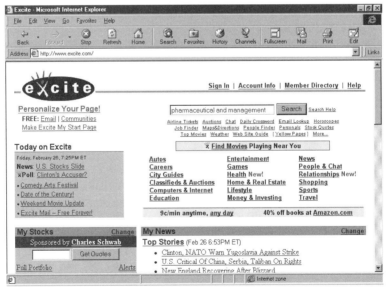

Excite is a trademark of Excite, Inc. and may be registered in various jurisdictions. Excite screen display Copyright © 1995–1999 Excite, Inc.

General Search Tips

▲ Use more than one word. Search for ideas and concepts instead of just keywords (be sure to use more than one word when you search). Excite uses Intelligent Concept Extraction (ICE) to find relationships that exist between words and ideas, so the results will contain words related to the concepts for which you are searching.

▲ Try "More Like This." If you find that one of the Web results better describes what you are searching for, click on "More Like This" next to the title. Excite Search will then use that document as the basis for a new search to find more sites similar to the result you selected.

▲ Be specific. Use specific words as opposed to general ones. For example, a search for "CFO" will return more targeted results than a search for "manager."

▲ Use "List by Web Site." Excite's list of search results may present several pages from the same site. When you click on the "List by Web site" link, your list will compress to show the names of the sites and relevant documents within them.

▲ Try a Power Search. Excite's Power Search feature makes it simple for you to perform an advanced search without having to use advanced syntax. You can also control how many search results are returned and what type of content you want to search against. For your search, choose among the different sources of information such as World Wide Web, Selected Web Sites, Current News, Excite Germany, Excite France, Excite UK, Excite Sweden, and Usenet Newsgroups.

Advanced Search Tips

▲ Try using plus (+) and minus (−) signs. These signs indicate which terms must (+) and must not (−) be present in the returned documents. When using these options, do not leave any space between the sign and the word.

▲ Plus (+). If you put a plus sign directly in front of a word, all documents Excite retrieves will contain that word. So if you search for "+programmer +windows," you will be sure to get results with both those words in them. Remember, you must mark each word appropriately to have these tools work. For instance, if you type "programmer +windows," all of the documents returned will have "windows" in the text, but not necessarily "programmer."

▲ Minus (−). If you put a minus sign directly in front of a word, Excite will *not* retrieve documents containing that word. So if you search for " + programmer-cobol-fortran," you will be spared documents that emphasize the programming languages (or the same words with different meanings) of "cobol" and "fortran."

▲ Try using Boolean operators. Boolean operators tell Excite's concept-based search mechanism to turn off, allowing you to search for documents that contain exactly the words you are looking for. Boolean operators include AND, AND NOT, OR, and parentheses. These operators *must* appear in all caps, with a space on each side in order to work.

 ▲ AND   Documents found must contain all words joined by the AND operator. For example, to find documents that contain the words "programmer," "windows," and "sql," enter: programmer AND windows AND sql

 ▲ OR   Documents found must contain at least one of the words joined by OR. For example, to find documents that contain the word "programmer" or "hacker," enter: programmer OR hacker

 ▲ AND NOT   Documents found cannot contain the word that follows the term "AND NOT." For example, to find documents that contain the word "programmer" but not "hacker," enter: programmer AND NOT hacker

 ▲ ( )   Parentheses are used to group portions of Boolean queries together for more complicated queries. For example, to find documents that contain the word "programmer" and either the word "oracle" or "sybase," enter: programmer AND (oracle OR sybase)

Search Results

▲ Directory Matches. Think of these as the best sites on the Web that fit your search criteria. Excite has a dedicated staff of content-area experts who browse through the Web to bring you the best information, then organize, categorize, and give it to you in the search results as Directory Matches.

▲ News Articles. Excite searches the Web for articles continually throughout each day, collecting thousands of the most current articles from more than 300 of the Web's best newspapers and magazines, including *The New York Times, Forbes,* and *Entertainment Weekly.* The most current articles are displayed in the News Articles area.

▲ Web Results. Excite lists ten search results at a time, with the most relevant documentation listed first. For each site you will see the title and relevancy ratings. Click on the title to go to a site. Use the More Like This link to search for sites similar to the result you selected.

▲ List by Web Site. When you click on List by Web Site, your list will be compressed to show the names of the Web address and the relevant hits within them. Suppose you queried for technology stocks. When Excite searches, it may find sites all around the Web that discuss technology stocks. By clicking the List by Web Site link, you can quickly see which sites contain the most Web pages from the top forty results, and then just go to the site with the most information.

▲ Relevance Rating. Search results are listed in decreasing order of relevance. The percentage sign to the left of each result is the relevance rating. The closer the rating is to 100 percent, the more confident Excite is that the document will fit your needs. The relevance ratings are automatically generated by the search engine, which compares the information in the site against the information in your query.

▲ Show Summaries/Show Title Only. Clicking Show Summaries will display the site summaries of your results (this is the default mode). This is a toggle switch, so to eliminate display of site summaries, simply click Show Title Only.

Why Some Links Seem Not to Work

The Internet is a constantly changing place. To address this, Excite tries to rebuild its index once a week. Even at this frequency, things can change. If a link does not seem to work, a site is temporarily down, very busy and not taking on new visitors, or may have even moved or gone. Such changes should correct themselves on the next index.

Other Online Search Tools

In addition to using the popular Web search engines described previously, there are also an increasing number of other Internet search tools available to you. Many of them are finding their niche in providing more specialized search services than the typical Web search engines. The following are a few examples of these search tools:

▲ AccuFind (www.nln.com). AccuFind provides a single interface to a number of different search engines for a veritable plethora of content. While it is possible to do searches through popular search engines from

AccuFind's home page, it is also possible to search a number of other databases, including Reference.com, Veronica, and others.

▲ InfoSeek Professional (www.professional.infoseek.com). InfoSeek Professional is a separate (from the InfoSeek search engine) service that provides up to 200 hits on Web searches, and allows access to many other databases, including wire services such as the Associated Press, PR Newswire, and Business Wire; company profiles; and movie, book, and video reviews (see Figure 12.6).

▲ Open Text Index (www.opentext.com). Open Text claims to offer some of the most advanced search options of any Internet search service. The simple search allows users to search by exact phrase ("this exact Phrase ..."), or with the Boolean operators AND ("All of these words ...") and OR ("Any of these words ..."). The Power Search interface allows a wide variety of Boolean operators (AND, OR, NOT, NEAR, FOLLOWED BY) and the ability to search different fields of the database: summary, title, contents first header tag, and Web address. It is also possible to weight search terms by the number of times they appear, or whether a term is

Figure 12.6 Infoseek screen.

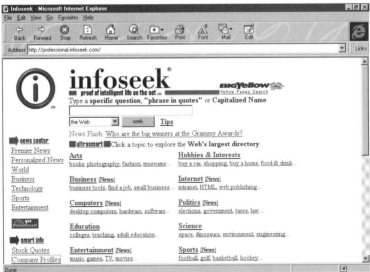

Reprinted by permission. Infoseek, Ultrasmart, Ultraseek, Ultraseek Server, Infoseek Desktop, Infoseek Ultra, iSeek, Quickseek, Imageseek, Ultrashop, the Infoseek logos, and the tagline "Once you know, you know." are trademarks of Infoseek Corporation which may be registered in certain jurisdictions. Other trademarks shown are trademarks of their respective owners.

Copyright © 1994–1999 Infoseek Corporation. All rights reserved.

present or absent. When search results are displayed, it is possible to "find similar pages" as well as to see your keywords in context. Though these search options may sound complex to beginning searchers, the user interface is very intuitive and user friendly.

Accessing Web Pages Containing Hot Link Lists

Another important aid in finding information on the Internet is to use the pages on the World Wide Web that contain links to (and often short descriptions of) other information sites on the Net. Some of these hot-link pages demand that users register and charge for the service, while most are still free. Hot-link pages may be provided by companies, universities, or individuals. They attempt to create some order in the massive amount of information out there, and they usually do so by sorting hot links by topics and subtopics. This might be an easier way of finding what you are looking for, rather than using a general search engine. Some of the most famous Web sites that categorize and list Web sites are Argus (Clearinghouse) and WWW Virtual Library (VL).

▲ The Clearinghouse for Subject-Oriented Internet Resource Guides (www.clearinghouse.net). The Clearinghouse for Subject-Oriented Internet Resource Guides provides a central access point for value-added topical guides that identify, describe, and evaluate Internet-based information resources. Guides are organized by subject, and you can search for the topic of your interest. The guides are created by various Net denizens, often experts on the subject, and are evaluated and selected by the Clearinghouse staff (see Figure 12.7).

▲ The VL (www.w3.org/hypertext/DataSources/bySubject/Overview.html). The VL is probably the oldest catalog of the Web. Unlike commercial catalogs, it is run by a loose confederation of volunteers who compile pages of key links for particular areas in which they are experts. Even though it is not the biggest index of the Web, the VL pages are widely recognized as being among the highest-quality guides to particular sections of the Web.

Individual indexes live on hundreds of different servers around the world. A set of catalog pages linking these pages is maintained at Stanford University (California). Mirrors of the catalog are kept at Penn State University (United States), East Anglia (United Kingdom), Geneva (Switzerland), and Argentina (see Figure 12.8).

Figure 12.7 The Argus Clearinghouse screen.

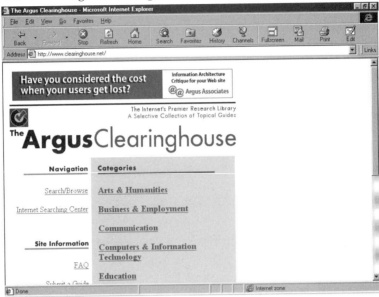

Figure 12.8 The Virtual Library screen.

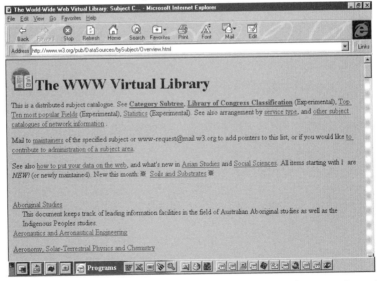

Intelligent Agents

Intelligent agents started emerging on the World Wide Web in 1996, and a number of different innovative software firms have now created programs that can be labeled Intelligent Agents. Behind this somewhat mysterious label is regular software that actively can search the Internet for information, usually based on keywords that you provide. The results can be provided to you as links to Web sites containing the keywords you listed, as e-mail messages to your e-mail address, or as summaries being presented in a "news" application on your screen.

An example of the latter is MSNBC's News Alert service. The service is free (because it is sponsored by advertising) and you can download its news software for free from www.zdnet.com. You create your initial profile through its Web site and specify what topics and keywords its computers should use in order to find the news stories you are interested in. The news will be delivered automatically to your desktop PC (of course provided that your PC is on and that you are hooked up to the Internet) as short summaries. To see the full story behind any news brief you can click on a link and it will bring you to its Web site and let you read the story in full length.

Other Information Tools Useful for Internet Search

The information that follows is in no way meant to be comprehensive, because the speed of development of new search tools and related technology is now so great that no book can stay updated for very long before new tools have emerged. However, it should give you an idea of some of the new and potentially powerful ways to find information on the Internet.

▲ A Business Compass (www.abcompass.com). A Business Compass, L.L.C., has launched a new service for indexing and abstracting business articles published on the World Wide Web. The new service complements the company's directory of leading Web-based sources of business information and research. A Business Compass's editorial team selects and creates detailed profiles of Web sites that offer information resources relevant to business researchers. Examples of such resources include full text of newsletter, journal, or magazine articles; research reports, white papers, and working papers; extensive directories of other Internet sites on a particular business topic; company sales and financial information; and interactive features. A Business Compass then creates informative abstracts of the most important documents on the sites.

Although a Business Compass's abstracts are informative in themselves, a Business Compass also provides access to the original full text of documents via hyperlinks to the original sites. The Internet changes constantly, often causing problems and frustrations for users. A Business Compass tracks down files that move and updates their link. They are also arranging with content providers to archive their full text on the a Business Compass service. That way, even if a file disappears completely from its original site, it remains available to researchers.

▲ Brainwave (www.n2kbrainwave.com). This service is provided by N2K Telebase, a provider of business and consumer information resources. Brainwave provides business professionals and researchers with an immediate and cost-effective means of accessing more than 250 of the world's most powerful commercial databases through an easy-to-use Web interface or a Windows-based software package.

Brainwave covers thirty broad subject areas and offers a wide range of in-depth information, including business credit reports, biographical information, financial news, professional journals, industry newsletters, engineering and scientific research, international trade and marketing data, and more.

▲ Citizen 1 (www.citizen1.com). In 1996, Citizen 1 Software, Inc., introduced a technology to help people locate information on the World Wide Web more efficiently. Called Citizen 1, the software package organizes and provides desktop access to thousands of the best databases on the Internet. Users receive updates each week delivered directly to their PC. Citizen 1 helps transform the Web into a desktop reference as immediately useful as a dictionary, almanac, or encyclopedia.

Citizen 1 takes a logical approach to information searches on the Web. It organizes subject areas into a hierarchy and enables users to retrieve specific, highly useful information—from airplane schedules to drink recipes to current mortgage rates—all from within the application. Users access the most valuable information sources directly and can avoid wasting time sifting through results from a search engine. A new version of the product is available for download at www.citizen1.com.

The following discussion tells how Citizen 1 works. Citizen 1 was among the first search and retrieval products to use Multi-Search—a technology that enables a user to query different information providers simultaneously. This allows a user to view one retrieved document while others load in the background. In practice, it means an investor can search for a company snapshot, stock quote, Securities and Exchange Commission (SEC) filing, and annual report—each from a different provider—all at the same time.

Citizen 1 utilizes two kinds of structured information resources on the Web: databases and link lists. Web-based databases, of which there are already many thousand covering a wide range of information areas, function as specialized search engines. They provide dynamic and often comprehensive coverage of very narrow topic areas. Using a Web-based database, a user can locate, for example, a specific university program, an interest rate quote, a recipe, or a trade show. The product also utilizes selected link lists—structured lists of pointers to Web content. Citizen 1 has developed technology that enables a user to access selected link lists as if they were searchable databases. Queries are forwarded to the Citizen 1 server, which scans the appropriate index and retrieves the desired information.

To select and compile these resources, Citizen 1's staff monitors the Web, seeking out the most valuable new information resources as they come online. Electronic updates are then regularly sent to the user's PC.

▲ Internet.Org (www.internet.org). This product is created by the company Imperative! and is a WWW search engine designed to make it easier to retrieve detailed information on companies that have a presence (as a rapidly increasing number of companies now do) on the World Wide Web.

Internet.Org provides a single source of information on a company's Internet usage by combining proprietary Internet data with SIC codes American Business Information and other geographic and market data (see Figure 12.9).

Internet.Org's database currently includes information on more than 100,000 companies, segmented by SIC codes. The program also allows users to search companies and organizations by WWW domain name (registered Web address).

▲ PointCast (www.pointcast.com). PointCast broadcasts national and international news, stock information, industry updates, weather from around the globe, sports scores, and more from sources like CNN, CNNfn, *Time, People,* and *Money* magazines, Reuters, PR Newswire, Business Wire, Sportsticker, and Accuweather! Even your local newspaper might be on PointCast—*Los Angeles Times, New York Times, Boston Globe, San Jose Mercury News,* and more. Headlines move dynamically across the screen, the colors pop, and all you have to do is keep your eyes open.

PointCast is completely customizable. When you are interested in news in your particular industry, PointCast will send you just the news and information you care about. The service is advertising supported and you can use it free of charge. You can download the necessary software from its Web site (www.pointcast.com) (see Figure 12.10).

Figure 12.9 Internet.org screen.

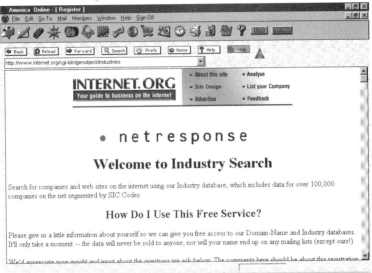

Figure 12.10 PointCast screen.

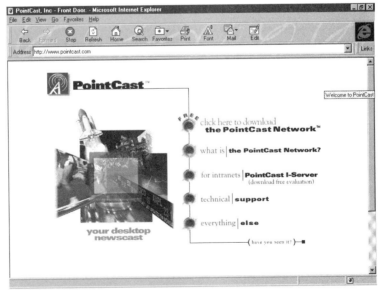

▲ Wajens Internet Group (www.wajens.no). This company has created a Web site where you can find links to all the phone directories in the world that are available on the Internet. The phone directories include both white pages and yellow pages.

Finding People on the Internet

Mailing Lists (listserv)

There are thousands of mailing lists on the Internet, covering a huge number of both professional and other topics. These lists are sometimes edited by a person who oversees the content of each e-mail that is contributed to the list, while others are unedited and all contributions are distributed automatically to all the members of the list.

How can a listserv help you find information about attractive job candidates and the companies where they work today? Recently, with the enormous growth in popularity of the Internet, researchers have started to discover that some of the mailing lists covering the fields where they are looking for talented people are very good places to find candidates and also to learn about some of their skills. Active participants (that is what most mailing lists expect their members to be; otherwise there would be no content to distribute) are often involved in heavy discussions on topics of interest or expertise, and very often they leave both name and address at the bottom of their contributions to a mailing list. This means that if, for example, you are looking for an international accounting executive, you could read a mailing list on the topic of international accounting, and watch for interesting people who contribute there.

Finding a Mailing List
There are a number of ways to find mailing lists. Lots of Internet books list them, and as always, you can find overviews on the Internet itself. Following are some Web addresses where you can find overviews of mailing lists:

www.alabanza.com/kabacoff/Inter-Links/listserv.html
www.liszt.com
www.neosoft.com/internet/paml
www.tile.net/lists

Subscribing to a Mailing List
For administrative requests about a list (such as getting added or deleted, asking about archive files, etc.), write to the address listed under

"Subscription Address" *not* the "List Address." "Subscription Address" gets you to the list owner or an automated list processor, rather than to the membership of the entire mailing list. Avoid sending an administrative message to the entire mailing list—use the subscription address for administrative requests.

If the subscription address is:

Package	*Command*
LISTSERV	subscribe *listname yourfirstname yourlastname*
LISTPROC	subscribe *listname yourfirstname yourlastname*
MAILBASE	join *listname yourfirstname yourlastname*
MAJORDOMO	subscribe *listname*

The command should be placed in the *body* of the message to the subscription address. Most automated list servers will send back an explanation of the correct command structure if you happen to get it wrong in your request.

If the list you subscribe to is a publicly available list, you should now start to receive e-mails as members of the list make their contributions. There are also a number of easy ways to retrieve historical contributions to a list (you will normally receive written instructions about this procedure the first time you subscribe to a list).

Reading Newsgroups

Newsgroups are different from mailing lists in that they are not distributed to their readers. On the contrary, the reader opens a newsgroup with a so-called newsreader (simple software included in many Internet browsers) and reads all the entries posted there. The contributions that users post to a newsgroup can include pictures as well as text.

Just as you can monitor listservs, you can follow a newsgroup covering a topic where attractive candidates might show off their skills. Monitor a particular newsgroup for a while, and it will become pretty clear which participants in the discussion are knowledgeable. You can then contact them directly (their e-mail addresses are listed with every posting to the newsgroup) to get more information.

One way to locate newsgroups is to use an Internet browser that includes a newsreader, or to get stand-alone software (many can be downloaded from the Internet for free—so-called shareware) and then access

Figure 12.11 Dejanews screen.

the newsgroup server of your Internet access provider to start searching for those that might be of interest (see Figure 12.11). If you have a PC with Windows 95 or Windows 98, you probably also have a Microsoft application called Outlook Express. It contains a newsreader that allows you to read newsgroups. You can also go to a Web site like www.dejanews. com and search newsgroups from there, or you can use the newsgroup features in America Online.

Finding Personal Information on Web Sites

It is almost surprising to see how much data some companies and organizations publish on their Web sites for anybody on the Internet to read. In addition to general corporate and product/service information, you can often find material about employees, their current and past projects and work tasks, and even how you can get in touch with them if you have any questions or inquiries. Many organizations have realized that this type of public access to information about their employees also has made it easy for competitors and headhunters to find what they are looking for, and thus they often remove personal information from their Web sites. In addition to the information you can find in corporate or personal Web sites, a number of newspapers have placed all or parts of their printed editions on the Web. Often you can browse and search for data in more than a year's worth of editions in a matter of seconds, and when using keywords for people or companies you can get great feedback in a matter of seconds. Many of these services are free, and will probably continue to be so because of advertising on their Web sites or until the World Wide Web has matured for a few more years.

Internet White Pages

Similar to regular paperback phone books where people's phone numbers and addresses can be looked up, there are more and more "white pages" sites on the Internet, where you can search for a person's name in order to get his or her e-mail address, phone number, and other information.

▲ Four 11 (www.four11.com). This service claims to be one of the Internet's largest white-pages directories, with more than 6.5 million listings.

▲ The Switchboard (www.switchboard.com). The Switchboard Internet directory is a very popular Web site where people and businesses can find each other on the Internet. Switchboard broke new ground when it went live in February 1996 by giving Internet users a single site for finding friends, family, and colleagues nationwide. Switchboard, which provides 106 million residential listings and 11 million business listings, was the first online directory to help people rendezvous on the Internet while protecting their privacy.

Switchboard has more than 15,000 sites linked to its Web address (www.switchboard.com). These links include corporate Web sites, special interest groups, and associations and regional ISPs (Internet Service Providers). Switchboard is also one of the Internet's hottest sites for people seeking information on businesses, with more than 250,000 business look-ups per day.

Anyone with a Web browser can look up the names, phone numbers, and street addresses of friends, colleagues, and businesses. All of this information is publicly available. Each week, more than 15,000 new people update and add information to their Switchboard listings.

Switchboard protects e-mail address privacy while enabling people to make themselves easily reachable via e-mail. Switchboard's users can take advantage of the site's "knock-knock" feature, which serves much like Caller-ID for e-mail. Knock-knock, a privacy screen, lets people unveil the e-mail portion of their listings. Switchboard, acting as an intermediary, forwards the e-mail. The address is revealed to the correspondent only if the individual responds to the message.

▲ WhoWhere (www.whowhere.com). Among many other things, this site allows you to find people based upon past or current affiliations such as schools, interest groups, and occupations and look up e-mail addresses, phone numbers, and addresses of more than ninety million U.S. residents. It also offers online yellow pages with geographic mapping. For your company research check out WhoWhere's Companies Online. It claims to be "the most extensive worldwide directory of company whereabouts on the Net."

Other Internet White Pages

Following is a list of some of the other Web sites that let you do people searches:

www.yahoo.com/search/people
www.theultimates.com/white
www.infospace.com
www.worldpages.com (see Figure 12.12)

Figure 12.12 WorldPages screen.

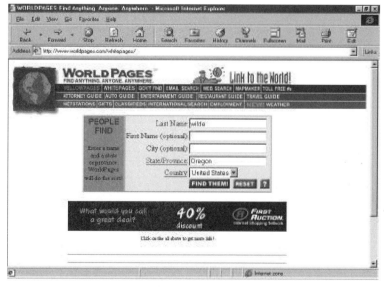

Futurestep

The Wall Street Journal and the executive search firm Korn/Ferry International provide an Internet recruiting tool called Futurestep (see Figure 12.13) (www.futurestep.com). Their goal is to help corporations fill vacant positions with the most qualified midlevel managers as quickly as possible.

Futurestep uses the Internet to register job candidates, who are then matched to available positions at leading corporations around the world. Using Futurestep, the time it takes hiring managers and human resources (HR) executives to find an appropriate candidate should be reduced to about thirty days, according to Futurestep. Online and print advertisers can streamline response management and categorize candidates using the Futurestep system. Linking to careers.wsj.com, *The Wall Street Journal*'s free career Web site, Futurestep can be used to help fill management jobs advertised in *The Journal* and previously handled by human resource executives.

Recruitment advertisers in *The Wall Street Journal* and careers.wsj.com can choose from a range of services to help them manage candidates' responses, from résumé evaluation to complete management of the entire recruitment process.

Futurestep utilizes an effective matching algorithm that incorporates job-related factors such as work history and management experience as

Figure 12.13 Futurestep screen.

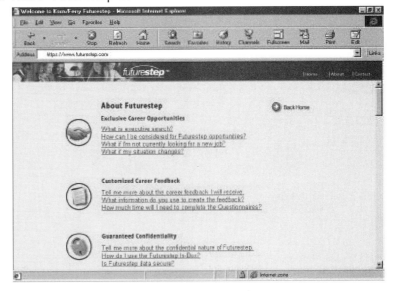

well as candidate motivators such as career path and managerial style preferences. This matching algorithm enhances the recruiter's ability to develop the fit between a candidate's qualifications and goals and a client's needs and organizational culture.

Futurestep focuses on filling positions in accounting, finance, sales, marketing, information technology, HR, operations, engineering, and general management across all industries as well as professional services.

Industry and Company Resources on the World Wide Web

The following is a list of some of the sites on the WWW where you can find industry and company information.

▲ 100hot (www.100hot.com). Provides links to many of the best sites and lists many directories and companies.

▲ Associations on the Net (AON) (www.ipl.org/ref/AON). AON is a collection of more than 700 Internet sites. It provides information on many professional and trade associations, cultural and art organizations, political parties and advocacy groups, labor unions, academic societies, and research institutions.

▲ BEST Catapult (www.jobweb.org/catapult/emplyer.htm). A site with many links to valuable company, industry, and job-search information.

▲ BEST LDOL CareerNet Reference (www.ldol.state.la.us/career1/ HP_REFER.HTM). The Louisiana Department of Labor has provided a lot of useful research information on this site: search engines, directories, the Internet Public Library, a congressional bill-tracking database, the ERIC, LOUIS, and CARL databases, and links to a number of good sites.

▲ BEST Sales Leads USA (www.abii.com). A great site for conducting company research, sponsored by American Business Information. You can find at least some information on almost any business in the United States. Its business profiles include the "company name, address and phone number, name of the owner or top decision-maker, number of employees, estimated annual sales, credit rating score, and primary and secondary lines of business."

▲ BigBook (www.bigbook.com). Calling itself "a new kind of yellow pages," BigBook lets you search for any one of sixteen million businesses

Figure 12.14 Companies Online screen.

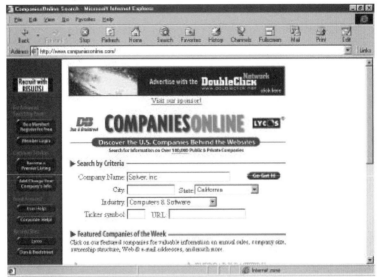

by name, or by industry group, and/or geography. Along with company names and addresses, you can get a map, although these are sometimes outdated or do not have enough detail.

▲ BizWeb (www.bizweb.com). Lists hundreds of companies indexed by product.

▲ Business Sources on the Internet (www.simsbury.lib.ct.us/business.html). This site provides many links to approximately thirty-eight popular business and career sites.

▲ CompaniesOnline (see Figure 12.14) (www.companiesonline.com). CompaniesOnline is a service provided by Dun & Bradstreet in cooperation with Lycos (Internet search service). CompaniesOnline is free to end users. There are no costs or fees involved. Users are encouraged to register for additional free information about companies, such as annual sales, number of employees, and much more.

The CompaniesOnline service is built to be very powerful, yet flexible in sorting through the thousands of records of company information its database contains. For text input fields (Company Name, City, Web address, or Ticker Symbol), you may enter whole or partial words or phrases. The CompaniesOnline search engine will find all companies in its database that match the word fragments you supply. Additionally, pull-down boxes allow you to narrow your search criteria by state and industry, and (for registered users) by annual sales and the number of employees. You may search on any one or any combination of these criteria.

▲ Dun & Bradstreet (www.dnb.com/). The Dun & Bradstreet Commercial site has information about the services provided by this company. In particular, it specializes in company information retrieval.

▲ Edgar (www.sec.gov/edgarhp.htm). This site is run by the U.S. government and is one of the most visited sites for business research on the Internet. The site contains SEC corporate filings and gives online access to annual reports and other documents filed by all publicly held companies in the United States. Usage of the service is free.

▲ Engineering Information Inc. (Ei) (www.ei.org). Ei is a popular engineering-focused service that has links to information retrieval services, newsgroups, and listservs. It offers unique services that take advantage of the Web, Gopher, e-mail, and other Internet technologies to provide an electronic bookshelf. It also offers services from engineering consultants to help you find what you are looking for (see Figure 12.15).

▲ FindLinks (www.findlinks.com/index.html). FindLinks—Industry-Specific Web Links—contains a comprehensive list of links to industry-

Figure 12.15 Ei (Engineering Information) screen.

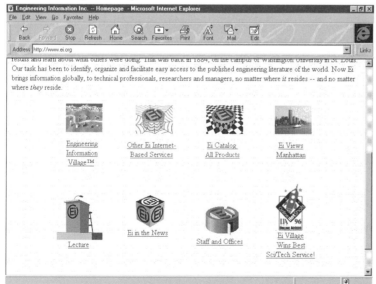

Figure 12.16 Hoover's screen.

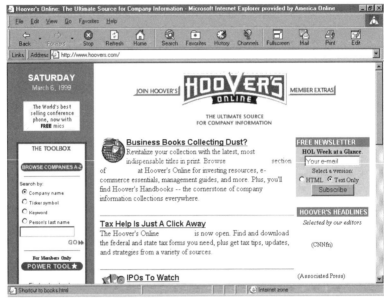

Courtesy of Hoover's Online (www.hoovers.com).

specific World Wide Web news, links and classifieds, and directories of World Wide Web sites.

▲ Forbes "Annual Report on American Industry" (www.forbes.com/forbes/archives). Published annually in the first January issue. The report covers more than 1,100 of the largest public companies in twenty major industry groups. The report ranks companies against their competitors, companies in similar or related industries, and against all other companies.

▲ Hoover's Online (www.hoovers.com). This site gives detailed information about more than 400 large U.S. companies, and is based on the famous Hoover's Handbook (see Figure 12.16).

The information includes corporate history, products and services, financial information, employee statistics, and more. The site also gives information on how you can subscribe to the full Hoover's Online Company Database, with about 1,700 international corporations included.

▲ Hotlinks (www.abracadabra.com/hotlinks.html). Here you can find links to industries such as the following: automotive, aviation, business marketing and management, chemicals and polymers, electrical and electronics, HVAC and refrigeration, industrial automation, paints and coatings, and recycling and mining.

▲ IBM InfoMarket Service (www.infomarket.ibm.com). Contains much detailed information on thousands of companies. This is a fee-for-service site.

▲ INC. 500 Almanac (www.inc.com/incmagazine/archives/ 14950381.html). Fully searchable list of the INC. 500 companies.

▲ Internet Business and Industry News (www.lib.lsu.edu/bus/biz news.html). Internet Business and Industry News provides economic and corporate research reports, industries, international, local, regional, state, and national periodicals on public policy.

▲ KnowX (www.knowx.com). Atlanta-based Information America (IA) has introduced "KnowX," a unique Internet public-records information service. This service enables individuals to uncover background data, assets, adverse filings and other public information on companies and individuals more easily and inexpensively than with many other electronic public-information services. Customers pay only for the precise information they need, and know precisely what that information will cost before they purchase it, according to the IA.

Companies that might earlier have been limited to on-site public records research or higher-cost monthly online services have an affordable Internet alternative with this service.

KnowX has no initial sign-up or connect-time fees, and provides users with unlimited searching of databases and viewing of search-summary lists at no charge. The only cost is for full detail records that customers access from a specific database, and this is priced on a per-record basis.

KnowX's databases, provided by IA, include state, corporate, and limited partnership records, liens, judgments, death records, bankruptcy records, lawsuits, and assets (boats, aircraft). Other IA databases, such as real property records, are now also being added.

Founded in 1982, IA has developed one of the world's largest services that combines public records with information from proprietary sources to address the relationship between businesses, people, and their assets. With twenty-three U.S. locations, IA provides online information and document retrieval services to legal firms, banks, government agencies, and Fortune 500 corporations throughout the country and internationally.

▲ Mansfield University Cybrarian (www.mnsfld.edu/depts/lib/ index.html). Nicely laid out and easy to navigate, the Cybrarian offers much online information including government documents, links to EDGAR, Hoover's, a number of Internet resources, and much more. A good general research site.

▲ National Yellow Pages (www.ypo.com). Eighteen million business listings.

▲ Starting Point (www.stpt.com/buine.html). Starting Point gives you a number of directories from which to choose. After you get to the site, click on *business,* and you can choose from multiple business and career directories.

▲ SunSITE LibWeb (www.sunsite.berkeley.edu/libweb). A good general research site, SunSITE is maintained by Berkeley Digital Library. It is a good source for locating academic, public, and national libraries currently online. Many of these libraries have their own valuable research resources.

▲ The Switchboard (www.switchboard.com). The Switchboard Internet directory is a very popular Web site where people and businesses can find each other on the Internet. The Switchboard provides more than eleven million business listings. These links include corporate Web sites, special-interest groups, and associations and regional ISPs. Anyone with a Web browser can look up the names, phone numbers, and street addresses of businesses.

▲ *Wall Street Journal* (www.wsj.com). The interactive version of the *WSJ* is great—but full text is only available through online paid subscriptions.

▲ Whois.Net (www.Whois.org). Whois.Net allows you to search for a company's Web address based on a keyword search. A database containing all Web addresses containing that word will be listed. It is a great way to find a Web address if you already have the name of the company you are looking for.

Web Sites With Salary Statistics and Surveys

▲ JobSmart (see Figure 12.17) (www.jobsmart.org/tools/salary/sal-surv.htm). Contains information for more than 150 salary surveys from general surveys and profession-specific salary surveys. This site is updated regularly.

▲ Pencom Career Center (www.pencomsi.com/java_career.html). Pencom gives you an interactive salary guide.

Figure 12.17 JobSmart screen.

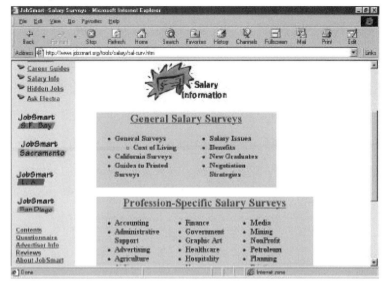

Examples of Executive Search Companies on the World Wide Web

Just like most other businesses these days, executive search companies are setting up their own Web sites to provide current and prospective clients and job candidates with information.

Some of the world's largest executive search firms and their Web sites are:

Boyden (www.boyden.com)
Egon Zehnder International Inc. (www.zehnder.com)
Heidrick & Struggles, Inc. (www.h-s.com)
Korn/Ferry International (www.kornferry.com) (see Figure 12.18)
LAI Ward Howell (www.laix.com) (see Figure 12.19)
Ray & Berndtson (www.prb.com)
Russell Reynolds Associates, Inc. (www.russreyn.com)
Spencer Stuart and Associates (www.spencerstuart.com)

Figure 12.18 Korn/Ferry screen.

Figure 12.19 LAI Ward Howell screen.

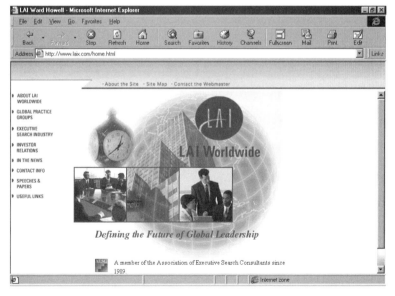

Career Magazine (www.careermag.com/classifieds/recruiters/ index.html), a home page run by Career Magazine, has an extensive list of executive recruiting firms and contact information as well as a brief description of its specialties (see Figure 12.20).

Figure 12.20 Directory of Executive Recruiters screen.

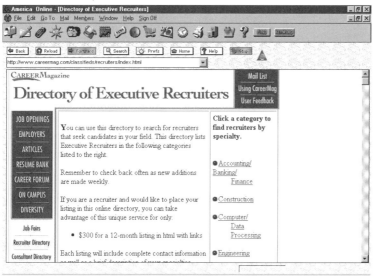

Part IV

Country Profile Overview

13 | Country Profiles

Most of the country profiles contain the following:

Country Information

Internet link to country information
International dialing code
Population
Ethnic divisions
Religions
Language(s)
Labor force

Capital
Economic overview
Industries
Currency

Culture

Business culture
Cultural factors affecting executive search
Foreign nations with similar cultures

Key Research Resources

Company directories
Specialty directories
Libraries
News services

These countries were selected based on population, economy, geography, and several other factors. For information on countries not discussed in this book, please refer to your local library or online source.

Note: Only the most common directories and resources have been presented. Several other specialty directories and resources are also available that are not covered here (e.g., various membership directories issued by different associations).

Australia

Figure 13.1 Map of Australia.

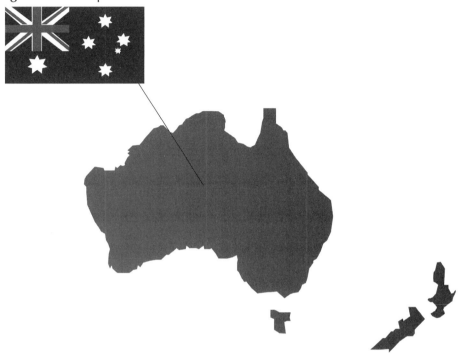

Country Information

Internet link to country information: www.aust.emb.nw.dc.us

International dialing code: +61

Population: 18,430,824 (July 1997 est.)

Ethnic divisions: Caucasian 95 percent, Asian 4 percent, aboriginal and other 1 percent

Religions: Anglican 26.1 percent, Roman Catholic 26 percent, other Christian 24.3 percent

Languages: English, native languages

Labor force: 8.4 million (December 1996); by occupation: finance and services 34 percent, public and community services 23 percent, wholesale and retail trade 20 percent, manufacturing and industry 17 percent, agriculture 6 percent (1997)

Capital: Canberra

Economic overview: Australia has a prosperous Western-style capitalist economy, with a per capita gross domestic product (GDP) comparable to levels in industrialized West European countries. Rich in natural resources, Australia is a major exporter of agricultural products, minerals, metals, and fossil fuels. Primary products account for more than 60 percent of the value of total exports, so that, as in 1983–84, a downturn in world commodity prices can have a big impact on the economy. The government is pushing for increased exports of manufactured goods, but competition in international markets continues to be severe.

Industries: Mining, industrial and transportation equipment, food processing, chemicals, steel. Agriculture accounts for 5 percent of the GDP and more than 30 percent of export revenues; world's largest exporter of beef and wool, second largest for mutton, and among top wheat exporters; major crops—wheat, barley, sugarcane, fruit; livestock—cattle, sheep, poultry.

Currency: 1 Australian dollar (AU$) = 100 cents; exchange rates: Australian dollars (AU$) per US$1—1.67 (October 1998)

Figure 13.2 Major cities, industries, and corporations.

City	Center of
Adelaide	Automotive and defense
Brisbane	Tourism
Darwin	Oil and gas
Hobart	Agriculture and fishing
Perth	Oil and gas, mining, shipyard
Sydney	Financial services

Company	Industry
A.N.Z. Bank	Banking
BHP	Minerals, steel, oil and gas
Coles/Myer	Retail
Commonwealth Bank	Banking
Elders IXL	Agriculture, brewing
Fletcher Challenge	Pulp and paper, construction
I.E.L. Holdings	Mining, retail
National Australia Bank	Banking
Telecom	Telecommunication
Wespac	Banking

Culture

Business Culture

BUSINESS PROTOCOL: Do as you would at home, with the same courtesies and attention to hierarchy and etiquette. Handle all correspondence as promptly as possible, and always arrive on time for an appointment. With regard to manner, Melburnians are slightly more conservative than their peers elsewhere in the country. It is always best to err on the formal side in business dealings until the Australians present indicate otherwise.

PREPARATION FOR THE MEETING: Appointments should be made as far in advance as possible. Although Australians can appear casual, you should be prompt for scheduled meetings. If you are going to be late, call ahead. Lunch meetings are common, as are afternoon drinks if the meeting is late in the day. As in the United States, prepared brochures, as well as videotapes and other audiovisual presentations, are common. Always bring business cards; it is important to exchange them, but without ceremony.

WORKING WOMEN: Australian women work in most fields and their status is nearly equivalent to that of North American women. Australians tend to be more chauvinistic than their American counterparts, and women should not be too put off by what seems like bawdy banter. The women partake in this as much as the men, and rarely is it meant offensively. Women are always included in after work activities.

WORK ETHIC: Australians are conscientious workers, though they like to play as hard as, if not harder, than they work. Foreign companies will find Australians easy to work with and reliable.

ATTITUDE TOWARD FOREIGNERS: For the most part Australians are open, friendly people who like foreigners and enjoy meeting and getting to know them.

Cultural factors affecting executive search: Australia is fairly relaxed and informal, but normally the first candidate contact by telephone is kept semi-formal.

Antidiscrimination laws exist in Australia, so discretion is necessary during the course of conversations with candidates when seeking personal information. In Australia, you cannot legally ask age, marital status, racial background, or any questions that relate to sexual orientation or that may be considered discrimination in this regard.

Stability and financial security are important issues within the work environment in Australia. Lifestyle considerations are important, and many people would choose not to accept a higher salary if it meant moving to another part of the country and disrupting the family. Australians often choose a certain state capital for lifestyle reasons. Great distances and relatively large cost-of-living differentials between the state capitals often mean that people are reluctant to change cities because of family and financial reasons.

Foreign nations with similar cultures: United Kingdom and New Zealand

Key Research Resources (see Figure 13.3 beginning on page 181).

Figure 13.3 Research resources.
General Company Directories

Name of Service	Medium	Vendor Address	Description	Price
Business Who's Who	Book	Dun & Bradstreet 19 Havilah St. Chatswood NSW 2067 Australia Ph.: 61 2 9935 2700 Fax: 61 2 9935 2777	A listing of all major businesses in Australia, with company status, contact details, office holders, product information, list of directors.	AU$ 400 per year
Business Who's Who of Australia	CD-ROM	Dun & Bradstreet 19 Havilah St. Chatswood NSW 2067 Australia Ph.: 61 2 9935 2700 Fax: 61 2 9935 2777	Electronic database with details on companies in Australia, giving information on contact details, company directors, nature of business including products and services, number of personnel, parent company information, SIC codes.	Single User: AU$ 1,345 (Full version updated annually) Single User: AU$ 1,895 (Full version updated semi-annually)

Specialty Directories

Name of Service	Medium	Vendor Address	Description	Price
National Guide to Government	3 books published annually	Information Australia Publication Company 75 Flinders Lane Melbourne, VIC 3000 Australia Ph.: 61 39654 2800 Fax: 61 39654 6532	Updates to all federal and state governments and departments of Australia, covering the following specific areas: federal and state departments; administrative arrangements (acts passed); Governor-General; parliament; political parties; foreign representation and freedom of information procedures.	AU$ 350

(Continued)

Figure 13.3 *(Continued)*

Name of Service	Medium	Vendor Address	Description	Price
The Australian Media Guide	Book	Information Australia Publication Company 75 Flinders Lane Melbourne, VIC 3000 Australia Ph.: 61 39654 2800 Fax: 61 39654 6532	Up-to-date resource of all media found in Australia, covering all national, state, and regional newspapers; magazines; radio; television. Also media regulatory bodies; federal parliamentary press; overseas press representatives; news/feature/photo agencies; ethnic press; personnel involved in media; distribution maps of radio/television; circulation figures, frequency, editor/specialist writers for newspapers and magazines.	AU$ 350
The Directory of Australian Associations	Book	Information Australia Publication Company 75 Flinders Lane Melbourne, VIC 3000 Australia Ph.: 61 39654 2800 Fax: 61 39654 6532	Covers a wide spectrum of associations throughout Australia, including international and foreign national associations with offices/branches in Australia; state associations; metropolitan associations (associations within the capital cities of each state or territory in Australia) and other organizations, e.g., foundations and marketing bodies.	AU$ 350

Who's Who	Book	Information Australia Publication Company 75 Flinders Lane Melbourne, VIC 3000 Australia Ph.: 61 39654 2800 Fax: 61 39654 6532	The Australian version of the international standard reference book.	AU$ 200 per year
Who's Who in Business	Book	Information Australia Publication Company 75 Flinders Lane Melbourne, VIC 3000 Australia Ph.: 61 39654 2800 Fax: 61 39654 6532	Biographies of leading business people. Two volumes, one the biographical and contacts reference to Australia's leaders in every field of business and the other on organization and contacts reference.	AU$ 295 per year
Who's Who of Australia	Book	Information Australia Publication Company 75 Flinders Lane Melbourne, VIC 3000 Australia Ph.: 61 39654 2800 Fax: 61 39654 6532	Reference to notable people in Australia, recording the biographies and achievement of prominent Australians and provides information about past/present community leaders in a range of areas.	AU$ 120

News Services

Ausinet	Online service	Ausinet GPO Box 506 Sydney NSW 2001 Australia Ph.: 61 2 9282 1583 Fax: 61 2 9299 4507 www.ausinet.fairfax.com.au	Covers all major business press in Australia. Service can be accessed by a variety of providers, or direct. Publications include major national newspapers, e.g., *Australian Financial Review*, *Sydney Morning Herald*.	AU$ 40–150 per month depending on usage time. Standard database rate is AU$ 6 per minute.

(Continued)

Figure 13.3 *(Continued)*

Name of Service	Medium	Vendor Address	Description	Price
Dialog	Database	Australian Agents for Knight-Ridder Information, Inc. Insearch Limited Level 2 187 Thomas St. Haymarket NSW 2000 Australia Ph.: 61 2 9514 2151	Dialog specializes in business, science and technology, and intellectual property. Other major areas of focus are: ▲ Agriculture, food, and nutrition ▲ Biosciences and chemistry ▲ Business news and industry analysis ▲ Company information and financial data ▲ Computers, software, and engineering ▲ Energy and environment ▲ Government, public affairs, and law ▲ Medicine, health care, and drug information ▲ News and complete-text publications ▲ Patents, trademarks, and copyrights ▲ People, books, consumer news, and travel ▲ Physical science and technology ▲ Social sciences and humanities	Annual Service Fee: AU$ 60.53

Major Libraries

National Library of Australia
Parkes Place
Canberra, ACT 2600
Australia
Ph.: 6 262 111
Fax: 6 257 1703
Web address: www.ula.gov.au
E-Mail (reference and search services): docs@nla.gov.au

University of Sydney Library
Sydney, NSW 2006
Australia
Ph.: 2 351 2990
Fax: 2 351 2890
Web address: www.usyd.edu.au

Brazil

Figure 13.4 Map of Brazil.

Country Information

Internet link to country information:
   www.demon.co.uk/Itamaraty/body.html
International dialing code: +55
Population: 164,511,366 (July 1997 est.)
Ethnic divisions: Caucasian (includes Portuguese, German, Italian, Spanish,
   Polish) 55 percent, mixed Caucasian and African 38 percent, African
   6 percent, other (includes Japanese, Arab, Amerindian) 1 percent
Religions: Roman Catholic (nominal) 70 percent
Languages: Portuguese (official), Spanish, English, French

Labor force: 57 million (1989 est.); by occupation: services 42 percent, agriculture 31 percent, industry 27 percent

Capital: Brasilia

Economic overview: The economy, with large agrarian, mining, and manufacturing sectors, entered the 1990s with declining real growth, runaway inflation, an unserviceable foreign debt of $122 billion, and a lack of policy direction. In addition, the economy remained highly regulated, inward-looking, and protected by substantial trade and investment barriers. Ownership of major industrial and mining facilities is divided among private interests—including several multinationals—and the government. Most large agricultural holdings are private, with the government channeling financing to this sector. Conflicts between large landholders and landless peasants have produced intermittent violence. The current governmental focus lies on the implementation of sweeping market-oriented reform, privatization, deregulation, and elimination of barriers to increased foreign investment. Brazil's natural resources remain a major, long-term economic strength.

Industries: Textiles, shoes, chemicals, cement, lumber, mining (iron ore, tin), steel making, machine building—including aircraft, motor vehicles, motor vehicle parts and assemblies, and other machinery and equipment

Currency: 1 real CR = 100 centavos; exchange rates: CR per US$1—1.189 (October 1998)

Figure 13.5 Major cities, industries, and corporations.

City	Center of
Belo Horizonte	Minerals, precious stones
Blumenau	Textile and other products
Recife	Fishing and seafood
Rio de Janeiro	Shipyards, offshore industry
Salvadora and Bahia	Petrochemical industry
São Paulo	Automotive, manufacturing
Bamerindus	Banking
BCN	Banking
Bradesco	Banking

(Continued)

Figure13.5 *(Continued)*

Company	Industry
Camargo Correa	Construction
Economico	Banking
Itausa	Banking
Nacional	Banking
Real	Banking
Safra	Banking
Varig	Banking

Culture

Business Culture

BUSINESS PROTOCOL: When meeting a group of people, shake hands with each person on entering and leaving. A general "hello" or "goodbye" to everybody in the room or office is not acceptable. Address a man as a Senhor (Seen-YOHR) plus his surname and a woman as Senhora (Seen-YOH-ruh) plus her surname. Brazilians use first names very quickly, but let them use your first name before addressing them by theirs. Doctors, professors, and priests usually go by their titles plus their first names. Physicians, lawyers, and persons with university degrees are addressed as Doutor (Doh-TOHR). Business discussions are often accompanied by cafezinho, a strong, very sweet Brazilian coffee served in demitasses, usually finished in a few sips. You should accept.

PREPARATION FOR THE MEETING: Prior appointments are always necessary, and bilingual business cards are helpful; cards should be of good quality, but simple. The best hours for appointments are from 10:00 A.M. to 12:00 noon and again from 3:00 P.M. to 5:00 P.M. Be prompt for appointments; the mañana attitude is a thing of the past within business circles in Rio and São Paulo. Always schedule appointments at offices. Never suggest meeting in a restaurant or bar. Business is usually not conducted over lunch. The best time for travel is from April through October. Avoid travel from mid-December to late February, when it is hot and people are on vacation; also avoid Carnival time, the few days preceding Ash Wednesday. If your colleague writes you a letter, reply in the language he or she uses. Never use presentation materials in Spanish. Bring enough copies so the materials can be distributed to the top management personnel.

WORKING WOMEN: Women occupy many prominent positions in Brazilian government, politics, and business. Foreign female executives should encounter no particular problems as long as they are professional in manner and appearance.

WORK ETHIC: Brazilian laborers take a rather breezy attitude toward life and work, and are unlikely to embrace workaholism. Nevertheless, Brazilian workers are considered well motivated, possessing both the capacity for hard work and a willingness to learn. Extremely paternalistic labor legislation and active unions cloud the attitude of the individual worker.

ATTITUDE TOWARD FOREIGNERS: Foreign executives and their families will not encounter overt hostility. The surest way to win over Brazilians is to try to speak Portuguese; they really appreciate such a gesture.

Cultural factors affecting executive search: In Brazil people are mostly accessible on the telephone—if you can bluff your way through the omnipresent secretary. You should wait for the potential candidate to decide when to be on a first-name level. There are no restrictions on the type of questions that can be asked of candidates.

Many good Brazilian executives tend to emulate American executives: Usually they have been trained in an American multinational company's subsidiary. As an example, Brazil's best business school, the Getulio Vargas Foundation, was set up by the Michigan Business School.

Foreign nations with similar cultures: Latin American countries

Key Research Resources (see Figure 13.6 beginning on page 190).

Figure 13.6 Research resources.
General Company Directories

Name of Service	Medium	Vendor Address	Description	Price
Brazil Company Handbook	Book	Hoover's, Inc. 1033 La Posada Dr., Ste. 250 Austin, TX 78752 Ph.: 800-486-8666 Fax: 512-372-4501	Presentation of 115 major companies.	US$ 49.95
Brazil Dez Mil	Book	Dun & Bradstreet Information Services, Dun & Bradstreet Corp. Three Sylvan Way Parsippany, NJ 07054-3896 Ph.: 201-605-6000 www.dnb.com	10,000 of the largest companies in Brazil. Standard Industrial Classification (SIC) code.	Please inquire
Brazilian-American Business Review/ Directory	Book	Brazilian-American Chamber of Commerce, Inc. 22 W. 48th St., Ste. 404 New York, NY 10036-1886 Ph.: 212-575-9030 www.brazilcham.com	Covers Brazilian and American businesses interested in developing trade and investment between the two countries. Arranged alphabetically.	US$ 50
Brazilian-American Who's Who	Book	Brazilian-American Chamber of Commerce, Inc. 22 W. 48th St., Ste. 404 New York, NY 10036-1886 Ph.: 212-575-9030 www.brazilcham.com	More than 1,300 firms, subsidiaries, and affiliates in both the United States and Brazil. Indexed according to company name, line of business, geography.	US$ 100
Dun & Bradstreet	CD-ROM	AV. Dr. Chucri Zaidan, 80, Bloco C 04583-110 Sao Paulo, SP Brazil Ph.: 11 532 8831 www.dnb.com	Complete information on industries and companies including activity, yearly billing, chief executives.	US$ 5,332.00 (10,758 companies) US$ 540.00 (1,000 companies)

Title	Type	Description	Price	Contact
Hoover's Master List of Major Latin American Companies	Book	Complete information on the top public, private, and state owned companies in eighteen Latin American countries.	US$ 79.95	Hoover's, Inc. 1033 La Posada Dr., Ste. 250 Austin, TX 78752 Tel.: 800-486-8666
Major Companies of Latin America	Book	Complete coverage of the 6,000 largest companies in Latin America. Full descriptions of company activities, brand names, key executives, and financial data. All companies are organized by SIC code.	US$ 630	Gale Research 835 Penobscot Bldg. Detroit, MI 48226-4094 Ph.: 313-961-2242

Specialty Directories

Title	Type	Description	Price	Contact
American Chamber of Commerce Yearbook [Information on all Corporate Members]	Book		Free to all members; CR$ 80.00 for nonmembers	Rua Alexandre Dumas, 1976 04717-004 Sao Paulo SP Brazil Ph.: 11 246 9199 www.brazilcham.com
Exame Magazine	Magazine	Articles of general interest about Brazilian industries, companies, prominent executives, new technologies, international business, economics, entertainment, publishing. Additional yearly publication on the 500 best and largest companies (giving information on yearly sales and profit, products, number of employees).	US$ 10 Yearly subscription in Brazil: US$ 100 Yearly subscription for the US: US$ 200	Address in Brazil: Editora Abril Av. Otaviano Alves de Lima, 4400 Frequesia do Q 02909-900 Sao-Paulo SP Brazil Ph.: 11 877 1322 Fax: 11 833 1437 Address in the USA: Editora Abril, Lincoln Bldg., 60 East 42nd St., Ste. 3403 New York, NY 10165-3403 Ph.: 212-557-5990/5993 Fax: 212-983-0972

Major Libraries

Biblioteca Central, Universidade de Brasilia
Campus Universitario, Asa Norte
70910 Brasilia, DF
Ph.: (61) 348-2402

Biblioteca Nacional
Av. Rio Branco 219-39
20040-008 Rio de Janeiro, RJ
Ph.: (21) 262-8255
Fax: (21) 220-4173

Figure 13.7 Internet snapshot of company information source for Brazil.

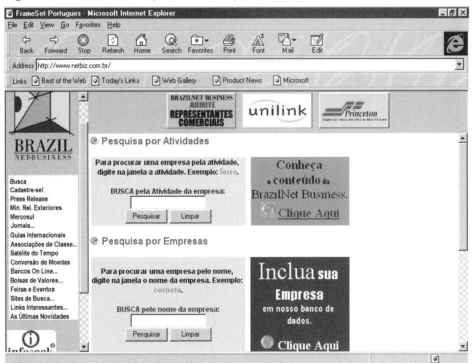

Canada

Figure 13.8 Map of Canada.

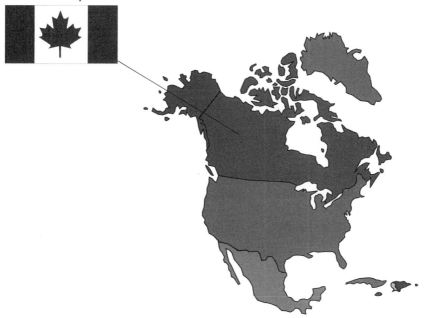

Country Information

Internet link to country information:
www.canada.gc.ca/canadiana/cdaind_e.html
www.city.net/countries/canada
International dialing code: +1
Population: 30,337,334 (July 1997 est.)
Ethnic divisions: British Isles origin 40 percent, French origin 27 percent, other European 20 percent, indigenous Indian and Eskimo 1.5 percent
Religions: Roman Catholic 46 percent, United Church 16 percent, Anglican 10 percent, other 28 percent
Languages: English (official), French (official)
Labor force: 15.1 million (1996); by occupation: services 74 percent, manufacturing 15 percent, agriculture 3 percent, construction 5 percent, other 3 percent (1994)
Capital: Ottawa
Economic overview: As an affluent, high-tech industrial society, Canada today closely resembles the United States in per capita output, market-oriented economic system, and pattern of production. Since World

War II, the impressive growth of the manufacturing, mining, and service sectors has transformed the nation from a largely rural economy into one primarily industrial and urban. In the 1980s, Canada registered one of the highest rates of real growth among the Organization for Economic Cooperation and Development (OECD) nations, averaging about 3.2 percent. With its great natural resources, skilled labor force, and modern capital plant, Canada has excellent economic prospects, although the country still faces high unemployment and a growing debt. Moreover, the continuing constitutional impasse between English- and French-speaking areas has observers discussing a possible split in the confederation; foreign investors have become edgy.

Industries: Processed and unprocessed minerals, food products, wood and paper products, transportation equipment, chemicals, fish products, petroleum, and natural gas

Currency: 1 Canadian dollar (Can$) = 100 cents; exchange rates: Canadian dollars (Can$) per US$1—1.50 (October 1998)

Figure 13.9 Major cities, industries, and corporations.

City	Center of
Alberta	Crude oil, natural gas
British Columbia	Information technology, coal, copper, fishing, pulp
Newfoundland	Fishing, pulp, mining
Ontario	Financial services, automotive, manufacturing
Quebec	Aerospace, transportation, paper/pulp, aluminum, telecommunication

Company	Industry
Alcan Aluminium	Aluminum
BCE (Bell Canada)	Telecommunication
Brascan	Holding company in finance and natural resources
Canadian Pacific	Pulp and paper, cellulose, railing/transportation, hotel
Chrysler Canada	Automotive
Ford Motor	Automotive
General Motors	Automotive
George Weston	Grocery stores, fish, paper
Imperial Oil	Oil
Norenda	Metal mining, pulp
Thompson	Media

Culture

Business Culture

BUSINESS PROTOCOL: Customs among Canadian businesspeople are similar to those in the United States or Britain, tending to be a little more formal in Ontario and Atlantic Canada, and more breezy in Quebec and the West.

PREPARATION FOR THE MEETING: The languages for business are English and French, depending on where the company is located. Many Quebec companies work entirely in French and refuse to reply if addressed in English. Canadians are generally more conservative than their neighbors to the south, and etiquette is more important. English Canadians from Ontario tend to be more reserved than French Canadians and Westerners, and do not welcome a lot of body contact or gestures in greeting or conversation.

WORKING WOMEN: Perhaps even more than in the United States and Britain, women are making their presence felt in business and government in Canada. While sexism and subtle barriers still exist, women are found in powerful positions in all walks of life. Visiting female executives can expect to be taken seriously.

WORK ETHIC: The work ethic among Canadians is generally as varied as in any other developed nation, with large immigrant communities generally reflecting the ambitions of their home countries. At the same time, the getting ahead ethic is strong, particularly among recent arrivals.

Cultural factors affecting executive search: First candidate contact is semiformal and rather easy (although not on a first-name basis, especially with French-speaking people). Senior executives are used to being called regularly by recruiters. A very small proportion insists on being called at home outside business hours. Several calls are made as contact or source calls only and people willingly refer their ex-colleagues, even current colleagues or their superiors, and talk about the job opportunity among themselves. A few conservative companies are strict about their executives looking at other opportunities but loyalty toward employees seems to have somewhat decreased in the past few years due to major layoffs and downsizing programs. After only a few minutes, candidates willingly divulge their exact compensation program (base salary, bonus, etc.).

The Quebec and Canada Charters of Human Rights preclude you from asking about age, language, ethnic origin, sex, sexual preferences, religious beliefs, and political opinions. All over, people are used to being asked about languages spoken as a large percentage of your assignments require bilingualism (French/English) as a basic criterion. More and more, international employers ask for a third or fourth language (Spanish, German, etc.).

Some young executives may tend to change the pattern and put emphasis on personal or family life but the market is still very demanding on the number of hours required from senior executives, and most continue to put a very strong emphasis on their career. Given the current unemployment rate, people are more and more insecure and reluctant to change jobs unless they have a very good reason to do so. Higher compensation is not the only incentive to change employers. Geographical mobility is becoming more difficult as spouses have increasingly well-paid jobs and fear not being able to find suitable work at the new location. Selling the house or finding good education for the children in the new location is also becoming a priority.

Foreign nations with similar cultures: United States and United Kingdom

Key Research Resources (see Figure 13.10 beginning on page 197).

Figure 13.10 Research resources.
General Company Directories

Name of Service	Medium	Vendor Address	Description	Price
Dun & Bradstreet	Book	Dun & Bradstreet 5770 Hurontario St. Missisaua, Ontario Canada Ph.: 905-568-6207 Fax: 905-568-6278	Business information for the largest Canadian companies; you can select by industry, size of company, SIC code, etc.	CAN$ 520 per year
Dun's Direct Access	Online	Dun & Bradstreet 5770 hurontario St. Missisaua, Ontario Canada Ph.: 905-568-6207 Fax: 905-568-6278	Online access to business information for more than nine million U.S. and Canadian companies; select by industry, size of company, headquarters-only etc.; up to fifteen executive's names are listed for each company; requires PC and modem.	CAN$ 1,000/year minimum investment
Financial Post Top 500	Book	Canada's Largest Companies, 184 Frontstr. East, Ste. 400 Toronto M5A 4N3 Ontario, Canada Ph.: 416-368-7237	Canada's largest companies ranked by *The Financial Post*.	Annual publications included with subscription

(Continued)

Figure 13.10 *(Continued)*

Name of Service	Medium	Vendor Address	Description	Price
Infomart Dialog	Online	Infomart 1450 Don Mells Rd. Don Mells, M3B 2X7 Ontario, Canada Ph.: 416-442-2198 Fax: 416-445-3508	Provides access to the products and services of both Infomart Online and DIALOG; services include online databases, CD-ROM and media monitoring products; contains thousands of sources including: worldwide company information, both directory listings and full financials (company background and financial data, Canadian financials, directory of directors; Dun & Bradstreet files, FP Corporate Survey, intercorporate ownership).	Price varies, depending on service; call 800-668-9315 or 416-442-2198 for info.
The Blue Book of Canadian Business	Book	Toronto, Ontario Canada Ph.: 416-422-4742 www.bluebook.ca	Reference guide to approximately 2,500 Canadian firms; includes in-depth profiles and ranking of major Canadian firms; photographs of CEOs.	CAN$ 159.95
The Globe & Mail	Book	Report on Business, Top 1000 Companies in Canada 444 Front St. West Toronto, M5V 2S9 Ontario, Canada Ph.: 416-585-5000 Fax: 416-585-5085	Top 1,000 companies in Canada.	Included with subscription

Specialty Directories

Canadian Trade Index	CD-ROM	Canadian Trade Index 75 International Blvd. Etobicoke, M9W 6L9 Ontario, Canada Ph.: 416-798-8000 Fax: 416-798-8055	CD-ROM version available in April 1996; a national listing of Canadian manufacturing companies having more than a local distribution for their products; also includes an exporters section. Consultant Service: The service is called Manufax; provides customized searches.	Price (update): CAN$ 400.00 for CD-ROM CAN$ 200.00 (for nonelectronic version only)
Directory of Directors	Book	Financial Post Data Group, 333 King St. East Toronto, MSA 4N2 Ontario, Canada Ph.: 416-350-6500 Fax: 416-350-6501	Lists addresses, executive positions and directorships of directors and executives of Canadian companies, with access by company and name of director.	CAN$ 134.95
Scott's Selectory—The Directory on Disc	CD-ROM	Scott's Selectory 1450 Don Mells Rd. Don Mells, M3B 2X7 Ontario, Canada Ph.: 416-442-2070 Fax: 416-442-2191	Manufacturing database of 17,500 estimated companies across Canada; more than twenty employees; eleven megabytes required; network and/or CD-ROM versions available.	CAN$ 1,300 annually
The Directory of Associations	Book	Micromedia Limited 20 Victoria Street Toronto, M5C 2N8 Ontario, Canada Ph.: 416-362-5211 Fax: 416-362-6161	Comprehensive list of associations in Canada; includes name, address, phone, service and contact name; sometimes publications provided and membership availability.	CAN$ 250

(Continued)

Figure 13.10 *(Continued)*

Name of Service	Medium	Vendor Address	Description	Price
Top Employers Data Base	Diskette	Metro Toronto Board of Trade 1 First Canadian Place P.O. Box 60 Toronto, N5X 1C1 Ontario, Canada Ph.: 416-366-6811 Fax: 416-366-2483	Database identifying more than 12,000 executives in the Toronto region's largest businesses and organizations; all organizations with 100 + employees; variety of industries; public and private companies, government, educational institutions, etc.; detailed company profiles provided with up to eleven key personnel per company.	CAN$ 695
Info-Globe	Online	Globe & Mail, Toronto Ph.: 416-585-5250 www.globeandmail.ca	Online access to variety of news and business information products: newspapers, news wires and magazines, reference and directory databases.	CAN$ 39.95 per month
The Globe & Mail Report on Business	Book	Report on Business, Top 1000 Companies in Canada 444 Front St. West Toronto, M5V 2S9 Ontario, Canada Ph.: 416-585-5000 Fax: 416-585-5085	Current news, ratios, and price performance charts, and annual and quarterly financial information for 503 major Canadian public companies; Toronto Stock Exchange 300; additional section of all companies that appeared in the July 1995 Report on Business (ROB) 1000 including public and private companies, crown corp., and cooperatives; each entry lists address, stock symbol, description of business, senior executive, assets, revenue, and net income from most recent annual report and rankings from the ROB 1000.	CAN$ 59.95

Major Libraries

National Library of Canada
395 Wellington St.
Ottawa, Ontario
K1A 0N4
Ph.: 613-995-9481
Fax: 613-996-7941
Web address: www.nlc-bnc.ca
E-Mail: reference@nlc-bnc.ca

University of Toronto Libraries
Toronto, Ontario M5S 1A5
Ph.: 416-978-5093
Fax: 416-978-7653
Web address: www.library.utoronto.ca

France

Figure 13.11 Map of France.

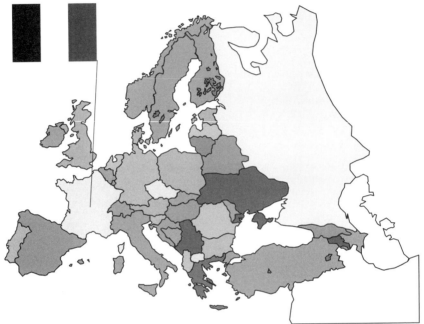

Country Information

Internet link to country information: www.france.com

International dialing code: +33

Population: 58,609,285 (July 1997)

Ethnic divisions: Celtic and Latin with Teutonic, Slavic, North African, Indochinese, Basque minorities

Religions: Roman Catholic 90 percent, Protestant 2 percent, Jewish 1 percent, Muslim (North African workers) 1 percent, unaffiliated 6 percent

Languages: French 100 percent, rapidly declining regional dialects and languages (Provencal, Breton, Alsatian, Corsican, Catalan, Basque, Flemish)

Labor force: 25.5 million; by occupation: services 69 percent, industry 26 percent, agriculture 5 percent (1995)

Capital: Paris

Economic overview: One of the world's most highly developed economies, France has substantial agricultural resources and a diversified modern industrial sector. Large tracts of fertile land, the application of modern technology, and subsidies have combined to make it the leading agricultural producer in Western Europe. Largely self-sufficient in agricultural products, France is a major exporter of wheat and dairy products. The industrial sector generates about one-quarter of the GDP, and the growing services sector has become crucial to the economy. Regardless, high unemployment still poses a major problem for the government. However, economic and financial integration within the European Union (EU) will presumably remain a major force in shaping the fortunes of the various economic sectors over the next few years.

Industries: Steel, machinery, chemicals, automobiles, metallurgy, aircraft, electronics, mining, textiles, food processing, tourism

Currency: 1 French franc (FFR) = 100 centimes; exchange rates: French francs (FFR) per US$1—5.62 (October 1998)

Figure 13.12 Major cities, industries, and corporations.

City	Center of
Aquitaine; Bordeaux	Chemicals, paper, pulp, conservatives
Ile-de-France; Paris	Public administration
Mid, Pyrénées; Toulouse	Aerospace and space industry
Nord-Pas de Calais; Lille	Textiles, mechanical industry
Provence, Alpes, Côte d'Azur; Marseille	Oil, chemicals
Rhône-Alpes; Lyon, Grenoble	Textiles, mechanical industry, electronics

Company	Industry
BNP	Banking
Carrefour	Trade
CGE	Electrical equipment
EDF	Electricity production
Elf Aquitaine	Petroleum
France Telecom	Telecommunication
Générale des Eaux	Water, construction
Peugeot	Automotive
Renault	Automotive
Total CPE	Petroleum
Usinor Sailor	Metallurgic industry

Culture

Business Culture

BUSINESS PROTOCOL: Punctuality is essential, even though meetings rarely start on time and a visitor may be kept waiting for half an hour or longer. If you are running late, it is advisable to call ahead and explain the delay. This is even more important in Lyon than in Paris. Lyonnais tend to be more reserved and formal in business relations than Parisians. When in France, do as the French do. They are quite possibly Europe's champions at handshaking—doing so at every meeting and parting. Men should wait for their superior to take the initiative in shaking hands; women should extend their hands first to a man, regardless of his position. Business cards should be exchanged at the first meeting. They should be both in French and in English, as should be any promotional material presented. The senior person should be addressed first, and often should be referred to according to his position, for example, "monsieur le director." Follow the lead of the French subordinates in this respect. Otherwise, last names should be used unless the visitor is invited to use first names. Opening conversation is usually brief and typically on a subject dealing with France—culture, travel—but not politics or personal or family matters, which are considered private. Conversation then turns quickly to business. Regret should be expressed at not speaking French.

PREPARATION FOR THE MEETING: Arranging an appointment with a French businessperson can take time and persistence, but the effort can be well worth it. The French appreciate good form and business manners. If there has been no previous contact, an intermediary known to both parties can be most helpful, especially if an introduction over lunch (ideal) can be arranged. Otherwise, contact should be initiated through a respectfully phrased letter. Appointments should be made well in advance—the best times are 11:00 A.M. to 3:30 P.M.—and it is advisable to confirm a day or so before. A visitor should be well aware of French business attitudes and procedures in advance. A business card should be presented to the secretary or receptionist upon arrival for an appointment.

WORKING WOMEN: According to French government statistics, some 60 percent of French women are in the workforce. The greater part are in lower-pay fields and lower-pay positions; their average earnings are about 75 percent of what their male counterparts make. Increasing numbers of women, however, are finding their way into business, especially in the service sector and into staff positions. Some women hold top positions in banks, insurance companies, the media, advertising, and retailing, and nearly everywhere women make an increasingly strong showing in middle and upper-middle management. Prejudice persists in industry, but there is progress in areas such as personnel, sales, and financial departments.

WORK ETHIC: French workers are among the most skilled and well trained in Western Europe. Their prior reputation of being volatile in relations with management and excessively strike-prone, especially in the public sector, has largely been shed during the past few decades of rapid economic growth and restructuring.

ATTITUDE TOWARD FOREIGNERS: The French are intensively aware who they are. They are proud of their long history and influential role in world affairs, and above all, of a culture they regard as the world's most brilliant. They do not regard their stature as a nation and civilization as diminished in any respect. Their reputation of being brusque and unfriendly with foreigners is not entirely deserved. This reputation is based, to a great extent, on the experiences of tourists in Paris, where the pressures of life take their toll in civility, as in many other busy places of the world. If approached with respect and consideration, the French will generally respond in a like manner. Friendships, once established, can be most rewarding.

Cultural factors affecting executive search: In France, the main problem when contacting a candidate is the secretary. She is considered a real obstacle. Once you can get through and you talk to the candidate, usually the candidate is nice and does not hesitate to give you some time.

According to the law you cannot ask about race, and very few people do so. Otherwise, personal questions, such as marital status, age, salary, can be asked when necessary.

In France the quality of the work and the company are very important for the candidates. Next in importance lies the salary, the organization of the company, and the location of the post.

Foreign nations with similar cultures: Belgium

Key Research Resources (see Figure 13.13 beginning on page 206).

Figure 13.13 Research resources.
General Company Directories

Name of Service	Medium	Vendor Address	Description	Price
Duns Marketing (Companies, France)	Online	Dun & Bradstreet France S.A. 345, Av. George Cleminceau 92882 Nanterre Cedex 9 France Ph.: 33 1 4135 1700 Fax: 33 1 4135 1777 www.dbfrance.com	More than 240,000 French companies with more than ten employees or annual turnover exceeding 10 million FFR. Brief company information, with key executives. Categorized by SIC code.	Please request
EURIDILE	Online	France Institut National de la Propriete Industrielle (INPI) 26 bis, rue de Leningrad F-75800 Paris Cedex 8 France Ph.: 33 1 5304 Fax: 33 1 4294 0209 www.INPI.fr	Contains descriptive and financial information on more than 2 million companies registered in France. Information available in French only.	Please request
French Company Handbook	Book	Hoover's, Inc. 1033 La Posada Dr., Ste. 250 Austin, TX 78752 Ph.: 800-486-8666	Profiles of companies quoted on the Paris Societe des Bourses Francaises (SBF) 120 index plus major bond issuers.	US$ 59.95
Kompass France	CD-ROM/Online	Kompass France S.A. 66, quai du Marechal Joffre 92415 Courbevoie Cedex France Ph.: 1 4116 5100 www.kompass.fr	115,000 French manufacturers, distributors, and service companies. Indexed by company and industry.	Please request

206

Title	Format	Contact	Description	Price
Top Management France	Book/CD-ROM	Alain Renier & Co. Ave. des Casernes 41A B-1040 Bruxelles Belgium Ph.: 2 646 2740 Fax: 2 646 2017 www.topmanagement.net	11,000 top French managers and 10,000 leading companies. Brief information on both people and companies.	FFR 2,300

Specialty Directories

Title	Format	Contact	Description	Price
American Chamber of Commerce in France—Membership Directory	Book	American Chamber of Commerce in France 21, Ave. George-V 75008 Paris France Ph.: 1 4723 8026	1,800 American businesses interested in developing trade and investment within and between France and the United States. Indexed by line of business and company name.	US$ 90
ESSOR Francais du Commerce International	Book/CD-ROM	Union Francaise d'Annuaires Professionals (UFAP) 13, Ave. Hennequin 78192 Trappes Cedex France Ph.: 1 3013 8200	30,000 exporting companies from all lines of businesses in France. Arranged by product/service.	Please request

Most of the resources are yearbooks issued by the alumni associations of business and engineering schools (more or less 220 reference books).

There are several hundred reference books concerning various sectors such as insurance, bank, retail, and industries.

It is very common to use school directories to find information concerning candidates.

Major Libraries

> Bibliothèque Nationale et Universitaire
> 6, place de la République
> BP 1029/F
> 67070 Strasbourg Cedex
> Ph.: 88 28 2800
> Fax: 88 25 2803
>
> Bibliothèque de la Sorbonne
> 47, rue des Ecoles
> 75230 Paris Cedex 05
> Ph.: 40 46 3027
> Fax: 40 46 3044

Germany

Figure 13.14 Map of Germany.

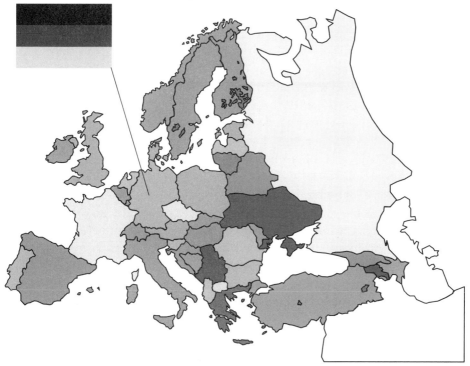

Country Information

Internet link to country information:
www.germany.net/index.html
www.rz.uni-karlsruhe.de/Outerspace/VirtualLibrary
International dialing code: +49
Population: 82,071,765 (July 1997 est.)
Ethnic divisions: German 95.1 percent, Turkish 2.3 percent, Italian 0.7 per-
cent, Greek 0.4 percent, Polish 0.4 percent, other 1.1 percent (made
up largely of people fleeing the war in the former Yugoslavia)
Religions: Protestant 45 percent, Roman Catholic 37 percent, unaffiliated
or other 18 percent
Languages: German
Labor force: 38.7 million; by occupation: industry 41 percent, agriculture 3
percent, other 56 percent (1995)
Capital: Berlin

Economic overview: Years after the fall of the Berlin Wall, progress toward
economic integration between eastern and western Germany is clearly
visible, yet the eastern region almost certainly will remain dependent
on subsidies funded by western Germany until well into the twenty-
first century. The economic recovery in the east is led by the construction industries, which account for one-third of industrial output, with
growth increasingly supported by the service sectors and light manufacturing industries. Eastern Germany's economy is changing from
one anchored on manufacturing to a more service-oriented economy.
Western Germany, with three times the per capita output of the eastern states, has an advanced market economy and is a world leader in
exports. Western Germany has a highly urbanized and skilled population that enjoys excellent living standards, abundant leisure time, and
comprehensive social welfare benefits. It is relatively poor in natural
resources, coal being the most important mineral. Western Germany's
world-class companies manufacture technologically advanced goods.
The region's economy is mature: Services and manufacturing account
for the dominant share of economic activities, and raw materials and
semimanufactured goods constitute a large portion of imports.

Industries: Western: Among the world's largest and most technologically
advanced producers of iron, steel, coal, cement, chemicals, machinery,
vehicles, machine tools, electronics; food and beverages
Eastern: metal fabrication, chemicals, brown coal, shipbuilding, machine building, food and beverages, textiles, petroleum refining

Currency: 1 deutsche mark (DM) = 100 pfennig; exchange rates: deutsche
marks (DM) per US$1—1.68 (October 1998)

Figure 13.15 Major cities, industries, and corporations.

City	Center of
Berlin	Industry and service
Bonn	Government administration, automotive
Düsseldorf or Köln	Administration
Frankfurt	Banking
Hamburg	Trade
München	Industry and service
Stuttgart	High technology industry and service

Company	Industry
BASF	Chemicals
Bayer	Chemicals

Company	Industry
Daimler-Benz	Automotive
DBP	Telecommunications
Deutsche Bank	Banking and finance
Hoechst	Chemicals
RWE	Energy
Siemens	Electronics
Tengelmann	Commercial industry
Veba	Energy and gasoline
Volkswagen (V.A.G.)	Automotive

Culture

Business Culture

BUSINESS PROTOCOL: When in Germany, do somewhat as the Germans do. The German executive, particularly of the younger generation, has become less formal and more relaxed in recent years. He (rarely she, despite the constitution's strictures on gender blindness) is, however, still inclined to be more conservative in attitude and attire than is the American norm. Business cards are expected. Punctuality is important. Handshaking is a national ritual. Meetings typically take place on company premises, in an office or conference room, and tend to be rather formal occasions. Polite small talk is customary before beginning to talk serious business. It is also important to be aware that in Germany, oral agreements or statements are often considered to be as binding as written contracts.

PREPARATION FOR THE MEETING: Appointments are essential and should be scheduled well in advance, preferably not for the later part of the afternoon. Hardworking as they typically are, Germans do not like to put in overtime. They are often at their desks early in the morning, and like to leave on time at the end of the working day. Punctuality is expected. If there is going to be a delay for any reason, a business visitor should call and explain the situation.

WORKING WOMEN: Although women have become an important part of the workforce and are increasingly prominent in political life and, to some extent, in the media, they are not a significant presence in business at the management or executive levels. German business and industry are still male dominated. German businessmen typically are very courteous, but as a rule do not take a woman as seriously as a decision maker for a foreign firm as they would a male representative.

WORK ETHIC: German workers have a well-deserved reputation for being hardworking. Concern has been expressed in the press and elsewhere that there has been some erosion in the work ethic as a consequence of the affluence in recent years. There is no evidence that productivity has been seriously affected, however. German labor costs have long been among the highest in the world, yet German products remain among the most competitive in the world.

ATTITUDE TOWARD FOREIGNERS: Xenophobia has increased disturbingly since unification. It is directed almost exclusively toward foreign workers resident in Germany and, most violently, at the flood of would-be immigrants from the Third World pouring into the country, seeking asylum as political refugees. Although most Germans decry the violence, polls show a large percentage of the public is antagonistic to the foreigners.

Cultural factors affecting executive search: First contact: Getting to the first contact is the problem in Germany. Identification is made next to impossible because, in most cases, companies are hesitant to give the names or information about their employees. Therefore, identification is itself a fine art for German researchers. When you finally get hold of a potential candidate, it is common that he or she does not open up early in the contact—written information on the position is often necessary as proof of legitimacy.

In Germany most people are rather formal. Everyone should be addressed on a second-name basis. Most people should be contacted and interviewed in their offices. There are, of course, cases when you have to call people privately because they cannot talk frankly in their offices. It is important to be upright and trustworthy on the phone. You can legally ask anything, but the candidate may not want to answer. The biggest problem is salary.

Status—usually in the form of a company car—is of the utmost importance to German candidates. You can almost tell how successful somebody is by the make of his or her company car.

In Germany, many people do not like to move from their homes, even if they are offered a great chance. The family must be integrated in the process of changing jobs. This special subject has to be separately and widely discussed with a candidate. Immobility has become less of an issue with the younger generation of managers.

Languages—apart from English, at least to a certain level—are not a strength of German candidates.

It has become more and more important to keep contact with a candidate after signing the contract in order to make sure that he or she really starts in the new job. Once a candidate has chosen to leave his or her current occupation, he or she will choose the most lucrative and viable option. Staying in contact ensures that both parties agree that your offer will be kept and not discarded for one perceived as more profitable. Any remaining doubts have to be openly discussed with the candidate and the client.

Foreign nations with similar culture: Austria

Key Research Resources (see Figure 13.16 beginning on page 214).

Figure 13.16 Research resources.
General Company Directories

Name of Service	Medium	Vendor Address	Description	Price
Bilanzdatenbank	CD-ROM	Verlag Hoppenstedt GmbH Wirtschaftsdatenbank Postfach 10 01 39 D-64201 Darmstadt Germany Ph.: 49 6151 3800 Fax: 49 6151 380360 www.hoppenstedt.com	Detailed standard balance sheets (balance and income) of more than 4,000 major German companies.	DM 16,000 (annual subscription includes six updates)
Creditreform	Online	Creditreform Dusseldorf Frorman KG Cantadorstrasse 13 D-40211 Dusseldorf Germany Ph.: 49 211 16710 Fax: 49 211 1671108	German company profiles and balance sheets.	DM 61, 70 per document
Dafine	CD-ROM	Burau van Dijk Electronic Publications GmbH Ziegelhuttenweg 43 D-60598 Frankfurt Germany Ph.: 49 69 9636650 Fax: 49 69 96366550 www.bvdep.com	Balance and income of German companies (25,000 companies).	DM 9,600 (annual subscription include six updates)

Title	Format	Publisher	Description	Price
Firmendatabank	CD-ROM	Verlag Hoppenstedt GmbH Wirtschaftsdatenbank Postfach 10 01 39 D-64201 Darmstadt Germany Ph.: 49 6151 3800 Fax: 49 6151 380360 www.hoppenstedt.com	More than 170,000 profiles of major German companies, banks, authorities, organizations, and industry associations.	DM 24,000 (annual subscription includes four updates)
Handbuch der mittelstandischen Unternehmen (mid- to small-sized companies)	Book	Verlag Hoppenstedt GmbH Wirtschaftsdatenbank Postfach 10 01 39 D-64201 Darmstadt Germany Ph.: 49 6151 3800 Fax: 49 6151 380360 www.hoppenstedt.com	One of the standard works, which every researcher sees as the "bible" (also available in paper and as CD-ROM/online). The company profiles give details of: turnover, employees, main activities, and names of top management (in most cases).	DM 600–700
Hoppenstedt	CD-ROM	Verlag Hoppenstedt GmbH Wirtschaftsdatenbank Postfach 10 01 39 D-64201 Darmstadt Germany Ph.: 49 6151 3800. Fax: 49 6151 380360 www.hoppenstedt.com	Firm profiles of approximately 23,000 of big companies of all sectors such as details like the name of company, address, bank details, name of members of the executive board, turnover, assets, product, subsidiary.	DM 800
Hoppenstedt– Handbuch der Grossunternehmen	Book	Verlag Hoppenstedt GmbH Wirtschaftsdatenbank Postfach 10 01 39 D-64201 Darmstadt Germany Ph.: 49 6151 3800 Fax: 49 6151 380360 www.hoppenstedt.com	Company data of around 23,000 German companies; revised annually.	DM 790

(Continued)

Figure 13.16 *(Continued)*

Name of Service	Medium	Vendor Address	Description	Price
Hoppenstedt–Mittelstandische Unternehmen	Book	Verlag Hoppenstedt GmbH Wirtschaftsdatenbank Postfach 10 01 39 D-64201 Darmstadt Germany Ph.: 49 6151 3800 Fax: 49 6151 380360 www.hoppenstedt.com	Company directory, Germany	DM 520
Kompass	Book	Kompass Deutschland Postfach 964 D-79111 Freiburg Germany Ph.: 49 761 452670 Fax: 49 761 452672 www.kompass.com	Company directory, Germany	DM 750
Kompass Deutschland	CD-ROM	Kompass Deutschland Verlags- und Vertriebsgesellschaft GmbH Postfach 964 D-79009 Freiburg I. Br. Germany Ph.: 49 761 452670 Fax: 49 761 452673 www.kompass.com	German company profiles with detailed products and services.	DM 5,200 (annual subscription includes one update)
Laser-D International	CD-ROM	Disclosure GmbH Mainzer Land-strasse 78 D-60327 Frankfurt, Germany Ph.: 49 692739 9180 Fax: 49 692739 9190 www.disclosure.com	Document retrieval system: full-text annual reports of major worldwide companies.	DM 50,000 per year (includes hardware leasing)

Markus	CD-ROM	Burau van Dijk Electronic Publications GmbH Ziegelhuttenweg 43 D-60598 Frankfurt Germany Ph.: 49 69 963665 0 Fax: 49 69 963665 5 www.bvdep.com	Short profiles of 600,000 German and Austrian companies.	DM 15,000 (annual subscription includes four updates)
Schimmelpfeng	Online	Dun & Bradstreet Deutschland Grossen Baumerweg 40472 Düsseldorf Germany Ph.: 49 2217 7370 Fax: 49 2115 1923 www.dbgermany.com	German and European company profiles and balance sheets.	DM 63–83 per document (depending on length)

Specialty Directories

Hoppenstedt, Leitende Manner und Frauen der Wirtschaft	Book	Verlag Hoppenstedt GmbH Wirtschaftsdatenbank Postfach 10 01 39 D-64201 Darmstadt Germany Ph.: 49 6151 3800 Fax: 49 6151 380360 www.hoppenstedt.com	Candidate information about top management.	
Hoppenstedt, Wer leitet?	Book	Verlag Hoppenstedt GmbH Wirtschaftsdatenbank Postfach 10 01 39 D-64201 Darmstadt Germany Ph.: 49 6151 3800 Fax: 49 6151 380360 www.hoppenstedt.com	Candidate information about middle management.	

(Continued)

Figure 13.16 (*Continued*)

Name of Service	Medium	Vendor Address	Description	Price
Wer liefert was?	CD-ROM	Wer liefert was? GmbH Normannenweg 16-20 D-20537 Hamburg Germany Ph.: 49 40 254400 Fax: 49 40 254401 www.wlw.online.de	Supply and product information.	DM 600

News Services

Süddeutscher Verlag Archiv (archive of "Süddeutsche Zeitung")	Book	Süddeutscher Verlag Archiv Sendlinger St. 8 D-80331 Munchen Germany Ph.: 49 89 2183 8394 Fax: 49 89 2183 8395 www.suddeutscher.de	Provides articles from past editions; search on key issues.	DM 30

Because of the enormous restrictions regarding the private sphere of the individual in Germany there is very little published on candidates themselves.

All the main newspapers provide a research service (minimum cost about DM 30–40) where individual or company press releases can be obtained.

Major Libraries

TIB, Technische Information Bibliothek
Postfach 6080
D-30060 Hannover
Germany
Ph.: 49 511 762 2268
Fax: 49 511 715936

Staatsbibliothek Preuss
Kulturbesitz
Haus 1 D-10102 Berlin/Haus 2
  D-10772
Berlin
Germany
Ph.: 49 30 2015 0
Fax: 49 30 2015 1459

HWWA Institut f. Wirtschaftsforschung Bibliothek
D-20347 Hamburg
Germany
Ph.: 49 40 3562 242

Bibliothek d. Institutes f. Weltwirtschaft, Kiel
  Deutsche Zentralbibliothek f. Wirtschaftswesen
D-24100 Kiel
Germany
Ph.: 49 431 8814 1
Fax: 49 431 8814 520
E-Mail: zbwa@zbw.uni-kiel.de

Hong Kong

Figure 13.17 Map of Hong Kong (Chinese province).

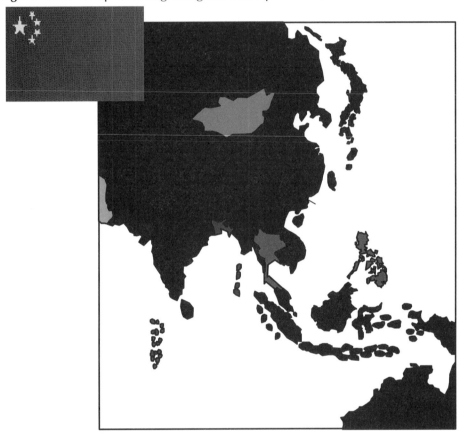

Country Information

Internet link to country information: www.asiawind.com/hkwwwvl
International dialing code: +852
Population: 6,547,189 (July 1997 est.)
Ethnic divisions: Chinese 95 percent, other 5 percent
Religions: Eclectic mixture of local religions 90 percent, Christian 10 percent
Languages: Chinese (Cantonese), English
Labor force: 3.251 million (1996); by occupation: manufacturing 14.2 percent; wholesale and retail trade, restaurants, and hotels 34.4 percent; services 19.8 percent; financing, insurance, and real estate 12.4 percent;

transport and communications 5.1 percent; construction 2.1 percent; other 12 percent (1994)

Capital: Victoria

Economic overview: Hong Kong has a bustling free-market economy with few tariffs or nontariff barriers. Natural resources are limited, and food and raw materials must be imported. Manufacturing accounts for about 17 percent of the GDP. Goods and services exports account for about 50 percent of the GDP. Unemployment, which has been declining since the mid-1980s, is now about 2 percent. A shortage of labor continues to put upward pressure on prices and the cost of living. Prospects for the next few years remain bright so long as major trading partners continue to be reasonably prosperous and so long as investors feel China will continue to support free-market practices in Hong Kong.

Industries: Textiles, clothing, tourism, electronics, plastics, toys, watches, clocks. Agriculture: minor role in the economy; local farmers produce 26 percent of fresh vegetables, 27 percent of live poultry; 8 percent of land area suitable for farming

Currency: 1 Hong Kong dollar (HK$) = 100 cents; exchange rates: Hong Kong dollars (HK$) per US$—7.73 (October 1998)

Figure 13.18 Major industries and corporations.

Company	Industry
Amway Asia Pacific Ltd.	The company distributes approximately 160 different products in four lines: personal care, home care, home tech, and health and fitness (nutrition).
China Light & Power Company Ltd.	Utility; electricity supplied to Kowloon and the New Territories in Hong Kong.
China Resources Development, Inc.	A holding company with major investments in agriculture in China.
CITIC Pacific Ltd.	Financial; investments in telecommunications, electricity, and aviation.
DSG International Limited	Manufactures and markets disposable diapers, disposable training pants, adult incontinence products, and feminine napkins.

(Continued)

Figure 13.18 *(Continued)*

Company	Industry
Hong Kong Telecommunications Limited	Provides more than three million phone lines to Hong Kong and southern mainland China and has more than 270,000 mobile customers.
Hopewell Holdings Limited	Has extensive holdings in real estate, including office buildings and hotels, in Hong Kong and mainland China. It is also a major infrastructure developer in Asia.
Hutchison Whampoa Ltd.	Has extensive interests in food processing and distribution, retailing, manufacturing, real estate, and telecom.
Peregrine Investments Holdings Limited	Financial; investment bank (#1 in Asia)
Singer Company N.V.	Manufactures, markets, and distributes sewing machines worldwide from its main base of operations in Hong Kong.
Swire Pacific Limited	One of the city's largest real estate owners and developers.
Tommy Hilfiger Corporation	Designs and sells designer men's sportswear and boys wear.

Culture

Business Culture

BUSINESS PROTOCOL: Generally, business dealings are much the same as in the West. Foreigners, the mainstay of Hong Kong's business, tourism, and media, are welcomed with open arms, although they are sometimes resented for their comforts. Your contacts are most likely to be Westernized, and Hong Kong has no formalities peculiar to itself. As elsewhere in Asia, age is revered and must be treated with respect. Dignity and stature are similarly valued. The foreigner should always be polite; losing your temper will cost you respect and possibly even the deal itself. Superstition (feng shui) is a widespread belief. Anyone planning to open an office is advised to hire a feng shui professional, or risk scaring off the local staff.

PREPARATION FOR THE MEETING: Presentation is very important. Bring plenty of promotional material along. Since some English instruction is compulsory in schools, it is not necessary to have everything translated into Chinese. Still, as a courtesy to potential candidates, have at least a summary rendered into Chinese that can be distributed at the start of the meeting. Appointments are essential, and it is wise to be prompt. Appointments, however, are often changed or canceled (sometimes by fax), as everyone in this city appears to be busy. Letters of inquiry count as well, although actual contacts and negotiations are direct and informal. Since Hong Kong has a long tradition of foreign trade, most businesspeople are used to dealing with foreigners. Business cards are essential. It is a good idea to have them printed in both English and Chinese with a Cantonese approximation of your name.

WORKING WOMEN: Largely because of American influence, women are becoming a greater presence in business careers, the professions, and politics. Some things are slow to change, though; secretaries are always female and the female staffers are still expected to get coffee. However, foreign businesswomen usually have little trouble getting equal treatment from Hong Kong executives. In this case, power is of more importance than gender. Blatant sexual overtures are considered bad form, so harassment like that common in other countries is almost unheard of.

WORK ETHIC: Wages are generally figured out on a time basis (hourly, daily, monthly), or on an incentive basis depending on volume of work. Women and children are restricted in the number of hours per week they can work (no more than forty-eight hours per week). The Chinese are hardworking and diligent. Factory workers are responsible, if unskilled.

ATTITUDE TOWARD FOREIGNERS: In general, foreigners with skills that are not readily available in Hong Kong can easily obtain work permits for entry. Bankers, entrepreneurs, and others capable of developing local employment and contributing to the economy are also considered for entry. Hong Kong is an extremely international city and foreigners are well received.

Cultural factors affecting executive search: Most contacts with candidates are initiated through the phone (i.e., cold calls). Whether you can be on a first-name basis depends on the kind of corporate culture that the potential candidate is in. If the potential candidate works for an American company, it is okay to start the conversation on a first-name level. However, if the potential candidate is from a local (Chinese) company, it is safer to address him or her formally as Mr. or Ms.

Generally, when speaking English, you are treated better and given information more readily. However, at times language is an issue and you need to speak Chinese in order to establish contact. Chinese secretaries are very tough—they overscreen calls—but if you do get through, most people are willing to speak to you.

There are no restrictions as to what questions you can ask, for example, married or single, age, race, what their family does, occupation of spouse, and other such personal information. Interviewing companies can expect to see this type of information on their candidate reports. Sometimes this type of information is necessary when a position involves, for example, a move to another country or to mainland China. In these cases, relocation expenses such as children's educational allowances are important to consider.

SPECIAL CHARACTERISTICS: Due to the fast-paced and competitive business environment of Hong Kong, people tend to be highly competitive, flexible, and ambitious. Generally, career advancement and family are their two major priorities. Social benefits from the government are very minimal, so Hong Kong people work very hard for long hours in order to better their living standards.

There is a high turnover among Hong Kong locals, especially at the lower to middle management levels. The changeover in 1997 to Chinese rule has affected the labor pool a great deal. Many of the management staff left to get overseas passports because life became uncertain and they wanted insurance for their future. Those who have stayed have adopted a more short-term attitude since a new job assignment with a move can easily increase their salary by 20 to 30 percent. Money is more important than lifestyle.

Job scope ranks second in importance. With the opening of China, most candidates are looking for regional exposures and larger responsibilities. They do not mind traveling extensively. However, this aspect may not apply to female executives, especially those married and with children. The husband's job still weighs more heavily than the wife's. Female executives do not mind working long hours, but they prefer minimal traveling and basing within Hong Kong.

Foreign nations with similar cultures: China and Taiwan

Key Research Resources (see Figure 13.19 beginning on page 225).

Figure 13.19 Research resources.
General Company Directories

Name of Service	Medium	Vendor Address	Description	Price
Asia Company Handbook	Book	Hoover's, Inc. 1033 La Posada Dr., Ste. 250 Austin, TX 78752 Ph.: 800-496-8666 www.hoovers.com	1,060 profiles of publicly traded corporations.	US$ 79.95
Asia's 7500 Largest Companies	Book/CD-ROM/ Online	ELC International 109 Uxbridge Rd. Ealing London W5 5TL England Ph.: 44 181 5662288 Fax: 44 181 5664931	Top 7,500 companies in selected countries in Asia. Brief company information.	£STG
Asia-Pacific Dun's Market Identifiers	Online	Dun & Bradstreet Ltd. 479 St. Kilda Rd. PO Box 7405 Melbourne, VIC 3000 Australia Ph.: 3 98283333 Fax: 3 98283300	More than 250,000 companies within Asia and the Pacific Rim. Full company information (SIC codes).	Please request
Business Directory of Hong Kong	Book	Current Publication Ltd. 1503 Enterprise Bldg. 228-238 Queen's Rd. Central Hong Kong Ph.: 22 5434702	More than 12,300 firms in Hong Kong classified by line of business.	US$ 180
Directory of Major Companies in South East Asia	Book	Gale Research 835 Penobscot Building Detroit, MI 48226-4094 Ph.: 313-961-2242 www.galenet.com	Detailed coverage of more than 1,500 indigenous and multinational corporations.	US$ 550

(Continued)

Figure 13.19 (*Continued*)

Name of Service	Medium	Vendor Address	Description	Price
Dun's Key Decision-Makers in Hong Kong Business	Book	Dun & Bradstreet Information Services, Dun & Bradstreet Corp. Three Sylvan Way Parsippany, NJ 07054-3896 Ph.: 201-606-6750 www.dnb.com	8,000 directors and senior executives from leading businesses in Hong Kong. Alphabetical by company and cross referenced by industry (SIC) and district.	US$ 380
Hong Kong Commercial/Industrial Guide	Book	GTE Directories (HK) Ltd. 25/F China Resources Bldg. 26 Harbour Rd. Wanchai, Hong Kong Ph.: 82 788668 www.gte.com	More than 200,000 suppliers of 2,000 products and services in Hong Kong. Arranged by product/service.	HK$ 30
The Thornton Guide to Hong Kong Companies	Book	Hoover's, Inc. 1033 La Posada Dr., Ste. 250 Austin, TX 78752 Ph.: 800-496-8666 www.hoovers.com	500 profiles of Hong Kong companies.	US$ 69.95

Specialty Directories

Name of Service	Medium	Vendor Address	Description	Price
American Chamber of Commerce in Hong Kong—Membership Directory	Book	American Chamber of Commerce in Hong Kong 19/F Bank of America Tower 12 Harcourt Rd. Central Hong Kong, Hong Kong Ph.: 2526 0165 www.amcham.org.hk	American and Hong Kong firms interested in developing trade and investment within and between the two countries. Indexed by line of business and company name.	US$ 181
Hong Kong Exporter's Association—Members Directory	Book	Hong Kong Exporter's Association Star House, Rm. 825 3 Salisbury Rd. Tsimshatsui	About 300 member firms, primarily manufacturers or exporters of goods from Hong Kong. Indexed by product.	US$ 48

Regarding candidate research, it is normal to focus on active identification of prospects in the market. Again, membership directories are the main source of candidate information.

Other people are usually the best sources of information in this very network intense town.

Major Libraries

Kowloon Central Library
5 Pui Ching Rd.
Homantin, Hong Kong
Ph.: 852 2926 4055
Fax: 852 2711 3126

City Hall Public Library
3/F, High Blk., City Hall
Central Hong Kong
Ph.: 852 2921 2555
Fax: 852 2877 2641

Figure 13.20 Internet snapshot of company information source for Hong Kong.

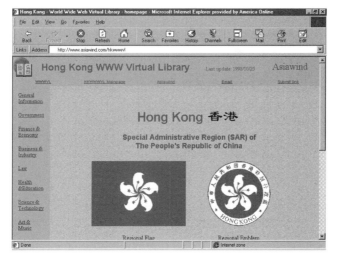

Japan

Figure 13.21 Map of Japan.

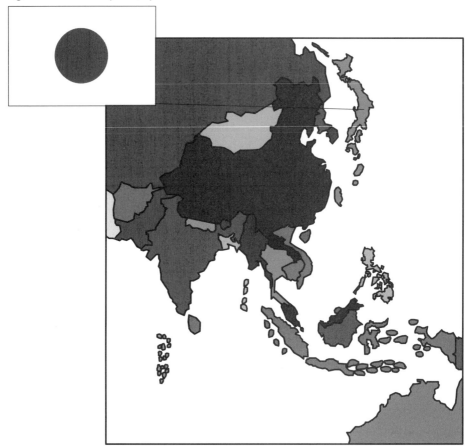

Country Information

Internet link to country information: www.ntt.co.jp/japan
International dialing code: +81
Population: 125,732,794 (July 1997 est.)
Ethnic divisions: Japanese 99.4 percent, other 0.6 percent (mostly Korean)
Religions: Observe both Shinto and Buddhist 84 percent, other 16 percent
    (including 0.7 percent Christian)

Languages: Japanese

Labor force: 67.23 million (March 1997); by occupation: trade and services 50 percent; manufacturing, mining, and construction 33 percent; agriculture, forestry, and fishing 6 percent; government 3 percent; utilities and communication 7 percent (1994)

Capital: Tokyo

Economic overview: Government–industry cooperation, a strong work ethic, mastery of high technology, and a comparatively small defense allocation (roughly 1 percent of the GDP) have helped Japan advance with extraordinary speed to among the most powerful economies in the world. Industry, the most important sector of the economy, is heavily dependent on imported raw materials and fuels. Usually self-sufficient in rice, Japan must import about 50 percent of its requirements of other grain and fodder crops. Japan maintains one of the world's largest fishing fleets and accounts for nearly 15 percent of the global catch. Overall economic growth has been spectacular: a 10 percent average in the 1960s, a 5 percent average in the 1970s and 1980s. However, government plans for administrative and economic reform, including reduction in the trade surplus are yet to be realized. The crowding of the habitable land area and the aging of the population are two major long-term problems.

Industries: Steel and nonferrous metallurgy, heavy electrical equipment, construction and mining equipment, motor vehicles and parts, electronic and telecommunication equipment and components, machine tools and automated production systems, locomotives and railroad rolling stock, shipbuilding, chemicals, textiles, food processing

Currency: yen (¥); exchange rates: yen (¥) per US$1—134.0 (October 1998)

Figure 13.22 Major cities, industries, and corporations.

City	Center of
Kobe	Imported goods
Nagoya	Toyota City, processing
Osako	Industry, trade
Sapporo	Trade
Tokyo	Finance, trade, industry
Yokohama	Imported goods

(Continued)

Figure 13.22 *(Continued)*

Company	Industry
Daiwa Securities Co.	Securities
Honda Corp.	Automotive
Nippon Telegraph and Telephone Corp.	Telecommunication
Nomura Securities	Securities
The Dai-ichi Kangyo Bank	Banking
The Fuji Bank	Banking
The Mitsubishi Bank	Banking
The Nikko Securities Co.	Securities
The Sanwa Bank	Banking
The Sumitomo Bank	Banking
Toyota Motor Corp.	Automotive

Culture

Business Culture

BUSINESS PROTOCOL: Your meeting will probably be in a conference room or one of the lounges scattered among the office desks. (A Japanese executive rarely receives outsiders at his desk, which is plain and may even be part of a large, open office.) The language of a meeting most likely will be Japanese, and the company will probably provide an interpreter. Even if the meeting is held in English, however, you would be advised to bring along a well-briefed Japanese-speaking associate. Silence is golden. Westerners are uncomfortable at lapses in the conversation, whereas Japanese often distrust someone who talks constantly.

You may address your new associates as "Mr. So-and-so," but "Mr. So-and-so-san" (adding the honorific "san" to the name) is preferable. The Japanese are formal in business matters and it is still recommended not to use their first names nor to suggest that they use yours. You may be greeted with an extended hand or with a bow; return the gesture. In a handshake, use only slight pressure; bow from the hips, or nod slightly. The exchange of business cards in the first meeting is an important ritual. The visitor goes first, after the bow or handshake, offering the English side up with both hands and facing the host so that he can read it immediately. Present your card only to those to whom you are introduced. To show respect (and learn the name), study the received card(s) carefully. Never pass on other people's cards without permission.

By custom, places are allocated around the table according to status.

Wait to be seated if in doubt. The meeting will begin with small talk to set the tone: the weather, your impressions of Japan, sports, and the like. Avoid personal questions; showing your appreciation of what you have seen in Japan will score points (try to take in a baseball game or a sumo match if possible).

State-of-the-art presentations that include graphs, charts, and bulleted major points on paper can help avoid misunderstanding and demonstrate your seriousness and the resources behind you. It is fine to show eagerness, but do not get excited or show strong emotion. Avoid negative statements or statements that require a negative answer. Japanese hate having to say "no" directly. They prefer expressions such as "let me think about it" or "I'm not sure."

PREPARATION FOR THE MEETING: Japanese are experienced generalists. They know a great deal of their company and its markets, and expect no less of the visitor. Learn all that you can about the company you will be dealing with and its competitors and be prepared to give a thorough account of your own company and its activities. Expect many meetings. The purpose of Japanese meetings is normally to exchange information and ideas, not to reach decisions and conclusions. Dress in formal business attire. The Japanese pay strict attention to dress and physical appearance. Men should wear dark suits, and women should wear restrained business dress, never pants.

WORKING WOMEN: The Japanese are slowly adapting to the idea of female executives. Foreign female executives will have far fewer problems than Japanese women. Women generally still play a more traditional role, so most Japanese executives are simply unaccustomed to dealing with women of status and power. If traveling as part of a group, make sure that rank and job function are clearly spelled out to avoid being ignored. After-hours entertainment is likely to present the most difficulty and awkwardness. Male Japanese executives do not invite their wives to these business-oriented drinking and socializing sessions. A Western female executive is likely to find herself as the only woman present.

WORK ETHIC: The Japanese work ethic could once be conveniently encapsulated in a few phrases: teamwork, strict adherence to seniority, decisions by consensus, long hours, total loyalty to employer, job security and lifetime employment. This is still, for the most part, true, but the younger generation seems to be changing toward a more individualistic, Western outlook. Punctuality is important: Even executives clock in, and senior staff members often come to work early.

ATTITUDE TOWARD FOREIGNERS: Many Westerners, though sometimes perceived by the Japanese as lazy and inferior businesspeople, are still considered valuable. Building a working, trusting relationship, however, takes time and patience. It is equally necessary for many foreigners to discard the preconceptions they may have developed toward the Japanese.

Cultural factors affecting executive search: When contacting candidates, you must make a lot of cold calls. Generally, people will open up more easily if you have been referred to them by someone they know. A good and efficient way to start the research and interview process is to do a mailing of the position specification to all your candidates, before you make any calls.

There are not many restrictions on what questions you can ask people. One of the few areas forbidden to probe is marital status. If this is a relevant fact to you, then you must use other techniques to get your answers without asking directly.

In general, Japanese professionals are very hardworking and do not mind sacrificing themselves by putting in overtime. There is, however, a new trend among young people that work is not the driving force in life.

Foreign nations with similar cultures: N/A

Key Research Resources (see Figure 13.23 beginning on page 232).

Figure 13.23 Research resources.
General Company Directories

Name of Service	Medium	Vendor Address	Description	Price
Affiliates and Offices of Foreign Corporations in Japan	Book	Affiliates and Offices of Foreign Corporations in Japan ('95) Nihon Keizai Shinbun Inc. 9-5, Ote-machi 1-chome Chiyoda-ku, Tokyo 100-66 Japan Ph.: 81 3 3270 0251 Fax: 81 3 5255 2648	Information on foreign corporations in Japan (3,319 companies): company names, English name, head office, establishment, outline, shareholder, parent company, board of directors, sales, characteristics, brand names, customers, bank reference, number of employees, offices, line of business, etc.	¥ 40,000 (annual issue)
Foreign Affiliate Companies in Japan: A Comprehensive Directory	Book	Tokyo Keizai Inc. 2-1, Nihonbashi Hongoku-cho 1-chome Chiyoda-ku, Tokyo 100 Japan Ph.: 81 3 3246 5655 Fax: 81 3 3241 5543 www.mediagalaxy. co.jp/tokyokeizei/index.htm	Information on foreign affiliated companies in Japan (3,130 companies): company name, line of business, English name, head office, telephone number, establishment, capital, shareholders, offices/plants, activities, suppliers, customers, brand names, bank reference, officers, important and export ratio, number of employees, performance, overseas parent company, characteristics and trends, etc.	¥ 15,000 (annual)

(Continued)

233

Figure 13.23 (Continued)

Name of Service	Medium	Vendor Address	Description	Price
Japan Company Handbook	Book	Tokyo Keizai Inc. 2-1, Nihonbashi Hongoku-cho 1-chome Chiyoda-ku, Tokyo 100 Japan Ph.: 81 3 3246 5655 Fax: 81 3 3241 5543 www.mediagalaxy. co.jp/tokyokeizai/index.htm	Information on 3,000 listed and unlisted companies in Japan: corporate name, order of listing, characteristic, outlook, income data, sales breakdown, stock prices, stock price chart, stocks, finance, financial data, facility investment, references, date of establishment, etc.	Quarterly edition: Japanese version—Listed ¥ 1,400, unlisted ¥ 1,850. English version—First Section ¥ 4,600, Second Section ¥ 4,600
Nihon no Kigyo (Japanese companies)	Book	Nikkan Kogyo Shinbun Ltd. 8-10, Kudan Kita 1-chome Chiyoda-ku, Tokyo 102 Japan Ph.: 81 3 3222 7110 Fax: 81 3 3764 0845	Information on 100,000 Japanese companies: company name, head office and branches, line of business, capital, sales, outlook, number of employees, board of directors, bank reference, president profile, etc.	¥ 159,000
Nikkei Company Profile	Online	Nikkei Company Profile Nihon Keizai Shinbun, Inc. 9-5, Ote-machi 1-chome Chiyoda-ku, Tokyo 100-66 Japan Ph.: 81 3 3270 0251 Fax: 81 3 5255 2648	Information of listed and unlisted companies in Japan (23,000 companies): corporate name, address, accounting period, capital, income data, outline, board of directors, customers, bank reference, stockholder, balance sheet, profit and loss, etc.	¥ 15,000 (monthly basic charge) plus unit charge

Nikkei: Annual Foreign Corporation Reports	Book	Nihon Keizai Shinbun Inc. 9-5, Ote-machi 1-chome Chiyoda-ku, Tokyo 100-66 Japan Ph.: 81 3 32270 0251 Fax: 81 3 5255 2648	Information on leading world companies in forty-one countries (3,676 companies): company name, head office, officers, number of employees, issued shares, capital, characteristics, shareholders, financial data, income data, outlook, etc.	¥ 53,000 (annual issue)
Teikoku Databank	Online	Teikoku Databank Ltd. 5-20, Minami-Aoyama 2-chome Minato-ku, Tokyo 107-8680 Japan Ph.: +81 3 3404 4311 Fax: +81 3 3475 4973 www.tdb.co.cco.jp	Same as previous entry (1,100,000 companies)	¥ 15,000 (monthly basic charge) plus unit charge
Tokyo Shoko Research	Online	Tokyo Shoko Research Shin-Ichi Bldg. 9-6, Shinbashi 1-chome Minato-ku, Tokyo 105 Japan Ph.: 81 3 3574 2211 Fax: 81 3 3571 5165	Information on listed and unlisted companies in Japan (670,000 companies): corporate name, address, president, telephone number, facsimile number, establishment, capital, number of employees, board of directors, shareholders, bank reference, suppliers, income data, ranking, president profile, etc.	¥ 15,000 (monthly basic charge) plus unit charge

(Continued)

Figure 13.23 (*Continued*)

Name of Service	Medium	Vendor Address	Description	Price
Specialty Directories				
Kaisha Shokuinroku	Book	Diamond Inc. 4-2, Kasumigaseki 1-chome Chiyoda-ku, Tokyo 100-60 Japan Ph.: 81 3 3504 6250 Fax: 81 3 3502 2614 www.diamond.co.jp	Personnel data on listed 2,246 companies in Japan, unlisted 4,957 companies in Japan: company names, position, name, home address, telephone number, date of birth and place, education, year of employment, etc.	Listed— ¥ 40,000 Unlisted— ¥ 30,000
Nikkei Corporate Who's Who	Book	Nihon Keizai Shinbun Inc. 9-5, Ote-machi 1-chome Chiyoda-ku, Tokyo 100-66 Japan Ph.: 81 3 3270 0251 Fax: 81 3 5255 2648	270,000 personnel data of 3,608 companies in Japan: company name, position, name, date of birth and place, year of employment, home address, telephone number, education, hobbies, etc.	¥ 55,000
Nikkei Who's Who	Electronic	Nihon Keizai Shinbun Inc. 9-5, Ote-machi 1-chome Chiyoda-ku, Tokyo 100-66 Japan Ph.: 81 3 3270 0251 Fax: 81 3 5255 2648	290,000 personnel data of companies, governments, and universities: company name, position, name, date of birth and place, year of employment, home address and telephone number, education, hobbies, etc.	¥ 8,000 per one company ¥ 15,000 (monthly basic charge) plus unit charge
WHO	Electronic	Nichigai Associates Inc. No. 3 Shimokawa Bldg. 23-8, Omori-kita 1-chome Ota-ku, Tokyo 143 Japan	370,000 personnel data that were run in Japanese newspapers, periodicals, and books: name, position, date of birth, education, business	

236

Major Libraries

National Diet Library
10-1, Nagata-cho 1-chome
Chiyoda-ku, Tokyo
Japan
Ph.: 81 3 3581 2331
Fax: 81 3 3581 0989
Web address: www.ndl.go.jp

Tokyo Metropolitan Central Library
7-13, Minami-Azabu 5-chome
Minato-ko, Tokyo
Japan
Ph.: 81 3 3442 8451
Fax: 81 3 3447 8924

Hibiya Library
1-4 Hibiyakoen
Chiyoda-ku Tokyo
Japan
Ph.: 81 3 3502 0101

The Netherlands

Figure 13.24 Map of The Netherlands.

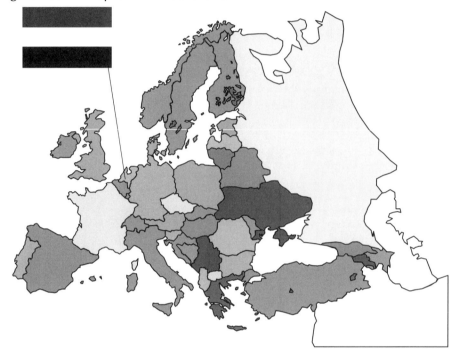

Country Information

Internet link to country information: www.netherlands.org

International dialing code: +31

Population: 15,649,729 (July 1997 est.)

Ethnic divisions: Dutch 96 percent; Moroccans, Turks, and other 4 percent (1988)

Religions: Roman Catholic 34 percent, Protestant 25 percent, Muslim 3 percent, other 2 percent, unaffiliated 36 percent (1991)

Languages: Dutch

Labor force: 6.4 million (1993); by occupation: services 73 percent, manufacturing and construction 23 percent, agriculture 4 percent (1994)

Capital: Amsterdam; The Hague is the seat of government

Economic overview: This highly developed and affluent economy is based on private enterprise. The government makes its presence felt, however, through many regulations, permit requirements, and welfare programs affecting most aspects of economic activity. The trade and financial services sector contributes more than 50 percent of the GDP. Industrial activity provides about 25 percent of the GDP and is led by the food-processing, oil-refining, and metalworking industries. The highly mechanized agricultural sector employs only 4 percent of the labor force, but provides large surpluses for export and the domestic food-processing industry. The Netherlands rank third worldwide in value of agricultural exports, behind the United States and France.

Industries: Agroindustries, metal and engineering products, electrical machinery and equipment, chemicals, petroleum, fishing, construction, microelectronics

Currency: 1 Netherlands guilder, gulden, or florin (HFL) = 100 cents; exchange rates: Netherlands guilders, gulden, or florins (HFL) per US$1—1.89 (October 1998)

Figure 13.25 Major cities, industries, and corporations.

City	Center of
Amsterdam	Trade
Den Haag	Government administration
Rotterdam	Shipping, offshore, port, oil refinery
Utrecht	Distribution (rail and trucking)

Company	Industry
Ahold	Consumer goods
Akzo	Chemical products
DSM	Chemical products
Exxon Netherland	Oil and offshore
Philips	Electrical articles
PTT-Netherland	Post and telecommunication
Shell Group	Oil, offshore, petroleum
SHV Holdings	Consumer goods
Unilever	Consumer goods
Vendex International	Consumer goods

Culture

Business Culture

BUSINESS PROTOCOL: Dutch people are generally very courteous and earnest, stick to business for the most part, and avoid personal questions. As elsewhere in Europe, handshaking is a ritual. Business cards are a must and are exchanged during introductions or at the conclusion of a discussion. First names are usually not used until a firm friendship has been struck. Most visitors find that once trust and confidence are established, they can count on a Dutch colleague's full cooperation. Close personal contact should be maintained with a Dutch colleague for constant exchange of information and ideas. Business courtesy is very important, particularly prompt replies to quotes, orders, and general correspondence. Terms of sale, delivery dates, and other details of an agreement should be strictly observed. As in Germany, oral agreements or statements are often considered to be as binding as written contracts.

PREPARATION FOR THE MEETING: Prior appointments are a must. The Dutch businessperson travels frequently, so care should be taken to be informed as to a colleague's schedule before arranging a visit. Literature and any other information pertinent to a meeting should be sent well in advance. Punctuality is important.

WORKING WOMEN: Women participate in the workforce, but when unemployment is high their opportunities tend to be more limited than their male counterparts'. They are active in the professions, but their presence is minimal at middle and higher levels of management.

WORK ETHIC: The historical reputation of the Dutch is of a hardworking, productive people. In recent decades, however, much of the workforce appeared to relax their hardworking ethics. Steep taxes on wages and an overly generous system of social benefits took most of the pain out of joblessness. This had the unintended effect of encouraging a growing population of the permanently unemployed. A series of reform measures easing taxes and curbing benefits to align them with European Community (EC) norms began to turn things around in the late 1980s. Despite the recent excesses, the majority of Dutch workers are well educated and skilled.

ATTITUDE TOWARD FOREIGNERS: The Dutch are very aware that their small nation exists in an international context. This basic fact, that is, that they are part of a much larger world with which they must interact, shapes not only their political and economic policies, but also their attitude toward foreigners. The opposite of xenophobic, they are especially hospitable in most cases toward English-speaking visitors. They regard their own open, democratic society as having strong bonds with the English-speaking democracies, which serve as a useful balance to the influence of some of their larger European neighbors such as France or Germany.

Cultural factors affecting executive search: The first contact with a possible candidate is made by telephone. First contact can be direct, but not at first-name level. Until four to five years ago—because of privacy—candidates were contacted at their home and not at work. Nowadays it is fully accepted that a candidate is called at the office. After you introduce yourself, the candidate will usually indicate whether the call is convenient at that moment. If not, he will call you back or you can call him later at his private number.

In Holland there is no limit to asking for appropriate personal information. It is even possible that a candidate called in the blind might be willing to give information on her salary and personal circumstances within five minutes. However, younger managers (ages twenty-five to thirty-five) seem to be growing a bit more reluctant and conservative with this type of personal information.

A higher salary is not necessarily the decisive factor when your candidate is evaluating a new opportunity. Common factors for consideration are geographic location, challenges and contents of position, and the opportunity for management positions.

Foreign nations with similar cultures: United Kingdom

Key Research Resources (see Figure 13.26 beginning on page 242).

Figure 13.26 Research resources.
General Company Directories

Name of Service	Medium	Vendor Address	Description	Price
ABC Netherlands	Online	ABC voor Handel en Industrie C.V. PO Box 190 2000 AD Haarlem The Netherlands Ph.: 31 23 531 9031 Fax: 31 23 532 7033 www.abc_1.nl	53,000 profiles of Dutch companies in all lines of business. Brief company information. Updated quarterly.	Please inquire
ABC voor Handel en Industrie	Online	ABC voor Handel en Industrie C.V. PO Box 190 2000 AD Haarlem The Netherlands Ph.: 31 23 531 9031 Fax: 31 23 532 7033 www.abc_1.nl	24,000 profiles of Dutch manufacturers, importers, import agents, and their goods. Brief company information. Updated quarterly.	Please inquire
ABC/Dienstverleners	Online	ABC voor Handel en Industrie C.V. PO Box 190 2000 AD Haarlem The Netherlands Ph.: 31 23 531 9031 Fax: 31 23 532 7033 www.abc_1.nl	24,000 Dutch service companies. Brief company information. Updated quarterly.	Please inquire

Name	Type	Contact	Description	Price
Dun's 20,000 Netherlands	Book/ CD-ROM	Dun & Bradstreet Information Services Three Sylvan Way Parsippany, NJ 07054-3896 Ph.: 201-605-6000 www.dnb.com	20,000 industrial, trading, banking, insurance, and service companies in the Netherlands. Primary and secondary SIC code.	Please inquire
Kompass Netherlands	Book	Kompass Netherland BV Hogehilweg 15 1101 CB Amsterdam The Netherlands Ph.: 31 20 697 4041 Fax: 31 20 696 5603 www.kompass.nl	3,000 manufacturers, distributors, and service companies.	Please inquire

News Services

Name	Type	Contact	Description	Price
het financieele Dagblad (Dutch Financial Times)	Online (Newspaper)	Het financieele Dagblad Amsterdam The Netherlands Ph.: 31 20 592 8888	This online database contains several databases: ▲ Full-text online database (available from 1985); Dutch language only ▲ Database In Brief: the small English summaries section in the newspaper (English) ▲ Database: The Netherlander Dutch business weekly (English)	Subscription HFL 3.000 (annual fee) Rate per hour HFL 200 (Price offline service: HFL 65 per search plus HFL 3.50 per document)

Major Libraries

Amsterdam University Library
Singel 421-425
1012 WP Amsterdam
The Netherlands

PO Box 19185
1000 GD Amsterdam
The Netherlands
Ph.: 20 525 2301
Fax: 20 525 2311

Library of the State University
Witte Singel 27
PO Box 9501
2300 RA Leiden
The Netherlands
Ph.: 71 272 801
Fax: 71 272 836

Koninklijke Bibliotheek
PO Box 90407
NL-2509 LK the Haage
The Netherlands
Ph.: 31 70 314 0911
Fax: 31 70 314 0450
Web address: www.kobib.nl

New Zealand

Figure 13.27 Map of New Zealand.

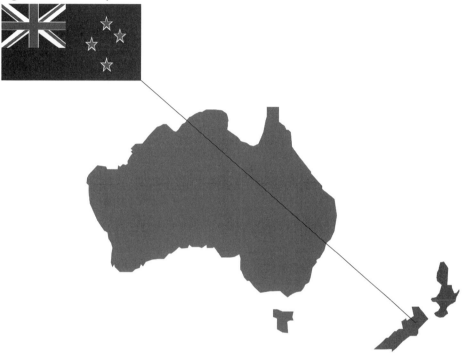

Country Information

Internet link to country information: www.govt.nz

International dialing code: +64

Population: 3,587,275 (July 1997 est.)

Ethnic divisions: European 88 percent, Maori 8.9 percent, Pacific Islander 2.9 percent, other 0.2 percent

Religions: Anglican 24 percent, Presbyterian 18 percent, Roman Catholic 15 percent, Methodist 5 percent, Baptist 2 percent, other Protestant 3 percent, unspecified or none 33 percent (1986)

Languages: English (official), Maori

Labor force: 1,634,500 (September 1995); by occupation: services 64.6 percent, industry 25 percent, agriculture 10.4 percent (1994)

Capital: Wellington

Economic overview: Since 1984 the government has been reorienting an agrarian economy dependent on a guaranteed British market to a more industrialized, open free-market economy that can compete globally.

The government has hoped that dynamic growth would boost real incomes, broaden and deepen the technological capabilities of the industrial sector, reduce inflationary pressures, and permit the expansion of welfare benefits. The initial results were mixed: inflation was down, but growth was sluggish until the early 1990s. In 1992–93, growth picked up to 3 percent annually, a sign that the new economic approach was beginning to pay off. Business confidence strengthened in 1994, and export demand picked up in the Asia-Pacific region, resulting in 6.2 percent growth. Inflation remains among the lowest in the industrial world.

Industries: Food processing, wood and paper products, textiles, machinery, transportation equipment, banking and insurance, tourism, mining

Currency: 1 New Zealand dollar (NZ$) = 100 cents; exchange rates: New Zealand dollars (NZ$) per US$1—1.98 (October 1998)

Figure 13.28 Major cities, industries, and corporations.

City	Center of
Auckland	The largest city and chief commercial center
Christchurch	The urban center for the South Island
Wellington	The national capital and transport link between the islands

Company	Industry
Fletcher Challenge Ltd.	New Zealand's largest group of companies. Its four companies (which each trade separately) are built around operations in paper, energy, forests, and building materials and construction.
Telecom Corporation of New Zealand Ltd.	The principal provider of telecommunications services in New Zealand.
Tranz Rail Holdings Ltd.	Transportation: rail freight transport and distribution and passenger services in New Zealand.

Culture

Business Culture

BUSINESS PROTOCOL: Business customs in New Zealand are similar to those in the United States and less formal than in Great Britain. Use of first names is common, especially if there has been previous phone contact. It is best to follow the New Zealander's example, which most likely will be fairly casual. Bring business cards, as the practice of exchanging them is becoming more common.

PREPARATION FOR THE MEETING: Meetings should be arranged well in advance. New Zealanders take long vacations (most often in January, up to a month or six weeks) so planning is necessary. Be prompt for meetings, as New Zealanders tend to be on time. Breakfast meetings are rare, whereas lunch meetings are quite common. Evenings and dinners are reserved for entertaining rather than for heavy business.

WORKING WOMEN: Women are commonly found in business and attitudes are generally comparable to those in North America and much of Western Europe. Dress, however, tends to be more middle of the road—less formal than conservative business suits, but more formal than slacks.

WORK ETHIC: New Zealanders have a responsible attitude toward their work and careers and approach their jobs with seriousness. Some companies offer awards and incentives, but this is not common policy for most businesses.

ATTITUDE TOWARD FOREIGNERS: The workforce is strongly geared toward trade unions, although workers are no longer required to join a union. Attitude toward foreign investment can vary from industry to industry, but in general, relationships with foreign-run companies are much the same as with other employers.

Cultural factors affecting executive search: In New Zealand the initial contact with a candidate is usually made by telephone. It is common practice to address the candidate by his or her Christian name. If the candidate uses a shortened version of his or her name (e.g., Tim for Timothy), you would address the candidate by this name. Although the style of approach is reasonably informal, professional conduct must be maintained at all times.

New Zealanders are very friendly and relaxed. First phone contact is always on a first-name level. People are fairly open to the approach and are generally happy to listen. Even if they are not interested they often offer to think of recommendations.

The small population of New Zealand means that candidates are very concerned with confidentiality. Therefore, it is necessary to ensure that lines are secure before either leaving a voice-mail message or sending a fax. In addition, where relevant, it may be necessary to check with the candidate that it is okay to leave messages with a personal assistant or secretary. In some cases the candidate will not want the personal assistant to have this information. The use of private unlisted numbers ensures that absolute confidentiality is observed. These lines are never answered with information that could identify either the company or the interviewer.

As in the United States, employers are prohibited by the Human Rights Act to discriminate against an individual on the basis of gender, marital status, age, ethnic background, religion, disability, political opinion, family status, and sexual orientation. Therefore, any question that relates to these aspects must be avoided. There are, however, two notable exceptions:

Interviewers may want to know the marital status, family status, health, and age of the candidate, even though this contravenes legislation. Some researchers continue to tell candidates that their answers will have no bearing on the selection decision, and that this information simply serves as additional background on each candidate. Generally candidates do not have a problem with this.

When interviewing a candidate who identifies himself as being Maori, it is accepted and indeed appropriate to ask which tribe he belongs to. Once again, the individual cannot be discriminated against on the basis of this information.

Lifestyle is very important to New Zealanders. It is one of the reasons many foreigners move to this country. New Zealanders looking to relocate offshore would need to be tempted by a much greater salary to compensate for less favorable living conditions in their eyes, that is, less populated cities, less pollution and traffic, and a wider range of outdoor activities.

In New Zealand, candidates are generally quite happy to discuss their TREM (total remuneration), even at an initial interview. It is not considered inappropriate to mention remuneration to a candidate even when making an initial approach.

Due to the uneven geographic concentration of New Zealand's population, the majority of the opportunities arise in the three main centers—Auckland, Wellington, and Christchurch—which are spread across the two islands. As a consequence three distinctive markets with their own unique characteristics have developed within New Zealand.

AUCKLAND: In Auckland, located on the North Island, senior executives are far more mobile (within New Zealand) and willing to relocate than they used to be. Two issues commonly affect an executive's willingness to relocate.

Where families are involved, the availability of quality schooling is important. Therefore, provided that the professional opportunity is perceived as desirable, families are more willing to relocate from a larger center to a provence if it has good educational facilities.

Second, New Zealanders are generally concerned with career development. Candidates are often attracted to an opportunity on the basis of its potential for career development, as opposed to the remuneration. Executives are frequently prepared to relocate if the opportunity is perceived to have the future potential to reward their efforts, or alternatively, act as a stepping stone to a better opportunity.

WELLINGTON: The Wellington market, also located on the North Island, is characterized by its concentration of service as opposed to consumer-based industries. Government and all public-service head offices are located here as well as head offices of major telecommunication, financial, and information technology industries.

CHRISTCHURCH: New Zealanders in general are concerned with the lifestyle that a particular opportunity will afford them. For example, New Zealand is currently experiencing a flight of young families from the larger centers in the north to Christchurch on the South Island. These individuals are attracted by the promise of excellent schools, low crime rates, shorter commuting times and distances, more affordable real estate, and other perceived benefits. Executives are prepared to take a decrease in remuneration if the opportunity is in a location that offers them an attractive lifestyle.

Often a job assignment may be introduced to a candidate as an opportunity, in an effort to counteract resistance to relocate to certain areas within these three markets.

Foreign nations with similar cultures: Australia

Key Research Resources (see Figure 13.29 beginning on page 250).

Figure 13.29 Research resources.
General Company Directories

Name of Service	Medium	Vendor Address	Description	Price
Business Who's Who of Australia	Book	Riddel Info Services Pty. Ltd. PO Box 204 Chatswood New South Wales 2057 Australia	Details of Australian business: contact details, area of activity, staff numbers, names of directors and executives.	NZ$ 568
The NZ Business Who's Who	Book	NZ Financial Press PO Box 1881 Auckland, New Zealand Ph.: 64 9 307 1288	Details of NZ business: contact details, area of activity, staff numbers, names of directors and executives.	NZ$ 258

Specialty Directories

Ad Media Magazine	Magazine	Minty's Media, PO Box 93218 Parnell Auckland New Zealand Ph.: 09 379 4233 www.auckland.ac.nz/lbr/comm/buspuss.htm	Weekly business publication. Advertising news, news of personnel movements within the industry.	NZ$ 48
Commonwealth Universities Yearbook	Book	John Foster House 36 Gordon Square London WC1H 6PF England Ph.: 44 171 387 8572 www.acu.ac.uk	List of personnel by country in each university in the commonwealth. Includes title, name, and qualifications.	£STG 140

Key Personnel in Local Government	Book	Strategic Info Service PO Box 33-1039 Auckland, New Zealand Ph.: 64 9 309 3657	NZ$ 75
Key Personnel in the Public Health Service	Book	Strategic Info Service PO Box 33-1039 Auckland, New Zealand Ph.: 64 9 309 3657 Fax: 64 9 308 0191 www.strategicinfo.co.nz	NZ$ 75
Key Personnel in Top 50 NZ Companies	Book	Strategic Info Service PO Box 33-1039 Auckland, New Zealand Ph.: 64 9 309 3657 Fax: 64 9 3080191 www.strategicinfo.co.nz	NZ$ 75
Marketing Services Directory	Book	Minty's Media PO Box 93218 Parnell, Auckland New Zealand Ph.: 64 9 379 4233	NZ$ 48	List of contact details and key personnel for New Zealand media organizations, advertising agencies, magazines, design companies, photography companies.

(Continued)

251

Figure 13.29 *(Continued)*

Name of Service	Medium	Vendor Address	Description	Price
New Zealand Aotearoa Who's Who	Book	*New Zealand Book Aotearoa Who's Who* PO Box 99075 Wellesley St. Auckland, New Zealand Ph.: 64 9 522 2335 Fax: 64 9 524 5706	Famous people in New Zealand history with achievements/date of birth and family details.	NZ$ 96
New Zealand Government Directory	Book	Network Communications PO Box 9691 Wellington, New Zealand Ph.: 64 4 473 8876 Fax: 64 4 473 0467	List of government departments and key personnel.	NZ$ 95
New Zealand Society of Accountants Yearbook	Book	*New Zealand Society of Accountants Yearbook* PO Box 11342 Wellington, New Zealand Ph.: 64 4 4747840, Fax: 64 4 4600390		NZ$ 55
The Interdata Financial Handbook	Book	IPP Interdata Limited 9 Napier St., Ste. 5, North Sydney NSW 2060 Australia Ph.: 61 2 957 2881	List of financial services organizations, grouped by specialty, in New Zealand and Australia. Contact details, staff numbers, key personnel.	N/A

Major Libraries

University of Auckland Library
PMB 92019
Auckland, New Zealand
Ph.: 9 373 7999
Fax: 9 373 7565
Web address: www.auckland.ac.nz/lb_/libhome.htm
E-Mail: ma.crick@auckland.ac.nz

National Library of New Zealand
PO Box 1467
Wellington 6000
New Zealand
Ph.: 4 474 3000
Fax: 4 474 3035
Web address: www.natlib.govt.nz

Russia

Figure 13.30 Map of Russia.

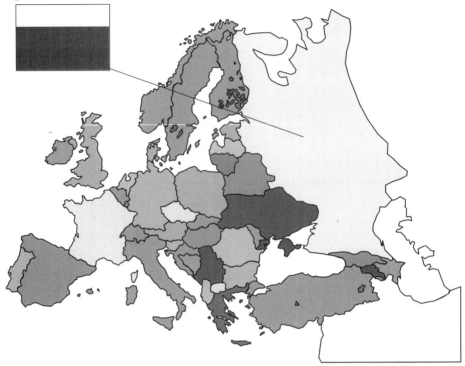

Country Information

Internet link to country information: www.russia.net/index.html
International dialing code: +7
Population: 147,305,569 (July 1997 est.)
Ethnic divisions: Russian 81.5 percent, Tatar 3.8 percent, Ukrainian 3 percent, Chuvash 1.2 percent, Bashkir 0.9 percent, Byelorussian 0.8 percent, Moldavian 0.7 percent, other 8.1 percent
Religions: Russian Orthodox, Muslim, other
Languages: Russian, other
Labor force: 73 million (1996); by occupation: production and economic services 83.9 percent, government 16.1 percent
Capital: Moscow
Economic overview: Russia, a vast country with a wealth of natural resources, a well-educated population, and a diverse industrial base, continues to experience formidable difficulties in moving from its old

centrally planned economy to a modern market economy. President Boris Yeltsin's government has made substantial strides in converting to a market economy since launching its economic reform program in January 1992 by freeing nearly all prices, slashing defense spending, eliminating the old centralized distribution system, completing an ambitious voucher privatization program, establishing private financial institutions, and decentralizing foreign trade. Russia, however, has made slow progress in a number of key areas that are needed to provide a solid foundation for the transition to full-market economy. Financial stabilization has remained elusive, with historically wide swings of inflation rates. Restructuring of industry is moving forward slowly due to a scarcity of investment funds and the failure of enterprise managers to make hard cost-cutting decisions.

In addition, Moscow has to fully develop a social safety net that would allow faster restructuring by relieving enterprises of the burden of providing social benefits for their workers, and has been slow to develop the legal framework necessary to fully support a market economy and to encourage foreign investment. As a result, output has not been optimal. Most Russians perceive that they are worse off now because of growing crime and health problems and mounting wage arrears.

Russia has made significant headway in privatizing state assets. Financial stabilization continues to remain a challenge for the government. Foreign sales—consisting largely of oil, natural gas, and other raw materials—have grown significantly. Imports are also up as demand for food and other consumer goods surges. Russia's physical stage continues to pose a challenge because of insufficient maintenance and new construction. Plants and equipment are on the average twice as old as those found in Western countries. Many years will pass before Russia can take full advantage of its natural resources and its human assets.

Industries: Complete range of mining and extractive industries producing coal, oil, gas, chemicals, and metals; all forms of machine building from rolling mills to high-performance aircraft and space vehicles; shipbuilding; road and rail transportation equipment; communications equipment; agricultural machinery, tractors, and construction equipment; electric power generating and transmitting equipment; medical and scientific instruments; consumer durables

Currency: 1 ruble (R) = 100 kopeks; exchange rates: rubles per US$1 = 15 (October 1998)

Figure 13.31 Major cities, industries, and corporations.

City	Center of
Arkhangelsk	Industry, forestry, and logging
Moscow	Governmental administration, trade
Murmansk	Fishing
St. Petersburg	Shipping, trade, and defense industry
Vladivostok	Fishing

Company	Industry
ABB (Swiss/Swedish)	Electronics
Coca Cola (USA)	Soft drinks
Gacprom (Russian)	Oil/gas
Mars Corp. (USA)	Candy
McDonald's (USA)	Fast food
Pepsi (USA)	Soft drinks
Rosneftegas (Russian)	Oil/gas
Svyaz Invest (Russian)	Telecommunications
US West (USA)	Telecommunications

Culture

Business Culture

BUSINESS PROTOCOL: Shaking hands during introductions and at the end of a meeting is typical. Defer to the senior Russian official to lead the meetings, and wait to be given the floor. Negotiations can be rather lengthy and involve socializing. Avoid impatience and a hard-sell approach. But try to get an agenda worked out before the meeting starts. Try not to use technical jargon or colloquialisms such as "ballpark figure" or "bottom line." Traditional Russian hospitality means that during negotiations you will be offered cookies and sweets. Heavy drinking is firmly entrenched in the Russian style of doing business. Avoid going to business meetings with an empty stomach. If you smoke, share generously with those around you. If you simply cannot tolerate smoking, business in Russia is not for you. Use formal titles like "Doctor" or "Professor" when addressing people. After a round of discussions, it is wise to sit down with your business contact and write out what was discussed, so there are no misunderstandings.

PREPARATION FOR THE MEETING: Business appointments are often arranged in advance through Russian representatives abroad. Be sure to take along written confirmation of dates. Russians are very status conscious,

so low-level experts should not initiate business contacts. Letters of introduction are helpful, and so are bilingual business cards. Setting up meetings with Russian business partners can sometimes be tedious because of
a lack of switchboards and secretaries to help you leave messages. You
will earn extra goodwill with your business contacts if you show interest
and some knowledge of Russian history and culture, and if you know at
least a few phrases of Russian. Get familiar with the nationality map of
Russia, and be careful of calling someone a Russian; the person you are
dealing with might be from Tatar or Bashkiria. Learn as much as possible
about the people you will meet with, their importance, background, and
the company history.

WORKING WOMEN: If it accomplished little else, Communism at least
made some inroads into the barrier between men and women in Russia.
Women in Russia are represented in most professions in the workforce.
Also, many older women in Russia work in traditional male jobs, since so
many men died in World War II. Having said that, Russian male chauvin-
ism can sometimes shock. Russian society has traditionally been broken
down in terms of sex and class. Much of this legacy of an agrarian economy
dies hard. There are many Russian men who simply will never be able to
take a female leader seriously. The younger generation seems more willing
to accept women in positions of power.

WORK ETHIC: The old Soviet labor quip, "As long as they pretend to
pay us we will pretend to work," may soon be coming to an end with
new times. Russians, in coming years, will be expected to take more pride
in their jobs as the effects of the free market continue to roll in. Many
professionals work very long hours. Russians possess great native talent
and ability, and individuals can be found who will develop into excellent
employees.

ATTITUDE TOWARD FOREIGNERS: Although Russians have historically
feared foreigners, they are now generally recognized as bringing prosper-
ity and democratic values to Russia. Russia's foreign community lives in
relative harmony with Russian citizens. Some Russians may resent their
presence, but most appreciate the efforts of foreigners to modernize the
local economy.

Cultural factors affecting executive search: Many potential candidates working
for Russian or even foreign companies in St. Petersburg are not very well
informed about existing executive search or personnel selection companies. This particular kind of service is new for most Russians. You will
need to present yourself properly and to explain the reason for your call
respectfully and in details. When approaching sources and candidates,

confidentiality is generally required as well. In Russia it is normal to address people by their first name and patronymic. Any information may be asked from a person; however, you may meet reluctance when asking his or her current compensation or some financial figures of the company he or she works for.

St. Petersburg locals will usually not move to another region or smaller city even when offered bigger compensation and benefits. People often care about office location within the city, medical insurance, and working-day organization (lunch, tickets for municipal transport, etc.).

Foreign nations with similar cultures: Russia is the most advanced Eastern country, which makes it more compatible with Western cultures than other Eastern European countries. Generally, Russians are quite compatible with Americans.

Key Research Resources (see Figure 13.32 beginning on page 259).

Figure 13.32 Research resources.
General Company Directories

Name of Service	Medium	Vendor Address	Description	Price
Business-Carta (Business Map)	Reference Book	Agency for Business Information 20 Gagarinsky Pereulok 121002 Moscow Russia Ph.: 7 095 241 7573 Fax: 7 095 956 3384	Series by regions, sectors of industry (30–35 volumes in each series). Russia and former USSR. Russian language.	US$ 6–10 per volume
Information Moscow	Book	Information Moscow Leninsky Pr. 45 117334 Moscow Russia Ph.: 7 095 135 1164 Fax: 7 502 22 47 111	10,000 businesses, press offices, embassies, and government offices in Moscow.	Please request
Reference and statistical issues and reviews	Book	State Committee for Statistics of Russia (Goscomstat) 39 Myasnitkaya St., 103450 Moscow Russia Ph.: 7 095 366 5531 Fax: 7 095 365 5547	Statistical data on Russian economy, industrial sectors, regions, and companies.	General info (address, location, telephone, production, output): 1 US$ per company. Detailed info: 100–150 US$ per company.

(Continued)

259

Figure 13.32 (*Continued*)

Name of Service	Medium	Vendor Address	Description	Price
Russian Exporters and Importers—Firm Directory	Book/CD-ROM/ Online	International Bureau for Information and Telecommunications (MBIT) Lenningradsky Ave. 80/2, p/b 44 125190 Moscow Russia Ph.: 7 095 1588000	4,300 leading Russian companies trading on the international market and their export/import product range. Arranged alphabetically by name of company, classified by line of business. Indexed by products/service.	Please request
Trading Partners USSR	Book	Trading Partners c/o Brendan Marketing PO Box 32467 Tucson, AZ 85751 Ph.: 602-722-5679	More than 1,900 enterprises in the Soviet Union interested in international trade. Classified by line of business.	Please request
WA-2 Register	Database	International Corporation WA-2 5 Lebedeva St. Moscow State University Moscow, Russia Ph.: 7 095 939 0287 Fax: 7 095 939 0288	Data and goods and services and their producers. Russian language. Hard copy available (cost: 60 US$).	90 US$

Major Libraries

Russian State Library (former All-Union State Library named after Lenin)
3 Vozdvizhenka St.
101000 Moscow
Russia
Ph.: 7 095 202 5790

State Public Library for Science and Technology (GPNTB)
12 Kuznetsky Most St.
103919 Moscow
Russia
Ph.: 7 095 925 9288

Figure 13.33 Internet snapshot of company information source for Russia.

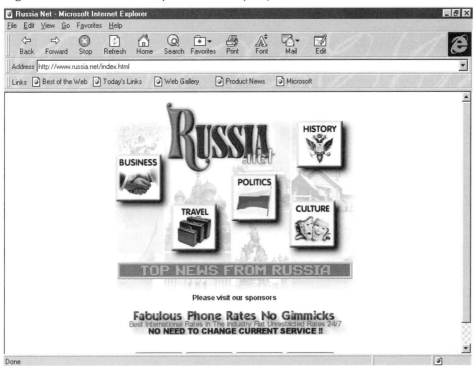

Scandinavia

Because of the economic and cultural similarities of the Scandinavian countries, as well as their geographic proximity, Denmark, Sweden, and Norway have been placed in this section under the heading Scandinavia. However, while it is easy to group Europe's Scandinavian countries together, each nation possesses a distinct personality and should be recognized as a separate entity from neighboring nations.

Denmark

Figure 13.34 Map of Denmark.

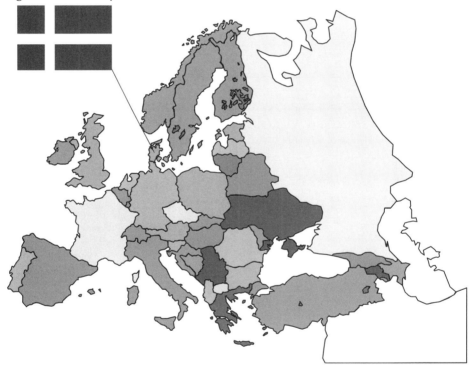

Country Information

Internet link to country information: www.info.denet.dk/denmark.html
International dialing code: +45
Population: 5,305,048 (July 1997 est.)
Ethnic divisions: Scandinavian, Eskimo, Faroese, German

Religions: Evangelical Lutheran 91 percent, other Protestant and Roman Catholic 2 percent, other 7 percent (1988)

Languages: Danish, Faroese, Greenlandic (an Eskimo dialect), German (small minority)

Labor force: 2.895 million (July 1997 est.); by occupation: private services 40 percent; government services 30 percent; manufacturing and mining 19 percent; construction 6 percent; agriculture, forestry, and fishing 5 percent (1995)

Capital: Copenhagen

Economic overview: This thoroughly modern economy features high-tech agriculture, up-to-date small-scale and corporate industry, extensive government welfare measures, comfortable living standards, and high dependence on foreign trade. Denmark is self-sufficient in food production. The coalition government concentrates on reducing the persistent high unemployment rate and the budget deficit as well as maintaining low inflation and a current account surplus. In the face of recent international market pressure on the Danish krone, the coalition has also vowed to maintain a stable currency. Denmark hopes to boost industrial competitiveness through labor market and tax reforms, increased research and development funds, and improved welfare services for the neediest. Reforms will focus on adapting Denmark to the criteria for European integration by 1999. Denmark is, in fact, one of the few EU countries likely to fit into the European Monetarian Union (EMU) on time.

Industries: Food processing, machinery and equipment, textiles and clothing, chemical products, electronics, construction, furniture and other wood products, shipbuilding

Currency: 1 Danish krone (DKR) = 100 oere; exchange rates: Danish kroner (DKR) per US$1—6.38 (October 1998)

Figure 13.35 Major cities, industries, and corporations.

City	Center of
Århus	Industry
Copenhagen	Finance, industry
Esbjerg	Offshore and shipping, fishery
Herning	Textiles
Kolding	Metal industry
Odense	Shipyard
Vejle	Preservative industry

(Continued)

Figure 13.35 *(Continued)*

Company	Industry
A.P. Møller Group	Shipping, offshore, aerospace, industry, and trade
Danisco	Preservatives and alcohol
FLS Industries	Mechanics and cement
FNB (Brugsen)	Trade
ISS Int. Service System	Industry and institutional cleaning
Lauritzen	Shipping, industry
MD Food	Preservatives
Post & Telegrafvæsnet	Post and telecommunications
United Breweries	Brewing, licensing

Culture

Business Culture

On initial contact the Danes might be somewhat forward until a closer relationship is established. Although they seem to be open-minded, it is not always so in reality. Punctuality is a must in Denmark. Business cards are expected. Prior appointments are the rule, and one should call if for any reason she must be delayed. Proper business attire is required. Danes are inclined personally to be more relaxed and less formal than some of their neighbors, but still very direct in business situations. Little business is done in the late afternoon, and a dinner invitation is often a convenient and pleasurable way to extend a discussion. Weekends, however, are different. Danes regard these as quality time for their families and personal activities, and business not concluded on Friday usually waits until Monday. Like many of their fellow Europeans, Danish businesspeople usually speak several languages. Women account for almost half the workforce and are found at all levels of business, industry, and government. The Danes are the most continental European of all the Scandinavians, sharing the south border with Germany. The Danes culturally are seen as being on the borderline of Scandinavia with a very close relationship to central Europe. As a rule, business visits should be avoided in the peak vacation period from mid-June to the beginning of August, and during national holidays.

Cultural factors affecting executive search: Among the Scandinavian countries, Denmark, with its long trade history and closeness to the European continent, has the longest professional experience with executive search. Some of the largest worldwide firms have been located in Copenhagen for twenty-five to thirty years, covering all the Scandinavian countries. The emergence of local search firms has significantly changed this picture in the last five to ten years.

When conducting a search there is much emphasis on local network. Being continental, Danish executives are used to receiving telephone calls from executive search firms. When initial calls are made, it is very helpful to mention the company name and position to catch the right interest. Calls to previous colleagues of the potential candidate can be very useful in the screening process.

As in all Scandinavian countries, the cellular phone system, GSM, is regularly used by many executives so they can be reached regardless of where they are. Recorded cellular phone answering systems are highly accessible and give new opportunities for reaching executives.

Being a small community, the business society is quite closely woven and requires a lot of care in the original preparation and screening process.

Foreign nations with similar cultures: Norway and Sweden

Key Research Resources (see Figure 13.36 beginning on page 266).

Figure 13.36 Research resources.
General Company Directories

Name of Service	Medium	Vendor Address	Description	Price
Greens	Annual handbook Also available on CD-ROM	A/S Forlaget Borsen Montergade 19 DK-1140 Copenhagen K Denmark www.borsensforlag.dk	General information about all major Danish companies (approx. 4,000): location, ownership, board, management, subsidiaries, affiliated companies, five years annual accounts in summary version, key figures, etc. Special section with profiles of managers, board members, etc.; list of major industrial branch organizations.	Price per yearbook approximately DKR 4,000
Kompass (annual handbook) (2 books)	Book	A/S Forlaget KOMPASS-Danmark Overdodvej 5 DK-2840 Holte Denmark Ph.: 45 45 46 09 10	Brief description of major companies and products in Denmark.	DKR 3,000. Can also be used online (DKK 20.00 per minute, no establishment cost)
Kraks (annual handbook—4 books)	Book	Kraks Forlag A/S Virumgaardsvej 21 DK-2830 Virum Denmark Ph.: 45 45 95 65 00 Fax: 45 45 95 65 65 www.krak.dk	Very much like Kompass, but also information on branch organization, municipalities and other public institutions (covers 20,000 public and private institutions and 60,000 companies). Consultant service available: address services.	DKR 4,000
Publi-com, Erhvervs- og Selskabssty relsen	Book/online	Det Kongelige Bibliotek Christians Brygge 8 DK-1219 Copenhagen K Denmark Ph.: 45 33 47 47 47 Fax: 45 35 32 90 22	The public office for annual reports (can be purchased by unit—one makes a copy—or by subscription to online system). Consultant service available:	Per annual report approximately DKR 100. Online: first time free, 375 DKR then charged according to consumption

Major Libraries

Lunds Universitetbibliotek (Lund University Library)
PO Box 3, S-221 42 Malmø
Ph.: 46 222 0000

Handelshøgskolans Bibliotek (Library of Stockholm's School of Economics)
PO Box 6501, S-113 83 Stockholm
Ph.: 8 736 9700
Fax: 8 31 8213
Web address: www.hhs.se/library

Norway

Figure 13.37 Map of Norway.

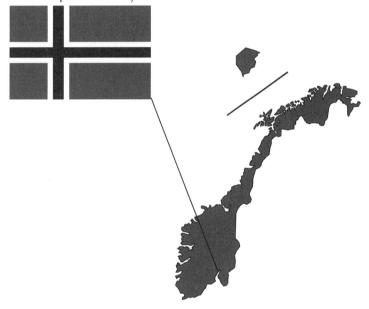

Country Information

Internet link to country information: www.norway.org
International dialing code: +47
Population: 4,399,993 (July 1997 est.)
Ethnic divisions: Germanic (Nordic, Alpine, Baltic), Lapps (Sami) 20,000
Religions: Evangelical Lutheran 87.8 percent (state church), other Protestant and Roman Catholic 3.8 percent, none 3.2 percent, unknown 5.2 percent (1980)
Languages: Norwegian (official); small Lapp- and Finnish-speaking minorities

Labor force: 2.13 million; by occupation: services 71 percent; industry 23
    percent; agriculture, forestry, and fishing 6 percent (1993)
Capital: Oslo
Economic overview: Norway has a mixed economy involving a combination
    of free-market activity and government intervention. The government
    controls key areas, such as the vital petroleum sector (through large-
    scale state enterprises) and extensively subsidizes agriculture, fishing,
    and areas with sparse resources. Norway also maintains an extensive
    welfare system that helps propel public sector expenditures to slightly
    more than 50 percent of the GDP and results in one of the highest
    average tax burdens in the world (54 percent). A small country with
    a high dependence on international trade, Norway is basically an ex-
    porter of raw materials and semiprocessed goods, with an abundance
    of small- and medium-sized firms, and is ranked among the major
    shipping nations. The country is richly endowed with natural re-
    sources—petroleum, hydropower, fish, forests, and minerals—and is
    highly dependent on its oil sector to keep its economy afloat. Norway
    imports more than half its food needs. Although one of the govern-
    ment's main priorities is to reduce its dependency, this situation is
    not likely to improve for years to come. The government also hopes
    to reduce unemployment and strengthen and diversify the economy
    through tax reform and a series of expansionary budgets.
Industries: Petroleum and gas, food processing, shipbuilding, pulp and
    paper products, metals, chemicals, timber, mining, textiles, fishing
Currency: 1 Norwegian krone (NKR) = 100 oere; exchange rates: Norwe-
    gian kroner (NKR) per US$1—7.41 (October 1998)

Figure 13.38 Major cities, industries, and corporations.

City	Center of
Bergen	Shipping, fishing
Drammen	Industry
Oslo	Headquarters for most major corporations, light industry, high tech, construction
Stavanger	Offshore, engineering
Trondheim	High tech, light industry

Company	Industry
ABB	General industry, power control systems
Aker	Cement, oil, gas, engineering
Den Norske Bank	Banking

Company	Industry
Gjensidige	Insurance
Hydro	Oil, offshore, petroleum, agriculture, chemicals
Kvaerner	Oil, gas, shipping, shipyards, energy, engineering
Orkla	Consumer products, chemicals, finance and investments
Statoil	Oil, offshore, petroleum
Telenor	Telecommunication products and services
Uni Storebrand	Insurance

Culture

Norwegians are very proud of their history, culture, and landscape. To endear yourself, make time to comment on the beautiful countryside or the rich culture. Your compliments will be highly appreciated. However, do not compare Norway to America or imply that America is better in any way. Boasting only alienates. Even if you are anxious to get your point across, always speak in a soft voice. The louder you talk, the less likely your ideas will be heard.

Be prepared to offer your heartiest handshake, not only to new contacts but even to people you have met many times before. This gesture is as important as saying hello, which, by the way, is translated in Norwegian as "Morn."

Do not ask "How are you?" without expecting to listen to an elaborate response. Typical Norwegians take this casual greeting quite literally and answer with a long, detailed tally of their health, mood, and whatever else may be remotely on their minds.

If you have a meeting scheduled at 7 A.M., be there at 7 A.M. Norwegians take punctuality for business meetings very seriously. Call if you are going to be late.

Norwegians consider some Americans to be too smooth-talking and polished. Do not fall into that trap but instead try to focus on sincerity and negotiations should go smoothly. Remember that modesty is the best policy. Norwegians do not flaunt their success, wealth, or material possessions, so refrain from boasting about your new Lexus or that summer home in Tahoe or The Cape.

If invited to the home of your Norwegian counterpart, bring a small gift, which will be opened upon receipt. If you are invited for dinner, send flowers to the hostess the morning of the dinner. However, avoid carnations and bouquets of only white flowers, which are reserved for funerals. Chocolates, wine, pastries, and liquor are also acceptable gifts.

In working situations, avoid all physical contact, except between relatives and close friends. Do not pat your Norwegian contact on the back or even touch his or her arm with affection.

Cultural factors affecting executive search: Executive search is a relatively young profession in Norway. The first companies in the field were established at the beginning of the 1980s. Since 1990, the profession has grown considerably and is now accepted as a major method of recruiting executives. Executives are open-minded when calls are made, provided you have a specific position in mind and you have a client relationship.

The first telephone calls should be formal (first names are not acceptable this early on). Successful executives are used to being called, but sometimes secretaries will shield and reject calls if the message is not clear about the reason for calling. Leaving messages can turn out to be unfruitful, so it is better to call again. If and when you get the prospective candidate on the phone, it is important to state what position you are calling him or her for. In Norway the cellular telephone system is very advanced, and most people can be reached any time through their cellular telephone (cellular phone voice mail) for return calls.

The business society in Norway is fairly small, and networking is an important way to locate candidates. In the initial stage of the search process, Norwegians are reluctant to inform you about their private life and family situation. What triggers the interest of potential candidates is the opportunity to move upward in organizational levels, often because of limited opportunities within their organization.

Reference checks about candidates are quite common before calling the potential candidates, in order to qualify the candidate and reduce the risk of not establishing a fit.

Although not forbidden, questions about race, religion, or other private areas should not be asked in initial telephone calls. Later in the process age is not a taboo subject since Norwegians write their date of birth on their CV.

Foreign nations with similar cultures: Sweden and Denmark

Key Research Resources (see Figure 13.39 beginning on page 271).

Figure 13.39 Research resources.
General Company Directories

Name of Service	Medium	Vendor Address	Description	Price
CD-Market	CD-ROM	Dun & Bradstreet Postboks 34 Økern 0508 Oslo Norway Ph.: 47 2291 5200 Fax: 47 2291 5303	CD-ROM covers information on 283,000 companies in Norway. Covers areas such as key executives, turnover, line of business.	NKR 5,000 (annual cost includes four yearly updates)
Hugin's annual reports	CD-ROM/Internet	Hugin As Mølla Næringspark Sagveien 19 0458 Oslo Norway Ph.: 47 2280 7980 Fax: 47 2280 7990 www.hugin.online.no	Full annual reports of most publicly traded companies in Norway, Sweden, Denmark, and Finland.	Free
Kompass	Book/CD-ROM	Kompass Norway Postboks 33 Linderud 0517 Oslo Norway Ph.: 47 2264 0575 Fax: 47 2264 7712 www.nettvik.no/ naeringsparken/kompass.no	Four-volume directory giving address, brief financial information, and name of key executives at 16,000 companies in Norway Vol. 1. Products and Services Vol. 2. Company Information Vol. 3. Finance Vol. 4. Contact People	NKR 2950 (annual cost per CD) Updated two times a year NKR 1650 (annual cost for set of four books) Updated once a year
Norge's storste bedrifter	Book/CD-ROM	Økonomisk Literatur Norge AS Langkaia 1 0150 Oslo Norway Ph.: 47 2247 4900 Fax: 47 2247 4901 www.ekolit.no	Key information on the 10,000 largest companies such as address, key executives, and financial numbers.	NKR 3200 for CD-ROM and set of two books. Includes two yearly updates of CD-ROM. NKR 1375 (two volumes)

(Continued)

Figure 13.39 *(Continued)*

Name of Service	Medium	Vendor Address	Description	Price
Telephone book	CD-ROM	Telenor Media Postboks 21 Øvre Ullern 0311 Oslo Norway Ph.: 47 800 33365 Fax: 47 800 33999 www.gulesider.no	The complete Norwegian telephone book including the so-called yellow pages (by industry), pink pages (companies alphabetized), white pages (private subscribers).	NKR 1495 (includes four yearly updates)

Specialty Directories

Membership guide for DND	Book	Den Norske Dataforening Postboks 8874 Youngstorget 0028 Oslo Norway Ph.: 47 223 64880 Fax: 47 223 63701 www.dnd.no	The annual book contains listing of all members in the Norwegian Data-Association. Listing is according to the company.	NKR 400

News Services

A-Tekst	Online/Internet	AIT Postboks 1178 Sentrum 0107 Oslo Norway Ph. 47 228 63832 Fax: 47 228 64290 www.aftenposten.no	Database with articles from leading newspapers in Norway. Major newspapers are: *Aftenposten, Dagens Naeringsliv,* and *Bergens Tidende.*	NKR 2500 for registration (includes Windows software) Thereafter the cost is NKR 5 per minute for search and NKR 10 for every article obtained in full text. If accessed through Internet there is no fee for registration or search time. Plus NKR 10 per article

Major Libraries

Deichmanske Bibliotek (Oslo Public Library).
Henrik Ibsensgate 1
0179 Oslo
Norway
Ph.: 47 220 32900
Fax: 47 221 13389

BI (Bedriftsokonomisk Institutt)
PO Box 580
1301 Sandvika
Norway
Ph.: 47 675 70777
Fax: 47 675 70787
E-mail: mainlibrary@bi.no
Web address: www.bi.no/library/main/index.htm

Figure 13.40 Internet snapshot of company information source for Norway.

Sweden

Figure 13.41 Map of Sweden.

Country Information

Internet link to country information: www.sweden.com

International dialing code: +46

Population: 8,864,051 (July 1997 est.)

Ethnic divisions: White, Lapp (Sami), foreign-born or first-generation immigrants 12 percent (Finns, Yugoslavs, Danes, Norwegians, Greeks, Turks)

Religions: Evangelical Lutheran 94 percent, Roman Catholic 1.5 percent, Pentecostal 1 percent, other 3.5 percent (1987)

Languages: Swedish; small Lapp- and Finnish-speaking minorities; immigrants speak native languages

Labor force: 4.552 million (84 percent unionized, 1992); by occupation: community, social, and personal services 38.3 percent; mining and manufacturing 21.2 percent; commerce, hotels, and restaurants 14.1 percent; banking, insurance 9.0 percent; communications 7.2 percent; construction 7.0 percent; agriculture, fishing, and forestry 3.2 percent (1991)

Capital: Stockholm

Economic overview: Aided by a long period of peace and neutrality during World War I through World War II, Sweden has achieved an enviable standard of living under a mixed system of high-tech capitalism and extensive welfare benefits. It has a modern distribution system, excellent internal and external communications, and a skilled labor force. Timber, hydropower, and iron ore constitute the resource base of an economy that is heavily oriented toward foreign trade. In the past, Sweden's favorable world economy picture of privately owned firms and increased imports and exports has been clouded by inflation, growing unemployment, and a gradual loss of competitiveness in international markets. However, Sweden has harmonized its economic policies with those of the EU.

Industries: Iron and steel, precision equipment (bearings, radio and telephone parts, armaments), wood pulp and paper products, processed foods, motor vehicles

Currency: 1 Swedish krona (SKR) = 100 oere; exchange rates: Swedish kronor (SKR) per US$1—7.9 (October 1998)

Figure 13.42 Major cities, industries, and corporations.

City	Center of
Goteborg	Automotive
Linkoping	Automotive
Malmo	Mechanical industry
Orebro	Agriculture
Stockholm	Electronics
Uppsala	Higher education

Company	Industry
ABB	Electronics
Electrolux	Electrical equipment
Ericsson	Telecommunication
KF	Food distribution center
Procordia	Multinational company with a variety of activities (pharmaceutical products, hotels, preservatives, and alcohol)
SAS	Airline
Skanska	Construction
Stora	Pulp and paper, flooring, packaging
Televerket	Telecommunication
Volvo	Automotive

Culture

Business Culture

When a foreign business traveler in Sweden refers to the country as Scandinavia, locals are offended. Swedes take pride in their country, and would rather not be grouped with Norway, Finland, Denmark, or Iceland. In all of Scandinavia, Swedes are the least laid back; therefore, keep the casual attitude out of the business setting.

Learn to pronounce the last name of your contact before arriving, as you will be using it a lot. Proper name calling is of dire importance; therefore, Mr., Mrs., Miss, or Dr. (preceding the last name) are appreciated whereas "hey, Sven" will most likely raise an eyebrow or foster a frown. As soon as a genuine attempt at constant formality is recognized, the host may insist on being called by his or her first name. Then you know you have made strides.

All parties involved in business meetings shake hands at both the opening and the close of negotiations. Get extra points with the Swedish by accompanying handshakes with a verbal greeting like "god dag" (pronounced goo dag) meaning good day or "god morgon" (pronounced goo MORN-ahn).

With extra-long winter nights and short summer evenings, trust clocks, not the sun, as business begins promptly at the prearranged time. Late arrival on your part can put your Swedish contact in a less than receptive mood.

Never wing it. Swedes carefully plan out their meeting agendas and expect the same from business counterparts. Following prompt arrival, expect to have a short period of casual small talk; then get down to the business at hand.

In winter months, Swedish culture is exhibited through what one might call "the etiquette of hats and coats" or "chivalry abounds." A gentleman frequently removes his hat when speaking to or passing a woman in the street. Concurrently, hats are always removed when entering a place of business, as are coats. Upon leaving, wait until you are out the door before putting on your coat. Otherwise, your northern European counterpart will think you are anxious to leave.

The Swedish love to socialize. Taboo subjects of discussion include politics and religion. Instead, talk about their beautiful countryside and cities, or ask how they spent their last vacation.

During social functions, Swedes rise to toasting tradition. Expect your host to lift a glass and proclaim "skoal" (translation: to your health). In turn, other party members raise their refreshment, make direct eye contact, and grin before downing a healthy swig. This silent gesture collectively indicates the same sentiment to the entire table.

Cultural factors affecting executive search: Relative to other Western countries, such as the United States and the United Kingdom, the executive search profession in Sweden is a more recent development, with the first firm establishments about twenty years ago. The profession has expanded greatly since the 1980s, with many new establishments in the larger cities.

People are very informal, and with the candidates you are almost at once on a first-name basis. You can ask any personal information you want, but try not to take too much time on the phone the first time. Rather try to have them send you their CV.

Swedish corporations often have very flat hierarchies, which makes it easy to get to the person you seek, no matter which level in the organization that he or she might occupy.

Swedish executives in general have an international perspective and are used to being approached by search firms. Initially, the atmosphere is polite but formal, and first calls should have a clear specification of the job opportunity that is at hand. Swedes are probably the most structured of all the Scandinavians in all business behavior and business performance, which is reflected in recruitment. In the search process, close attention should be focused on the initial approach when placing the first call. To catch the interest of the executive, you should be offering an upgrade in position. To get past the secretary and the level of indifference, the initial message should be very clear. Cellular phone systems such as GSM are now usually used and offer direct access to the people you want to reach.

An advance reference check of potential candidates is possible and highly recommended. When the first call is made, the potential candidate should know if they are, in fact, a candidate or just being scouted.

Foreign nations with similar cultures: Norway and Denmark

Key Research Resources (see Figure 13.43 beginning on page 278).

Figure 13.43 Research resources.
General Company Directories

Name of Service	Medium	Vendor Address	Description	Price
Bolagsfakta	CD-ROM	Brahegatan 9, Box 5371 10249 Stockholm Sweden Ph.: 46 8 6612130 Fax: 46 8 6678770 www.bolagsfakta.se	Annual reports from leading Swedish companies.	Free
Kompass	CD-ROM/Book	Kompass Sweden Torsgatan 21 11390 Stockholm Sweden Ph.: 46 8 7363000 Fax: 46 8 7363022 www.kompass.com	Three-volume directory giving address, brief financial information, and name of key executives at 19,000 companies in Sweden. Vol. 1. Products and Services Vol. 2. Company Information Vol. 3. Contact People	SKR 390 (annual cost for CD) Updated two times a year SKR 2490 (annual cost for set of three books) Updated once a year
Sveriges Aktiebolag	CD-ROM	Affärs-Data Torsgt. 21 11390 Stockholm Sweden Ph.: 46 8 73 65 919 Fax: 46 8 736 5555 www.ad.se	All Swedish companies including key facts and names of executives.	SKR 13,900 (annual cost) Updated four times a year

Specialty Directories

CF-Guiden	Book	The Civil Engineers Association Malmskilnadsgatan 48 11184 Stockholm Sweden Ph.: 46 8 61 38 000 Fax: 46 8 79 67 102	Guide of all member civil engineers.	SKR 350

News Services

Tidningsdatabasen	Online/Internet	Affärs-Data Torsgt. 21 11390 Stockholm Sweden Ph.: 46 8 73 65 919 Fax: 46 8 736 5555 www.ad.se	Database with articles from the leading newspapers and magazines in Sweden.	8 hours = SKR 7,909 20 hours = SKR 16,900 Same cost for CD-ROM and Internet

279

Major Libraries

Lunds Universitetbibliotek (Lund University Library)
PO Box 3, S-221
42 Malmø
Sweden
Ph.: 46 222 0000

Handelshøgskolans Bibliotek (Library of Stockholm's School of Economics)
PO Box 6501, S-113
83 Stockholm
Sweden
Ph.: 8 736 9700
Fax: 8 31 82 13
Web address: www.hhs.se/library/

Singapore

Figure 13.44 Map of Singapore.

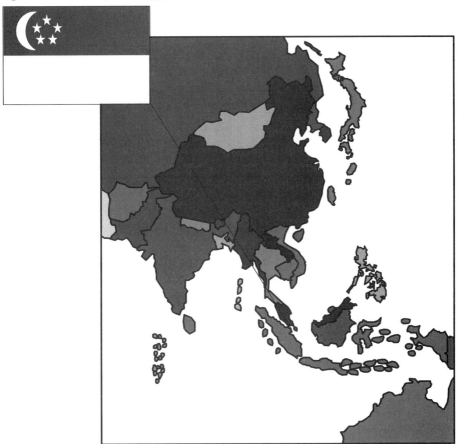

Country Information

Internet link to country information: www.singapore.com
International dialing code: +65
Population: 3,440,693 (July 1997 est.)
Ethnic divisions: Chinese 76.4 percent, Malay 14.9 percent, Indian 6.4 percent, other 2.3 percent
Religions: Buddhist (Chinese), Muslim (Malays), Christian, Hindu, Sikh, Taoist, Confucianist
Languages: Chinese (official), Malay (official and national), Tamil (official), English (official)

Labor force: 1.801 million (1996 est.); by occupation: financial, business, and other services 33.5 percent; manufacturing 25.6 percent; commerce 22.9 percent; construction 6.6 percent; other 11.4 percent (1994)

Capital: Singapore

Economic overview: Singapore has an open entrepreneurial economy with strong service and manufacturing sectors and excellent international trading links. Generally, the manufacturing, financial, and business service sectors have led to economic growth. Exports boom, led by the electronics sector, particularly the U.S. demand for disk drives. Rising labor costs continue to be a threat to Singapore's competitiveness, but there are indications that productivity is keeping up. In applied technology, per capita output, investment, and labor discipline, Singapore has the key attributes of a developed country.

Industries: Petroleum refining, electronics, oil drilling equipment, rubber processing and rubber products, processed food and beverages, ship repair, entrepot trade, financial services, biotechnology

Currency: 1 Singapore dollar (S$) = 100 cents; exchange rates: Singapore dollars (S$) per US$1—1.68 (October 1998)

Figure 13.45 Major industries and corporations.

Company	Industry
Asia Pacific Resources International Holdings Ltd.	Pulp and paper products
Asia Pulp & Paper Company Ltd.	Vertically integrated pulp and paper company
Creative Technology Ltd.	The world's leading maker of sound card and multimedia upgrade kits
Flextronics International Ltd.	Electrical components: printed circuit board assemblies for the computer, medical, consumer and communications industries
IPC Corporation	Computers: PCs; direct sales of PCs (IPC Technologies)
Neptune Orient Lines Ltd.	Transportation: shipping
Singapore Airlines Limited	Air transportation
Singapore Press Holdings Ltd.	Publishing: daily newspapers in Singapore (seven dailies in three languages) and magazines (Times Periodicals)

Company	Industry
Singapore Telecommunications Inc.	Telecommunications services: fixed-line, national, international, and mobile telecommunication services
Times Publishing Ltd.	Printing: commercial; bookstores (The Times Bookshop)

Culture

Although a very traditional community, the majority of Singapore's businesspeople tend to dress in Western garb. In spirit, though, each person sports a Confucian beard and a scholarly gown whether he or she is ethnically Chinese, Indian, Malay, Arab, or Anglo. This diversity saves Singapore from being merely modern and sterile. It is the soul of the sparkling clean city-state.

As with many aspects of life in this idiosyncratic Southeast Asian community, Singapore's native tongue belongs in the stranger-than-fiction category. While bowing to its Malaysian roots, the city-state's language-of-record (Malay) is only fully understood by a small number of today's Singaporean business communities.

Truly a melting pot, the island nation's diverse community of some three million is largely bilingual, conversing in different languages: Chinese (largely Puntonghua—common speech or Mandarin—or Cantonese), or Indian (mostly Tamil, but some Hindi and other dialects), or Malay and English. The latter, taught in all Singaporean schools, is compulsory, while the first is ethnically inspired. Be aware that this mix of languages has created some remarkable slang that you may come in contact with while traveling.

Because of its status as the unofficial international language, English has become modern Singapore's way to negotiate business opportunities. It is also the preferred mode for social communication, especially in international circles.

Perhaps the most fundamental clue offering insight into the typical Singaporean's essence is his or her desire to never lose face. A simile for maintaining peer status through respect and loyalty, "having face" means living up to everyone's expectations, a tall order for even the most scrupulous business traveler.

Westerners who understand this creed fare better than those who do not. If someone causes a Chinese Singaporean to lose face, he or she will likely ruin his or her own reputation, thus squelching any further business prospects. Further, in order to save face, the offended person will often seek revenge or retaliation. Dishonest behavior and not keeping a promise inevitably lead to someone losing face.

Cultural factors affecting executive search: It is best to call the executives directly and try to bypass the secretaries for the search confidentiality and to avoid jeopardizing the current position of the executives. If the executive is very senior, then it is best to ask a senior colleague (usually the principal consultant or partner) to make the call to honor the executives. In Asia, honoring seniority is an important part of the culture. In Singapore, it is usual to address candidates whom you deal with the first time by Mr. or Miss or Dr. Most of them are receptive to calls from interviewers as they are familiar with headhunting. If the executive is in middle to upper-middle management, a researcher can adopt a semiformal approach and a research associate can make the call.

In Asia it is very common and acceptable to ask an Asian about age, race, and family status. When speaking to an expatriate working in Asia, the approach has to be modified. It is important to ask these questions at the end of the conversation and explain the reasons why you need to know. However, do not push to get an answer.

Most Singaporeans and Asians who live and have settled in Singapore are not keen on relocating due to its significant impact on the family. They may consider opportunities if companies offer extremely attractive compensation, provide hardship allowance (for developing and underdeveloped countries), or relocate them to advanced cities such as Hong Kong or Taipei.

Singaporeans do not mind frequent travels because their families can still carry on their lifestyle and education without making many sacrifices. In compensation negotiation, transportation benefits are quite important because cars are very expensive in Singapore. For a senior executive, a good company car or a sizable car allowance is very important.

People in Singapore tend to put more importance on monetary terms and benefits, rather than longer annual leaves and free time for activities outside their work. Most Singaporeans are workaholics; however, they are beginning to realize the importance of recreation and family life.

Candidates normally do not feel comfortable revealing their exact remuneration package and their backgrounds over the phone. An estimated salary figure is usually given over the phone. It is usually not a problem talking about sex, age, education, race, and marital status either personally or over the phone. Face-to-face meetings are often very effective in finding out more information from the candidates.

Foreign nations with similar cultures: Malaysia and Hong Kong

Key Research Resources (see Figure 13.46 beginning on page 286).

Figure 13.46 Research resources. General Company Directories

Name of Service	Medium	Vendor Address	Description	Price
Asia's 7500 Largest Companies	Book/CD-ROM/ Online	ELC International 109 Uxbridge Rd. London W5 5TL England Ph.: 81 5662288	Top 7,500 companies in selected countries in Asia. Brief company information.	£STG 160
Asia-Pacific Dun's Market Identifiers	Online	Dun & Bradstreet Ltd. 479 St. Kilda Rd. PO Box 7405 Melbourne, VIC 3000 Australia Ph.: 3 8283333 www.dnb.com	More than 250,000 companies within Asia and the Pacific Rim. Full company information (SIC codes).	Please request
Dialog	Online service	Knight-Ridder Information, Inc. Universal Trade Center 3 Arbuthnot Rd. Hong Kong Ph.: 852 2868 0877 Fax: 852 2810 5861	Dialog contains hundreds of libraries covering a broad range of subjects. For company research, you can access different Asia and Pacific related databases as well as Dun & Bradstreet, Reuters, and occasionally Investext. Consultant service is available in Hong Kong.	Cost depends on number of connection times per month: approx. US$ 500–1,000 per month.
Kompass Singapore	Book/Online	Kompass South East Asia Ltd. 326-C King George's Ave. Singapore 0820 Ph.: 65 29696784 Fax: 65 2972 561	19,000 manufacturers, distributors, and service companies. Arranged by industry and company name.	US$ 239 (annual book)
Reuters Business Briefing	Online	Reuters Singapore Pty. Ltd. 18 Science Park Dr.	Business, corporate, market, and political news.	Please request

286

Name	Type	Contact	Description	Price
Singapore Trade Connection	CD-ROM	Singapore Trade Development Board 230 Victoria St. #07-00 Bugis Junction Office Tower Singapore 188024 Ph.: 65 3376628 Fax: 65 3376898	More than 6,000 Singapore companies active in electronics, major supporting industries, industrial machinery, international trade, and other areas.	US$ 300
The Thornton Guide to Singapore and Malaysia	Book	Hoovers, Inc. 1033 La Posada Dr., Ste. 250 Austin, TX 78752 Ph.: 512-374-4500 www.hoovers.com	250 profiles of companies in Singapore and 500 Malaysian companies.	US$ 69.95

Specialty Directories

Name	Type	Contact	Description	Price
Singapore Trade Connection	CD-ROM	Singapore Trade Development Board 1 Maritime Square #10-40 World Trade Center Telok Blangah Rd. Singapore 0409 Ph.: 2790451 www.tdb.gov.sg	More than 6,000 Singapore companies active in electronics, major supporting industries, industrial machinery, international trade, and other areas.	US$ 300

News Services

Name	Type	Contact	Description	Price
Reuters Business Briefing	Online	Reuters Singapore Pty. Ltd. 18 Science Park Dr. Singapore 118229 Ph.: 65 775 5088 www.reuters.com	Business, corporate, market, and political news.	Please request

Major Libraries

Trade Development Board Library
230 Victoria St. #07-00
Bugis Junction Office Tower
Singapore 0718
Ph.: 65 4334449
Fax: 65 3376898

The Monetary Authority of Singapore Library
10 Shenton Way
MAS Bldg.
Singapore 0207
Ph.: 65 2255577
E-Mail: btrg@mti.gov.sg

Figure 13.47 Internet snapshot of company information source for Singapore.

United Kingdom

Figure 13.48 Map of United Kingdom.

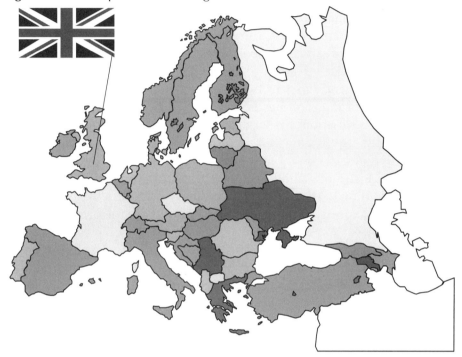

Country Information

Internet link to country information: www.neosoft.com/~dlgates/uk/ ukgeneral.html

International dialing code: +44

Population: 57,591,677 (July 1997 est.)

Ethnic divisions: English 81.5 percent; Scottish 9.6 percent; Irish 2.4 percent; Welsh 1.9 percent; Ulster 1.8 percent; West Indian, Indian, Pakistani, and other 2.8 percent

Religions: Anglican 27 million, Roman Catholic 9 million, Muslim 1 million, Presbyterian 800,000, Methodist 760,000, Sikh 400,000, Hindu 350,000, Jewish 300,000 (1991 est.). The United Kingdom does not include a question on religion in its census.

Languages: English, Welsh (about 26 percent of the population of Wales), Scottish form of Gaelic (about 60,000 in Scotland)

Labor force: 28.1 million (September 1996); by occupation: services 62.8 percent, manufacturing and construction 25.0 percent, government 9.1 percent, energy 1.9 percent, agriculture 1.2 percent (June 1992)

Capital: London

Economic overview: The United Kingdom is one of the world's great trading powers and financial centers, and its economy ranks among the four largest in Western Europe. The economy is essentially capitalistic; government has greatly reduced public ownership and contained the growth of social welfare programs. Agriculture is intensive, highly mechanized, and efficient by European standards, producing about 60 percent of the food needs with only 1 percent of the labor force. The United Kingdom has large coal, natural gas, and oil reserves, and primary energy production accounts for 12 percent of the GDP, one of the highest shares of any industrial nation. Services, particularly banking, insurance, and business services, account by far for the largest proportion of the GDP, while industry continues to decline in importance. Exports and manufacturing output are the primary engines of growth.

Industries: Production machinery including machine tools, electric power equipment, automation equipment, railroad equipment, shipbuilding, aircraft, motor vehicles and parts, electronics and communications equipment, metals, chemicals, coal, petroleum, paper and paper products, food processing, textiles, clothing, and other consumer goods

Currency: 1 British pound (£) = 100 pence; exchange rates: British pounds (£) per US$1 = 0.59 (October 1998)

Figure 13.49 Major cities, industries, and corporations.

City	Center of
Aberdeen	Offshore
Birmingham	Mechanical industry, automotive, railroad cars
Leeds/Bradford	Wool textiles, conservatives
London	Financial services, travel
Manchester	Chemicals, textiles
Newcastle upon Tyne	Shipyard, iron and steel industry, mechanical industry

Company	Industry
BAT Industries	Tobacco
British Aerospace	Aerospace, space technology
British Gas	Gas

Company	Industry
British Petroleum Co.	Oil and gas
British Telecommunications	Telecommunications
Grand Metropolitan	Brewing
Hanson	Mining, construction
Imperial Chemical Industries	Chemicals, pharmaceutical products
Sainsbury	Food, groceries
Unilever	Consumer goods

Culture

Business Culture

BUSINESS PROTOCOL: Office meetings are preferred, which normally begin and end with some social conversation. Coffee is generally served to visitors in the morning, tea in the afternoon break. There is much letter writing in British business. A formal letter addressed to someone by the title of his or her position rather than name should begin "Dear Sir" or "Dear Madam" and end "Yours sincerely." A letter addressed by name to someone not known to the writer should begin "Dear Mr." and "Dear Mrs." or "Dear Miss," depending on how she styles herself, otherwise "Dear Ms." Again, it should end "Yours sincerely." More personal endings, such as "With kind regards" may be used if writer and addressee are on a first-name basis, in which case the first name is also used in the address. Handshaking is common in the United Kingdom, but less of a ritual than in many other European countries. The accepted greeting is "How do you do?" to which the response is also "How do you do?" Detailed answers are not expected. On being introduced to a woman, she should extend her hand first. It is considered bad manners to speak loudly or to shout in public. Demonstrative gestures, especially physical touching, should be avoided. "Please" and "thank you" are used much more frequently than is customary among Americans. When in Britain, do as the British do to avoid appearing rude.

PREPARATION FOR THE MEETING: It is best to initiate a contact by letter rather than a cold telephone call, which may receive a cold response. Prior appointments are always preferred and punctuality is expected. In London and the South, executives are not usually at their desks before 9:00 A.M. and can seldom be reached after 5:30 P.M., when most switchboards close down.

WORKING WOMEN: Women in senior positions and even middle management are still rare in British business. The British businessman's attitude toward businesswomen, including foreign visitors, varies according to age and field. Older executives in traditional preserves such as banking may be condescending. There is much less prejudice among younger men and in newer growth businesses.

WORK ETHIC: Industrial relations in the United Kingdom were characterized by a bitter class-rooted antagonism between labor and management for much of the post–World War II period. The adversarial relationship, which produced frequent strikes, was a serious drag on productivity. The climate has greatly improved in more recent years. There is less of an "us against them" attitude and more cooperation, both on the shop floor and in labor negotiations.

ATTITUDE TOWARD FOREIGNERS: In the changed climate of the post–World War II world, the British have been compelled to submerge, if not entirely abandon, their traditional innate disdain for anything and anyone not British. They are much more receptive of foreigners. But distinctions are still drawn, subconsciously if not openly. A common language can be of help. North Americans are more likely to be accepted than continental Europeans. On a person-to-person basis, contact with British acquaintances and neighbors is likely to be very cordial.

Cultural factors affecting executive search: Candidate contact on the phone is usually semiformal (never first name), unless the candidate is well known to the researcher (e.g., a candidate from a previous job). Most potential candidates do not mind being called at work, although most in-depth conversations usually take place after office hours, when the candidate can be reached at home. As the market is very sophisticated, the term "executive search" is well known. Leaving a message mentioning the fact that you are seeking assistance in a search assignment and a rough idea of what you are looking for usually results in a return call from the prospective candidate.

Seeking information on sex or race is not allowed. Asking an individual's age is permitted. British people often like to work longer hours than is absolutely necessary to prove their dedication and indispensability.

Foreign nations with similar cultures: United States, Canada, Australia, and New Zealand

Key Research Resources (see Figure 13.50 beginning on page 293).

Figure 13.50 Research resources.
General Company Directories

Name of Service	Medium	Vendor Address	Description	Price
Corporate Register	Book	Hemmington Scott Publishing Ltd. City Innovation Centre 26-31 Whiskin St. London EC1R OBP England Ph.: 01 71 278 7769 Fax: 01 71 278 9808 www.hemscott.com	Detailed information on companies quoted on U.K. Stock Exchange. Gives address details and a list of key personnel.	£STG 200
Datastar	Online service	Knight-Ridder 78 Fleet St. London EC4Y 1NB England Ph.: 01 71 842 4000 Fax: 01 71 583 0519	Relevant databases on DataStar: Dun & Bradstreet, separate files for all countries of Western Europe. Information includes contact details, key personnel, sales, number of employees, history, SIC code.	
Disclosure	CD-ROM	Disclosure Ltd. 1 Mark Square Leonead St. London EC2A 4PR England Ph.: 01 71 278 7848 Fax: 01 71 566 1911	Information on the top public companies worldwide. It provides detailed financial information, stock price and share data, key financial ratios, and a list of the most recent press articles.	£STG 5,200 per year
Dun & Bradstreet Europe	Book	Dun & Bradstreet Ltd. Holmers Farm Way High Wycombe Bucks HP12 4UL England Ph.: 01 494 422000 Fax: 01 494 422260 www.dnb.com	Four-volume reference book. Information on 60,000 leading European companies. Gives basic details, e.g., address, financials, employee data, and parent or subsidiary information.	£STG 438

(Continued)

293

Figure 13.50 *(Continued)*

Name of Service	Medium	Vendor Address	Description	Price
Extel Card Database (EXTL)	Online service on DataStar	Knight-Ridder 78 Fleet St. London EC4Y 1NB England Ph.: 01 71 842 4000 Fax: 01 71 583 0519	Detailed annual balance sheet data and company information for U.K. and international companies, plus weekly corporate updates.	
Fame	CD-ROM	Bureau van Dijk 1 Great Scotland Yard London SW1A 2HN England Ph.: 01 71 839 2266 Fax: 01 71 839 6632 www.bwdep.com	Contains details of all U.K. registered companies with turnover of over £1 million. Gives income, balance sheet figures, and a number of key ratios. It also contains information on directors, holding and subsidiary companies.	£STG 6000 per year
FT Smaller Companies Handbook	Book	Extel Financial Information Ltd. Fitzroy House 13-17 Epworth St. London EC2A 4DL England Ph.: 01 71 825 8000 Fax: 01 71 251 2725	Two-volume reference book. A directory covering 1,500 smaller U.K. companies quoted on Main and unlisted Securities Market (those with market capitalization of under £250 million). Service is divided into two volumes, segmented by market capitalization.	£STG 165

Name	Type	Contact	Description	Price
Hoover's Handbook of World Business	Book	The Reference Press, (c/o William Snyder Publishing Associates) Five Mile Drive Oxford OX2 8HT England Ph.: 01 865 513186 Fax: 01 865 513186 www.hoovers.com	Current and historical financial and background information on the world's largest corporations and their competitors.	£STG 35.45
Key British Enterprises	Book	Dun & Bradstreet Ltd. Holmers Farm Way High Wycombe Bucks HP12 4UL England Ph.: 01 494 422000 Fax: 01 494 422260 www.dnb.com	Six-volume reference book. Addresses and overview (key personnel, brief financials) of the top 50,000 U.K. companies, ranked by geography, industry.	£STG 438
Kompass UK	Book	Reed Information Services Windsdor Court East Grinstead W Sussex RH19 1XD England Ph.: 01 342 326972 Fax: 01 342 335992 www.kompass.com	Three-volume directory giving address and brief financial information on U.K. companies that have advertised in it. Vol. 1—companies by location; Vol. 2—companies by product; Vol. 3—financial summaries.	£STG 290 (Vols. 1 and 2) £STG (Vol. 3, Financial Data)
Stock Broker Research (ICBR, INVE)	Online service on DataStar	Knight-Ridder 78 Fleet St. London EC4Y 1NB England Ph.: 01 71 842 4000 Fax: 01 71 583 0519	Full-text reports from British and international brokers and investment banks. This focuses mainly on companies although some industries are also covered.	

(Continued)

Figure 13.50 *(Continued)*

Name of Service	Medium	Vendor Address	Description	Price
Times 1000 (I)	Book	Harpercollins 77-85 Fulham Palace Rd. London W6 8JB England Ph.: 01 81 307 4158 Fax: 01 81 307 4813	Three-volume reference book. Tables of the United Kingdom's top 1,000, Europe's top 1,000, the top 100 for North America, Japan, Australia, New Zealand, and Southeast Asia.	£STG 35
Who's Owns Whom UK & Ireland	Book	Dun & Bradstreet Ltd. Holmers Farm Way High Wycombe, Bucks HP12 4UL England Ph.: 01 494 422000 Fax: 01 494 422260 www.dnb.com	Two-volume directory of U.K. and Irish companies showing the relationship between subsidiaries and parents.	£STG 338

Specialty Directories

Name of Service	Medium	Vendor Address	Description	Price
Bankers Almanac	Book	Reed Information Services Windsdor Court East Grinstead House, W Sussex RH19 1XD England Ph.: 01 342 326972 Fax: 01 342 335992 www.reedinfo.com	Three-volume reference book. Details of 4,000 major companies arranged alphabetically and geographically. Gives contact details, history and ownership, key personnel, balance sheet.	£STG 295

Directory of Directors	Book	Reed Information Services Windsor Court East Grinstead House, W Sussex RH19 1XD England Ph.: 01 342 326972 Fax: 01 342 335992 www.reedinfo.com	Two-volume reference book. Directory of information on 52,000 directors and their 150,000 board appointments.	£STG 195
Directory of Management Consultants	Book	AP Information Services Roman House 296 Golders Green Rd. London NW11 9PZ England Ph.: 01 81 455 4550 Fax: 01 81 455 6381 www.kennedypub.com/dmc.html	Alphabetical list of companies from small to major consultancies. Indexed by location, industry specialization, and practice area.	£STG 85
Directory of Management Consultants in Europe	Book	AP Information Services Roman House 296 Golders Green Rd. London NW11 9PZ England Ph.: 01 81 455 4550 Fax: 01 81 455 6381	Companies listed alphabetically by country and indexed as previous directory.	£STG 130
Dow Jones Telerate Bank Register	Book	Euromoney Publications Nestor House Playhouse Yard London EC4V 5EX England Ph.: 01 71 779 8888 Fax: 01 71 779 8617 www.telerate.com www.emwl.com	Three-volume reference book. Information on banks and financial institutions in more than 180 countries. Gives contact details, subsidiaries and affiliates, ownership and shareholders, advisers, statistics on employees, and branches.	£STG 150

(Continued)

Figure 13.50 *(Continued)*

Name of Service	Medium	Vendor Address	Description	Price
Marketing Managers Yearbook	Book	AP Information Services Roman House 296 Golders Green Rd. London NW11 9PZ England Ph.: 01 81 455 4550 Fax: 01 81 455 6381	Contains key personnel details of top U.K. companies, and details of advertising agencies, PR agencies, and other companies involved in marketing, advertising, and design.	£STG 57.25

News Services

Name of Service	Medium	Vendor Address	Description	Price
Reuters Textline (TXLN)	Online service on DataStar	Knight-Ridder 78 Fleet St. London EC4Y 1NB England Ph.: 01 71 842 4000 Fax: 01 71 583 0519	Full-text articles on companies and industries worldwide from newspapers, journals, regulatory news, and press releases.	Price dependent on usage.

There are very few directories relating to individuals because the U.K. market is so large. Those that are in existence such as Who's Who have information on major national figures only. Membership lists are sometimes available from relevant trade associations; the Directory of Associations is usually the best source for these.

Major Libraries

> British Library
> British Library Business Information Service
> 25 Southampton Building
> Chancery Lane
> London WC2A 1AW
> England
> Ph.: 0171 412 7457
> Fax: 0171 412 7453
> Web address: www.portico.bl.uk
>
> London Business School
> Sussex Place
> Regent's Park
> London NW1 4SA
> England
> Ph.: 0171 262 5050
> Fax: 0171 706 1897
> Consultant Service: Takes requests at £70 per hour plus costs.

United States

Figure 13.51 Map of United States.

Country Information

Internet link to country information: Please go to any of the major WWW search engines listed in Part III of this book.

International dialing code: +1

Population: 267,954,764 (July 1997 est.)

Ethnic divisions: white 83.4 percent, black 12.4 percent, Asian 3.3 percent, Native American 0.8 percent (1992)

Religions: Protestant 56 percent, Roman Catholic 28 percent, Jewish 2 percent, other 4 percent, none 10 percent (1989)

Languages: English, Spanish (spoken by a sizable minority)

Labor force: 133.943 million (includes unemployed) (1996); by occupation: managerial and professional 27.5 percent; technical, sales, and administrative support 30.3 percent; services 13.7 percent; manufacturing, mining, transportation, and crafts 25.5 percent; farming, forestry, and fishing 2.9 percent

Capital: Washington, D.C.

Economic overview: The United States has the most powerful, diverse, and technologically advanced economy in the world, with a per capita GDP of $25,850, the largest among major industrial nations. The economy is market oriented with most decisions made by private individuals and business firms and with government purchases of goods and services. Unemployment has declined gradually in recent years. The main issues for the U.S. government to address include inadequate investment in economic infrastructure, rapidly rising medical costs of an aging population, and sizable budget and trade deficit, which is currently in the process of being balanced.

Industries: Leading industrial power in the world, highly diversified and technologically advanced; petroleum, steel, motor vehicles, aerospace, telecommunications, chemicals, electronics, food processing, consumer goods, lumber, mining

Currency: 1 United States dollar (US$) = 100 cents

Figure 13.52 Major cities, industries, and corporations.

City	Center of
Atlanta	Industry in the South
Chicago	Industry in the Midwest
Detroit	Automotive
Houston	Oil and gas
Los Angeles	Industry in the Southwest
New York	Banking, finance, head office for many corporations
San Francisco	Computer industry
Washington, D.C.	Governmental administration

Company	Industry
American International Group, Inc.	Property and casualty insurance
Amoco Corporation	Integrated oil and gas
AT&T Corp.	Telecommunications services
Bank America Corporation	Miscellaneous financial
Blue Cross and Blue Shield Association	Accident and health insurance
Cargill, Incorporated	Miscellaneous food
Chevron Corporation	Integrated oil and gas
Chrysler Corporation	Automotive manufacturing
Citicorp	Banks—money center
ConAgra, Inc.	Miscellaneous food

(Continued)

Figure 13.49 *(Continued)*

Company	Industry
Dayton Hudson Corporation	Retail—major department stores
E.I. du Pont de Nemours and Company	Diversified operations
Exxon Corporation	Integrated oil and gas
Federal National Mortgage Association	Financial—mortgages and related services
Ford Motor Company	Automotive manufacturing
General Electric Company	Diversified operations
General Motors	Automotive manufacturing
Hewlett Packard Company	Mini- and microcomputers
International Business Machine Corporation	Computers—mini and mainframe hardware
J.C. Penney Company, Inc.	Retail—major department stores
Kmart Corporation	Retail—discount and variety
Koch Industries, Inc.	Integrated oil and gas
Lockheed Martin	Aerospace, aircraft equipment
Lucent Technologies Inc.	Telecommunications equipment
Merrill Lynch & Co., Inc.	Financial—investment bankers and brokerages
Metropolitan Life Insurance Company	Life insurance
Mitsubishi International Corporation	Diversified operations
Mobil Corporation	Integrated oil and gas
The Allstate Corporation	Property and casualty insurance
The Chase Manhattan Corporation	Banks—money center
The Dow Chemical Company	Diversified chemicals
The Kroger Co.	Retail—supermarkets

Culture

Cultural factors affecting executive search: Executive search originated in the United States. People are for the most part very open to being approached and are usually very receptive and helpful when contacted. The first candidate contact is important. Americans are very informal and first names are used immediately. Using "Mr." or "Mrs." is seen as too formal. Calls are completed most frequently with the use of a third party's name as a means of introduction. Probably 90 percent of all calls are received by an assistant or a secretary, who will either take a message or redirect you to voice mail. You can ask to leave a voice mail message in order to leave as much information as possible with the prospect to pique his or her interest. You can have a pretty good success ratio with those people returning calls. The people that you connect with usually want you to get to the point right away; they want the basic information in a brief amount of time—position, organization budget, search time line, major responsibilities, any issues or problems. Then, if interested and there is no catch for them, they usually want to be able to discuss the position in more detail later. There are also those who even want to see the position specification prior to talking over the phone.

You cannot ask for personal information regarding age, marital status, spousal or family employment, children, race, arrest record, and handicaps. Candidates usually offer or share this information with you anyway. There are ways of finding out personal information without asking for it. You can ask for year of degrees (for verification), a chronology of employment with years (for referencing), questions such as: Are there any personal considerations that would prevent you from moving? (A covert way of asking, Do you have children in school? Does your spouse have a job, etc.?)

People in the United States are motivated by money; however, lately an increasing number of people mention their quality of life as very important as well. They evaluate the entire job prospect and what it will mean for them and their family on top of financial considerations, especially when they are senior enough to be more particular about their career. Still there are always people who will not move to certain areas of the country, but it is hard to find out unless you ask them. Some areas of the country (i.e., Seattle, Boston, and San Francisco) are quite popular destinations, whereas other cities (i.e., New York, Cleveland, Los Angeles, Buffalo, and Detroit) are frequently less desirable locations. It is getting more difficult to move people, especially when family relocation plays a major role. Two-career marriages have been a limiting factor on relocation, and they have become more widespread.

Although career advancement is important, the prospect of higher future income linked with specific industries is of importance (equity participation and pay for performance are big issues). There are "sexy" fields such as bio-tech, which will attract people. There is a lot of mobility within the job market, and it is quite common that candidates are willing to move from corporate Fortune 500 environments to smaller companies if the compensation is right.

Foreign nations with similar cultures: Canada and the United Kingdom

Key Research Resources (see Figure 13.53 beginning on page 304).

Figure 13.53 Research resources.
General Company Directories

Name of Service	Medium	Vendor Address	Description	Price
Directory of Corporate Affiliations Library	Book/CD-ROM/ Online	Reed Elsevier 121 Chanlon Rd. New Providence, NJ 07934 Ph.: 800-521-8110 Fax: 908-665-2867 www.reedels.com/ nrt.index.html	Business profiles and corporate linkage for more than 121,000 of the world's leading companies with 286,000 key executives. SIC code.	Please inquire
Duns Million Dollar Disc Plus	CD-ROM	Dun & Bradstreet Information Services 461 From Rd. Mack Centre VI Paramus, NJ 07652 Ph.: 201-843-6555 Fax: 201-291-4848	240,000 public and private companies categorized by SIC codes. Key information about decision makers, and executive biographies. Updated four times per year. Can be installed on a local area network (LAN) or a PC.	The disc can be leased and must be returned when updated. A single user version costs US$ 7,900.
Standard & Poor's Register of Corporations, Directors, and Executives	Book/CD-ROM/ Online	Standard & Poor's 25 Broadway New York, NY 10004 Ph.: 212-208-8283 Fax: 212-208-8624 www.standardandpoors. com/rating	More than 55,000 public and privately held corporations in the United States, including names and titles of more than 400,000 officials. SIC code. Brief information on selected executives.	Please inquire

Title	Type	Description	Price
Ward Business Directory of U.S. Private and Public Companies	Book	132,500 U.S. companies categorized by SIC codes. Updated twice per year. Set of six volumes.	Set of books US$ 1,995

Specialty Directories

Title	Type	Publisher	Description	Price
Dun & Bradstreet Reference Book of Corporate Management	Book	Dun & Bradstreet Information Services Three Sylvan Way Parsippany, NJ 07054-3896 Ph.: 973-605-6000 Fax: 973-605-6930	Biographical directory covering nearly 200,000 corporate officers in 12,000 companies. Probably most extensive source of biographical data on corporate executives in United States, but generally more limited information than a Who's Who.	Annual US$ 785
Encyclopedia of Business Information Sources	Book	Gale Research 835 Penobscot Bldg. Detroit MI 48226-4094 Ph.: 313-961-2242	Covers 26,000 sources of information such as associations, periodicals, directories, handbooks, biographical directories, databases, etc., classified by highly specific subjects (often fields or industries)	Annual US$ 275
National Trade and Professional Associations of the United States	Book	Columbia Books 1212 New York Ave., NW, Ste. 330 Washington, DC 20005 Ph.: 202-898-0662 Fax: 202-898-0775 www.d-net.com/columbia	This directory covers about 7,400 trade associations, professional societies, and labor unions in the United States. Includes basic information, address, phone, membership, publications (including directories), chief executives.	Annual US$ 75

(Continued)

305

Figure 13.53 *(Continued)*

Name of Service	Medium	Vendor Address	Description	Price
Thomas Register	Book/ CD-ROM	Thomas Publishing 5 Penn Plaza New York, NY 10001 Ph.: 212-695-0500 Fax: 212-290-7365 www.thomasregister.com	Covers more than 149,000 manufacturing firms with limited corporate information and corporate contacts (including sales executives). Designed for targeting companies that produce or distribute specific industrial products.	Annual. US$ 240

News Services

LEXIS-NEXIS	Online	LEXIS-NEXIS 3445 Newmark Dr. Miamisburg, OH 45342 or PO Box 933-NR Dayton, OH 45401 Ph.: 800-544-7390 Fax: 937-865-1666 www.lexis-nexis.com	One of the leading sources for full-text legal, news, and business information. LEXIS-NEXIS is a database access provider for a large number of publications, magazines, newspapers, and company databases.	Cost is determined by number of searches conducted, online time, number of documents printed.

Major Libraries

Libraries with excellent research resources are found in all major cities and at every medium-to-large college and university. Info Trac-library will fax top 100 companies in the SIC code and individually produce a list of the companies with their address, phone number, chief officers, and annual sales. In addition, there are several publications that you can conduct a full text search for at Info Trac (public library, no fee). Check your local library for access information.

An excellent resource for information on all public U.S. companies is the Library of Congress in Washington, D.C. The company information in the Library of Congress has now also been made available at no cost on the Internet. The web address is: www.sec.gov/edgarhp.htm

Appendix

Internet and Technology Terms

baud   The speed at which signals are sent by a modem, measured by the number of changes per second in the signals during transmission. For example, a baud rate of 1,200 would indicate 1,200 signal changes in one second. Baud rate is often confused with bits per second (bps). See next entry.

bits per second (bps)   A measurement of the data transfer rate between two modems. The higher the bps, the higher the speed of the transfer.

bounced message   An e-mail message returned to sender, usually because of an address error.

corporate forums   One of the best ways for a company to gain visibility and interact with customers and suppliers by using an online service is to establish a corporate forum with the online service. Not all online services offer this service, and the establishment of such a forum involves a cost and agreements between the company and the provider. This forum is dedicated to the company and can contain bulletin boards, newsletters, order forms, support forums, chat areas (where users can have live, text-based discussions with each other or the company), and more.

e-mail   The abbreviation for electronic mail. E-mail is the most-used Internet tool today, and is electronic mail going from one person to one or more others. All parties need to have some sort of access to the Internet. Because it is so widespread, e-mail is currently one of the best resources available on the Internet. A person can use e-mail for inquiries, ordering, advertising, support, newsletters, and more. E-mail can be sent and received with regular e-mail programs, and it can be integrated into a company's home page on the World Wide Web, making it very easy for a user to make responses directly from the Web site.

FAQs   An abbreviation for Frequently Asked Questions, a file compiled for many Usenet newsgroups and other Internet services to reduce repeated posts about commonplace subjects in a newsgroup.

file transfer   Transfer of a file from one computer to another over a network.

forms   Area of a Web page with input fields where the user can be asked to fill in information. Whatever information is filled in will end up as e-mail or data in the company's mailbox or database connected to its Web site. Forms are excellent tools for allowing users to order products, request information, enter data that can be used in market research, and other uses.

gopher   A menu-based guide to directories on the Internet, usually organized by subject.

links   Distinct features of the World Wide Web (WWW). Any document published on the WWW can be linked to other documents present on the WWW. These links are colored text or graphics that the user can click on with a mouse. This drastically reduces the skills necessary to navigate around in a company's Web sites or to external Web sites that the company's links are pointing to.

listservs   Automated mailing lists where each member can publish information that is automatically distributed to all the members of the list (some listservs are edited by the owners, and usually only information considered to be of interest to most of the subscribers of the list is posted). There is normally no charge for a person to become a member of a list. All communication is done via e-mail on the Internet, and no other type of Internet service is needed to use listservs. A company can either subscribe to a listserv and become a member, or set up its own listserv (Internet access and listserv software is needed). A listserv will typically have a specific topic to which all contributions are expected to relate.

newsgroups   The Usenet message areas, organized by subject.

online services   The major online services consist of the Big Three: CompuServe, America Online, and Prodigy. In addition, there are a number of smaller online services. The online services have their own networks separate from the Internet, but they are also integrated with the Internet, giving their users access to different services such as e-mail, listservs, and the World Wide Web.

posting   The sending of a message to a newsgroup, bulletin board (an electronic message center usually serving special interest groups), or other public message area. The message itself is called a post.

real-time   The Net term for live, as in "Live from New York!" Generally applied to chat, where two or more people have a live real-time conversation online.

signature   A file added to the end of e-mail messages or Usenet posts that contains personal information—usually your name, e-mail address, postal address, and telephone number. Net etiquette dictates that signatures, or sigs for short, should be no longer than four or five lines.

URL   Abbreviation for uniform resource locator, the global address (also called Web address) of documents and other resources on the World Wide Web. The first part of the address indicates what protocol to use, and the second part specifies the Internet provider address or domain name where the resource is located. For example: ftp://www.pcwebopedia.com/stuff.exe or http://www.pcwebopedia.com/index.html

Usenet   A collection of networks and computer systems that exchange messages. It organizes these messages by subject in newsgroups.

Web site   A site (location) on the World Wide Web. Each Web site contains a home page, which is the first document users see when they enter the site. The site might also contain additional documents and files. Each site is owned and managed by an individual, company, or organization.

World Wide Web (WWW)   A hypertext system for searching the Internet that allows you to browse through a variety of Net resources, including Usenet newsgroups as well as FTP (file transfer protocol), telnet, and Gopher sites. You can access any of these resources directly from the WWW. The WWW is the fastest-growing network on the Internet. Since its introduction, the WWW has bypassed all other similar services on the Internet. Almost all businesses today that establish a presence on the information superhighway do so on the WWW.

Résumé Industry Codes

The codes described are used by Ward Howell International and many other leading executive search firms.

Agricultural/Forestry	AGRI
Construction	CONS
Financial	FINA
Bank	BANK
Insurance	INSU
Investment	INVE
Real estate	REAL
Government	GOVE
Manufacturing	MANU
Adhesive/Seals	ADHE
Aerospace	AERO
Apparel	APPA
Automotive	AUTO
Chemicals	CHEM
Cleaners	CLEA
Computer hardware	COMP
Cosmetics	COSM
Electric machines	ELEC
Food/Beverage	FOOD
Furniture	FURN
Instrument	INST
Machines, nonelectric	MACH

Medical equipment	MEDI
Miscellaneous	MISC
Petroleum	PETR
Pharmaceutical	PHAR
Plastic	PLAS
Primary metal	META
Publishing	PUBL
Rubber	RUBB
Textile	TEXT
Tobacco	TOBA
Transportation equipment	TRAN
Wood	WOOD
Natural Resources	RESO
Retail/Stores	RETA
Apparel	APPA
Auto	AUTO
Department	DEPA
Food	FOOD
Furniture	FURN
Hardware	HARD
Lumber/Construction	CONS
Miscellaneous	MISC
Services	SERV
Amusements	AMUS
Business	BUSI
Education	EDUC
Hotels	HOTE
Legal	LEGA
Miscellaneous	MISC
Not-for-profit	NOTP
Personal	PERS
Social	SOCI
Transportation	TRAN
Air	AIRX
Motor freight	MOTO
Passenger	PASS
Postal service	POST
Railroad	RAIL
Water	WATE
Utilities	UTIL
Electrical	ELEC

Gas	GASX
Pipelines	PIPE
Wholesaler	WHOL
Chemicals	CHEM
Commercial equipment	COMM
Lumber/Construction	CONS
Medical equipment	MEDI
Miscellaneous	MISC
Motor vehicle	MOTO
Office supplies	SUPP
Petroleum products	PETR

Résumé Function Codes

Banking	BANK
Corporate	CORP
Investment	INVE
Mortgage	MORT
Private	PRIV
Corporate Development	CORP
Engineering	ENGI
Chemical	CHEM
Electrical	ELEC
Industrial	INDU
Mechanical	MECH
Finance	FINA
Audit	AUDI
Controller	CONTI
Credit	CRED
Tax	TAXX
Treasurer	TREA
General Management	GENE
Administrative	ADMI
Consultant	CONS
Engineering	ENGI
Financial	FINA
Manufacturing	MANU
Marketing	MARK
Nonexecutive	NONE

Human Resources	HUMA
Benefit	BENE
Compensation	COMP
Labor relations	LABO
Organizational Development	ORGA
Training	TRAI
Legal	LEGA
Attorney	ATTO
General counsel	COUN
Mergers and acquisitions	MERG
Patent	PATE
Tax	TAXX
Management Information Systems	MISX
Manufacturing	MANU
Facilities/maintenance	MAIN
Operations	OPER
Plant management	PLAN
Marketing	MARK
Advertising	ADVE
Brand/Product Development	BRAN
Research	RESE
Sales	SALE
Public Relations	PUBL
Communications	COMM
Editor/Writer	EDIT
Investor/Shareholder Rel.	INVE
Purchasing	PURC
Logistics	LOGI
Materials	MATE
Quality	QUAL
ISO9000	ISO9
Research & Development	RESE
Sales	SALE
Marketing	MARK
Regional	REGI

Glossary

Terms Used Within Executive Search

assignment   A commission from a client to a headhunter to carry out a search to fill a specific position. The assignment officially begins when the client decides on a particular search firm and agrees to its initial brief.

associate   A ranking within a search firm, sometimes below consultant and certainly below partner.

Association of Executive Search Consultants (AESC)   Organized in 1959 as the Association of Executive Recruiting Consultants, Inc., the association brought together leading executive search consultants who established strict requirements for membership and standards of ethical practice for their professional field.

billings   A U.S. term used to denote the fee income, including expenses of search firms and individual consultants.

blockage   A problem faced by a search firm with too many clients within a limited sector, leaving no poaching grounds in which to search for candidates, because too many companies are off-limit or no-touch. This can cause severe limits to growth of volume business for a specialist company or a specialist headhunter.

boutique   An executive search firm that specializes in one or more relatively narrow niches in contrast to presenting a generalist image.

brief   In contrast with the initial brief, a detailed document that acts as a control on the search program and outlines the expected time span and the headhunter's fee. It follows the formal commission of the assignment.

business climate   The overall state of play of the economy. Headhunting thrives on changes in either upward or downward directions, and finds least work in a stable and static business climate.

business culture   The nature of a company in terms of what it is like to work there, the sort of people favored, and its attitude toward change. Companies with strong business cultures are keen on developing the skills of their own people and rarely use headhunters. They are seen as ideal poaching grounds, but are very difficult to penetrate, because they promote and gain strong company loyalty. Many of the key operators in these companies are clearly identifiable as a type, such as Xeroids, or for their Unileverness. They are subject to corporate guidelines for behavior and attitudes, such as the IBM Way. Understanding the nature of the business culture of a client is crucial to the researcher and consultant, as frequently the success of a candidate depends not just on his or her technical ability and qualifications, but on the ability to fit into the business culture of the new firm without undue culture shock.

business development Work promoting the activities of a search firm trying to gain more clients, by strategic mailings of brochures, cold-calling, business presentations such as beauty parades and making opportunities to join shoot-outs. This is crucial for new search firms, those that do not have a high level of repeat business, and those that are eager to expand their volume of assignments, such as transaction-oriented search firms.

candidate Definitions vary from all persons contacted in a wide trawl to fill an assignment (sometimes referred to as "prospect") to only those who have expressed a real interest in the job and in whom the client is interested (sometimes called "warm bodies"). Technically, candidates are just the frontrunners, or those who appear on the final short list.

candidate blockage Candidates who may not be considered for a position because they are active candidates in another search.

candidate reports The reports produced by the search firm for the client, providing background information on each candidate on the short list before the client enters the interview process. They add to the basic CV (curriculum vitae or résumé), suggesting why the headhunter thinks the candidate is especially suitable, perhaps emphasizing pluses and minimizing weaknesses, or at least preparing the client for them. Some candidate reports include photographs; some are accompanied by video interviews, especially for global searches where considerable expense is involved in the candidate meeting the client. Candidate reports are usually known as confidential reports.

client The company, firm, or organization employing the search firm.

client anonymity One of the principal reasons for using executive search. Client identity is usually not revealed to prospective candidates until well along in the process, except in general terms.

cloak-and-dagger headhunting An assignment where the search must be a particularly confidential one, because the person currently occupying the position must not know that his or her replacement is being sought.

code of business conduct Formal or informal code of conduct that headhunting firms operate by in order to establish a reputation and gain repeat business. Two of the most obvious rules are not poaching from one's clients for up to two years and maintaining strict confidentiality.

coding of candidate files A task of many researchers creating and maintaining an in-house data bank as a source of information on candidates and sources.

Information has to be coded so that it can be utilized to the maximum advantage by researchers and consultants, many of whom have their own screens and instant access to these files.

cold-calling   When a consultant or—more usually—a researcher has to make an initial call to a candidate or source not contacted before. The most effective cold calls follow extensive homework on the person. Often elaborate cover stories are needed to ascertain the name of the person to be cold-called. This is seen as one of the worst chores of headhunting, and is minimized by developing an expertise in a particular sector and, of course, by more experience in executive search generally.

compensation package   Total compensation can include various elements other than salary for senior executives: typically a mix of deferred income, incentive bonus, profit sharing, stock options, tax shelters (or some type of compensation that permits estate building), thrift plans, pension plans, life insurance, health insurance, long-term disability insurance, dental insurance, tuition assistance, payment for personal and family medical and dental expenses, cars, club memberships, loans, joining bonus, and other perquisites (including, increasingly, some form of hiring bonus).

completion rate   Percentage of retained searches that result in a hire. Estimated to be as low as 60 percent, claimed by some to be 100 percent. Be wary of the latter: No one is perfect, and the imponderables and intangibles in a search are many. Greatly affected by client lassitude in interviewing and following up with candidates, changes (written and subtle) in job specifications, internal client politics, organizational changes, as well as by recruiter performance and effectiveness.

confidential search   An assignment in which the consultant is not able to reveal the name of the client to candidates until the final stages, making the search process very difficult. It may be that the client needs cloak-and-dagger headhunting, but it may have perfectly sound and honorable intentions in wanting to keep the search very secret. Of course, all assignments are confidential to a greater or lesser degree, and many first cold calls do not reveal the client's name.

consultant   A general term loosely applied to all headhunters, as opposed to researchers. It can technically refer to a senior member of a headhunting firm before he or she becomes a partner.

contingency-based fees   Where the consultant's payment depends on the success of an assignment. Contingency work was common in the early days of headhunting, especially in the United States, but is now very unpopular among the search firms, who now do nearly all work on a retainer basis except for very exceptional circumstances.

cover stories, undercover research   Ploys by researchers to get information. A typical cover story is pretending that a conference is being organized for which names of invitees are sought. This, and other aspects of undercover research—any kind of inquiry in which the purpose is not made entirely clear—are frowned upon by many concerned about the ethics of headhunting, but it would be very difficult to obtain all necessary information without a minor form of semideception.

cross-vectoring   A term used by some researchers to describe discovering methods and pinning down suitable candidates by means of various research methods, both direct and indirect, to minimize the amount of cold-calling involved, and to reduce the time taken in homework on potential candidates and sources.

culture shock   Can be suffered by a successful candidate entering a new company with a different business culture, especially someone leaving a company with a strong business culture in which they have worked for some time.

CV (curriculum vitae)   Known as "résumé" in the United States, an outline of one's personal details, qualifications, and experience. A CV prepared for headhunters is not necessarily the same as one favored by potential employers; search consultants look for very brief outlines in a clear chronological order, not thematic appraisals that smack of career advisors and CV-producing companies. A CV for headhunters should always include salary details.

desire to hire   Intention on the part of a client engaging a search consultant to appoint a candidate to a specific position, as opposed to a client who is not necessarily interested in making a placing, but wants to appraise the quality of the market generally. Whether there is a desire to hire should always be made clear at the outset; otherwise candidates will become interested in a position and inevitably be disappointed. Client ethics should be seen as just as important as ethics of headhunting.

desk research   Refers to headhunting research—in books, the in-house sources, and online databases—before cold-calling and working the phones. Desk research includes the librarianship phase and sometimes includes telephoning.

employment agreement   Written terms of employment, as a protection to client organization and candidate. The employment agreement may take the form of a formal agreement or letter to the new executive, spelling out everything discussed and agreed upon: job specifications, reporting relationships, base salary, benefits, moving costs, and so on. The executive then replies, either by telephone or letter, and the deal is settled.

ethics of headhunting   A concern of most search firms when discussing their code of business conduct. Many claim to be consistently honest and open in their approach, denying the use of cover stories and undercover research. Companies most reluctant to use search frequently quote their suspicions about the ethics of headhunting as a reason for their caution. Some aspects of search, including poaching, are seen as most questionable in terms of ethics.

evaluation of candidate   At a convenient time and place, the recruiter interviews the prospective candidate to verify the original information gathered during sourcing and researching, to examine his or her background in depth, and to determine if the personal chemistry is appropriate. These appraisal interviews develop an in-depth picture of each candidate: employment background, business philosophy, career objectives, potential, and personality characteristics. Education and employment are verified, and a reference investigation is made of past performance. From the group of prospective candidates evaluated, several of the best qualified are selected for introduction to the client.

executive search   Used in the headhunting business synonymously with headhunting, but many firms much prefer this more formal and professional label, and never refer to themselves in any other way.

expenses   Charged by a headhunting firm to a client, counted within revenue but not fee income. The client commissioning the headhunter should seek an estimate of the expenses, at least as a percentage of the total bill for an assignment. This amount normally works out at between 15 and 25 percent of the total cost, but some headhunters have been known almost to double their bills through expenses.

external candidates   Candidates for a position to be filled who are working for an outside company, as opposed to internal candidates.

fallout   Term used to describe the following condition: After a placement has been made (or during the assignment), the client decides to hire one or more additional candidates who surfaced and were recommended by the recruiter. Some search firms demand full fee for each additional hire; others will not accept a fee.

fee income   The income a search firm receives from fees charged to the client, excluding expenses.

first-, second-, and third-generation research   The historical development of attitudes to research by search firms since the early days of headhunting. First-generation research depended largely on personal contacts within the old-boys' network. Second-generation research was supplemented by published secondary sources and circulation lists of particular business magazines and alumni, which, being rather imprecise, may be seen as fishing rather than trawling. Third-generation research is practiced in the most modern and successful firms today, involving systematic and creative cross-vectoring of a variety of sources, through desk research or the librarianship phase, online information, and cold-calling and telephoning existing contacts. Most search firms combine all three generations of research, but in varying proportions.

follow-up   The period after the successful completion of an assignment, after the candidate starts work, in which a good search consultant keeps in contact with both client and candidate to monitor the progress of both. Seen as good for business development and as a part of the search firm's code of business conduct.

front-runner   A candidate in the final short list who is presented to the client and has an equal chance with others of winning the position. Sometimes this term is used by the headhunter to refer to his or her favorite candidate, who is recommended most strongly to the client.

generalist headhunters   Consultants within search firms who do not specialize in any particular industry or functional sector and take on assignments in a range of areas. Generalist headhunters are becoming rarer in relation to specialist headhunters because of the increasing sophistication of business. Specialists are more tied to the fluctuations in the market, and some search firms have suffered heavy losses in business when a particular specialty becomes less profitable, such as the impact of the stock market crash of the fall of 1987 on headhunting in financial services.

guarantee   Offered by many search firms to clients in the case of an assignment that is not completed in a specific period of time, where none of the short-listed candidates is acceptable to the client, and if the successful candidate leaves within a period of twelve months or a year. Such guarantees usually take the form of an offer to continue or reactivate the assignment on an expense-only basis until a suitable candidate has been found.

headhunter/headhunting   The popular, slightly scurrilous, and irreverent term for consultants and executive search firms, used synonymously and interchangeably with the term *executive search.* The term is not particularly liked by those in the business, but is more or less accepted by them. The verb (to be headhunted) refers to a change in job due to an approach by a search consultant, not just being telephoned. An executive is headhunted by a client, using the search as an intermediary; but one cannot be strictly headhunted without the role of the search firm.

high-level search   Assignments at the top level of the salary range and in terms of responsibility, such as chief executives. These include searches at $100,000+, compared with middle-level searches of between $60,000 and $95,000, and lower-level searches of between $40,000 and $55,000 and below.

ideal candidate   A theoretical person exactly suited to the position to be filled, described in the job specification. Drawing up a profile of the ideal candidate is a popular approach to headhunting in the United States.

individual-oriented search firm   The opposite of a teamwork-oriented search firm: Consultants work on their own assignments, with a large degree of personal autonomy. Such a structure is favored in firms where the earnings of consultants are directly related to the business they bring in and the assignments they carry out.

in-house recruiting   When a client decides not to engage a search firm and tackle its own recruiting problems, either through the old-boys' network or by advertising. Not to be confused with internal candidates.

in-house sources   The research facilities available within the offices of a search firm, including the internal data bank, and as opposed to out-housed sources.

initial brief   A proposal letter from the search firm to the client, outlining its understanding of the assignment, and why the client should choose it. This is followed by either engagement to undertake the assignment or rejection. Not to be confused with the brief.

internal candidates   Candidates for a position to be filled who are already working within the client company, sometimes in competition with external candidates for the job.

internal database   The in-house sources of a search firm accessible from desktop terminals on consultants' and researchers' desks.

interview process   Part of the search process in which the consultant, then the client, interviews the candidate. This can also include testing and graphology.

job or position specification   An outline of the requirements of the ideal candidate, including experience, qualifications, background, and personal qualities.

lateral thinking   A quality needed by third-generation researchers in carrying out creative, efficient research, such as in cross-vectoring.

off-limits or no touch   Companies that are clients of a search firm may not be seen as poaching grounds in which to search for candidates. Too many clients in a certain sector can produce the problem of blockage, or lack of search areas.

old-boys' network   A system of personal contacts, based on knowledge of people one has met at school, university, the services, and in social gatherings; a very random and inexact way of finding candidates for positions that are declining in relative importance with the growing acceptability of headhunting.

online databases   Widely available sources, stored on large host computers and accessed remotely using a computer located at a search firm's offices. Interrogated information can be selectively downloaded to the computer's hard disk, where it can be edited and merged into in-house documentation.

out-housed sources   Sources such as specialist libraries and online databases used by researchers outside the offices of the search firm, as opposed to in-house sources.

placements   Successful assignments completed by a search firm, in which a candidate has been placed. Many headhunters talk of the numbers of placements in a certain period as a measure of their amount of business.

reference checks   Investigation of a candidate's résumé to ensure its accuracy. This term is also used in gaining outside references to a candidate's qualities and achievements from people he or she has worked with in the past.

repeat business   More assignments and work from existing clients of the search firm, seen as highly sought after since working for an existing client, where the headhunter already understands the business culture, is easier than taking on a completely new client. Many search firms quote their percentage of repeat business; this will be higher in the case of consulting-oriented search firms than transaction-oriented search firms. It is also inevitably higher in the older, established search firms than in the newer ones.

research manager   A member of the staff of a headhunting firm who has the responsibility for its combined research resources. The degree of involvement by the research manager in aspects of the search process varies considerably among firms.

research-oriented search firm   A firm where great emphasis is placed on the importance of research, which employs a large number of researchers—perhaps even more than the number of consultants—and has the most modern and comprehensive research resources. Within such firms, it is not uncommon for researchers to become consultants.

retainer-based fees   Whereby a search firm is paid in stages within the search process and where the payment of fees is not dependent on the success of the search in finding a suitable candidate, as in the case of contingency work.

rusing   See *unethical research.*

screening   Sifting through many preliminary candidates in order to arrive at a short list. Some screening must be carried out when cold-calling or by contacting sources. Otherwise screening may be possible through detailed desk research and by obtaining the candidate's résumé or background information.

selection   A method of recruitment whereby a selection firm undertakes the listing of a number of potential candidates through recruitment advertising and interviewing. As an agent of the client company, it undertakes its own telephoning, referencing, and further interviewing.

shoot-out   A competitive pitch for an assignment, nearly always at the client's offices, among a number of search firms—usually two to five—whereby the client may judge which it prefers.

short list   The final list of candidates presented by the consultant to the client, all of whom have expressed real interest in the position, and in whom the client is interested. The short list may contain as few as two names or as many as half a dozen or more, but three or four possible contenders is most common.

source   A person contacted by telephone by a consultant or researcher to suggest a possible candidate for an assignment. This may sometimes be interpreted as a roundabout way of approaching a potential candidate, but the leading firms do not favor this, and make clear when they make contact which of the two they consider they are addressing.

specialist company/headhunters   A search firm or individual consultant who specializes in recruiting and searching in one particular sector, either by industry or function.

success rate   The proportion of assignments successfully completed by a search firm, compared with those that had to be abandoned, either due to the failure of the search firm to find an acceptable candidate or to an unforeseen change in the job or position specification. Failed assignments (and hence a low success rate) are not always the headhunter's fault, but a good consultant does not undertake an assignment without having previously ascertained that it has a fair chance of success.

transaction-oriented search firms   Those firms seeking to maximize their volume business in terms of number of assignments, which do not necessarily enjoy a large portion of repeat business, and thus attach a great deal of importance to business development.

unethical research   Certain practices, such as phone-sourcing and "research" techniques, that involve misrepresenting the caller or purpose of the call. Considered by many to be unprofessional and are not tolerated by professional recruiters. These practices are also called *rusing*.

walk-ins   Would-be candidates who literally walk in to search firms' offices asking for career advice and how they can move on. Many leading firms will allow the walk-in to talk to a researcher, to give the researchers interviewing practice. Sometimes called *drop-ins*.

working the phones   A term used to describe telephoning sources and candidates, a task usually undertaken by a researcher, including cold-calling.

write-ins   Résumés sent by hopeful would-be candidates to search firms.

Bibliography

Basch, Reva. *Secrets of the Super Searchers* (Eight Bit Books, Wilton, CT, 1993).

Basch, Reva. *Secrets of the Super Net Searchers* (Pemberton Press, an imprint of Online, Inc., Wilton, CT, 1996).

Bjørner, Susanne. "Mercury Center: Fit for Supersearchers?" *Searcher* 2, No. 7, 1994, pp. 36–39.

Bredal, Johannes. *Den gyldne stol: Executive search som rekrutteringsværktøj* (Børsen Forlag, Copenhagen, 1988).

Byrne, John A. *The Headhunters* (Macmillan, New York, 1986).

Esholdt, Lars and Knut Isachson. *Headhunting* (TANO, Oslo, 1991).

Executive Search and the European Recruitment Market (The Economist Publications, London, 1990).

Gaffin, Adam. *Everybody's Guide to the Internet* (MIT Press, Cambridge, MA, 1994).

Hahn, Harley. *Internet Yellow Pages,* 2nd ed. (Osborne McGraw-Hill, Berkeley, CA, 1995).

Hahn, Harley and Rick Stout. *The Internet Complete Reference* (Osborne McGraw-Hill, Berkeley, CA, 1995).

Jones, Stephanie. *The Headhunting Business* (MacMillan, New York, 1989).

Jupina, Andrea A. *The Handbook of Executive Search Research* (Kennedy Publications, Fitzwilliam, NH, 1991).

Kennedy, Jim. *Getting Behind the Resume* (Prentice Hall Information Services, Upper Saddle River, NJ, 1987).

Korn, Lester. *The Success Profile: A Leading Headhunter Tells You How to Get to the Top* (Simon & Schuster, New York, 1988).

Lichty, Tom. *The Official America Online Tour Guide* (Ventana Press, Chapel Hill, NC, 1995).

Orenstein, Glenn S. and Ruth M. Orenstein. *CompuServe Companion: Finding Newspapers and Magazines Online* (Bibliodata, Needham Heights, MA, 1994).

Stoll, Clifford. *Silicon Snake Oil: Second Thoughts on the Information Highway* (Doubleday, New York, 1995).

Taylor, A. Robert. *How to Select and Use an Executive Search Firm* (McGraw-Hill Book Company, New York, 1984).

Wareham, John. *Secrets of a Corporate Headhunter* (Atheneum, Belmont, MA, 1981).

Yate, Martin. *Hiring the Best* (Adams Media Corp., Holbrook, MA, 1994).

Index